Social and Political Transformation In Iran Since 1979 : The Role of Islam

Social and Political Transformation In Iran Since 1979 : The Role of Islam

By

Dr. Shah Alam

Vij Books India Pvt Ltd
New Delhi (India)

Published by

Vij Books India Pvt Ltd
(Publishers, Distributors & Importers)
2/19, Ansari Road
Delhi – 110 002
Phones: 91-11-43596460, 91-11-47340674
Fax: 91-11-47340674
e-mail: vijbooks@rediffmail.com

Copyright © 2015, *Dr. Shah Alam*

ISBN (Pb) : 9789385563065 (2016)

All rights reserved.

No part of this book may be reproduced, stored in a retrieval system, transmitted or utilized in any form or by any means, electronic, mechanical, photocopying, recording or otherwise, without the prior permission of the copyright owner. Application for such permission should be addressed to the publisher.

The views expressed in the book are of author in his personal capacity.

CONTENTS

Preface		vii
1.	Islam: An Ideology	1
2.	Islamisation of Politics	63
3.	Economy in the Post-Revolution Iran	106
4.	Islamisation of Society	155
5.	Conclusion	188
Bibliography		197
Index		

PREFACE

The Islamic Revolution 1979 is a watershed in the history of Iran where Islam has played a dominant role in restructuring and reshaping society as a whole. The fusion of religion with politics and working as ideology is a unique in the history of Islam. The occurrence of revolution in the name of Islam shocked the whole world who ignored Islam as a political religion. The galvanization of Islamic idioms into action was clear indication that Iran is moving toward Cultural Revolution which had been aspired by Iranians for long time. The use of Islamic symbols and precepts and its conversion into action explicitly manifested that Iran is heading toward the Cultural Revolution. The revolution uprooted the monarchy and established the Islamic government in Iran.

The structural nature and functional scope of the three branches of the government has been changed along Islamic lines since the establishment of the Islamic Republic. Islam's penetration is so extensive that its manifestation has come up in the form of the institutionalized role of Islam. In the aftermath of the revolution, a new constitution was enacted which declared Twelver Shiism as state religion. Islam has profound impact on social, political and economic system of Iran.

The conversion of Islamic idioms into Islamic ideology marked the prelude of the Islamic Revolution where all segments of society sank their differences at least for time being against the despotic monarch and dethroned the Shah. The *ulema* mobilized the masses through using their social status and position which the Shah could not curb. The Islamic symbols and precepts were very effectively used by the *ulema* against the Shah.

The concept of *Velayat-e Faqih* is theorized by *Ayatollah Khomeini* is not his own innovation rather derived by him from the *Shia* political theory that is based on the concept of the *Imamate* system. According to *Shia* political theory, an *Imam's* functions are to guide the community and preserve God's law. It implies that *Imam* is a representative of God on earth and to run system as a whole. The concept of *Twelfth Imam* and its occultation put all responsibilities on the religious community to govern society because in the absence of the *Imam* leaderless community needs a leader to lead society. *Imam Khomeini* brilliantly put forward the concept of *Velayat-e Faqih* on this basis. Khomeini's leadership notion reflects that he was very much influenced by the *Maktabi* School (the old style of Islamic School).

The *Velayat-e Faqih* has overwhelming power in the Iranian political system where all branches of the government are under its supervision and surveillance. The president is directly elected by the people, yet next to the leader (spiritual leader). The *Velayat-e Faqih* has vast power in all matters and his word is final. His stature in the Iranian political system is so high that no one is even parallel to him. The entire system is rotating around this post because it is only source of the legitimacy.

Iranian economy has also been restructured along Islamic line. Its influence has deep and far-reaching in the economic system of Iran. The Iranian economy's changing nature has been perceived clearly different in both pre-plan period and plan period. During pre-planned period, Iranian economy was state-controlled economy the state adopted interventionist policy and created state-capitalism. In the process of creation of state-capitalism, it nationalized the heavy industries and banks etc. because Iranian economy was facing severe crisis due to the revolution and the Iran-Iraq war. During the war, Iranian economy was in difficulties, revenues accrued from oil were spent in purchasing war materials and other essential goods. The populist state policy was adopted by state during war to ward off economic severity which was bound to affect the people.

After the Iran-Iraq war and *Khomeini's* death, the five-year-plan began to reconstruct war-ravaged economy. The war with Iraq had profound impact on the Iranian economy. Iran was facing the severe financial crunch during this period when money was badly needed to reconstruct its fragile economy. In the process of reconstruction of the war-ravaged economy,

Preface

Rafsanjani government began economic liberalization policy. Before the government, there was no option other than to liberalize its economy and to invite foreign companies to help in the reconstruction of the war-ravaged economy. In this way the government reversed its many earlier policies which were taken during the Iran-Iraq war and Khomeini era. The process of liberalization of economy was in the way of integration into world economy. The basic thrust of the economic policy of government during this period was to reconstruct the war-ravaged economy and to mobilize maximum resources for development.

The Islamic Revolution 1979 is not only a political revolution against the monarchy but a Cultural Revolution also which has affected society as a whole. The Islamic ideology has penetrated in all spheres of society. In the aftermath of the revolution, the new regime has Islamized society by divorcing Western culture, norms and traditions which was adopted by the earlier regimes. The intrusion of western culture, norm and tradition in Iranian society has undermined Iranian culture. So, Islamisation of society has been adopted in all aspects to create an Islamic society. The government has been taking various measures in the process of Islamisation and promoting and strengthening the Islamic culture. Iran has imposed public veiling to women and has banned alcoholic drink, night club and so on. The Government has brought reform in the educational system and mass media along Islamic lines.

Islamisation of social and political system has far-reaching impact at all levels. Now the Islamic Republic has been trying to project a liberal face of Islam. The effects of Islam are dwindling in Iran and have many profound impacts.

My indebtedness to numerous persons and institutions is in fact much more than I may really express in words, yet I would attempt to do so in my most humble way. First of all I owe my sincere gratitude to Prof. A. K. Pasha for his scholarly guidance. I would like to thank Prof. A. H. H. Abidi, Prof. Mohammad Saqid, Prof. Gulshan Dietl, Prof. Girijesh pant, Prof. P. C. Jain and Dr. Mohammad Azhar who helped me in stages of this study. I extend thanks to Dr. M. H. Ilias and Dr. Jawaid Ahmed Khan for their help.

Without the courteous assistance of the staff of the libraries of Jawaharlal Nehru University (JNU), A. M. U Aligarh, the British Council, the American Culture, Sapru House, Iranian Cultural House, New Delhi, and Institute for Defence Studies and Analyses (IDSA), this study could not have been completed. I duly acknowledge their help, and thank all of them.

Last but not the least I thank Ismail and Mahmood Ali for patiently typesetting the study.

—**Shah Alam**

ISLAM: AN IDEOLOGY

The Islamic Revolution 1979 was a watershed in Iranian history where Islam had been redefined from a universal religion to a political ideology with universal claims. The corner-stone of this metamorphosis was Islamic ideology. This ideology in all its political and revolutionary dimensions was not only a unique Iranian or *Shiite* phenomenon. The conceptual and semantic roots of the metamorphosis were already present in the work of architects of the revolutionary pan-Islamists such as Jamal al-Din al-Afghani (1865-1935), Mohammad Abduh (1849-1905), Rasid Rida (1865-1935), Hasan al-Banna (1906-49), and Abd al-Hakim Khalifa. Abd al-Hakim Khalifa published a book entitled Islamic ideology.

Ayatollah Khomeini and Ali Shariati were the most articulated proponents of this concept in Persian, *ideology-e Islami* (Islamic ideology). However, in the Iranian modern history, the roots of this concept go back to Jalal Al-e Ahmad. The term has also been used in the literature of *Mujahidin-e Khalq Organization*. But the official use of this term is extensive in the Islamic Republic of Iran.

Islam is a religion which is not only for the particular purpose and aim but a total way of life. Prophet Mohammad, the founder of the Islamic Society was not only the leader of the *umma*,[1] but final authority vested in him in all matters of state and society. The primordial fusion of religion and politics is a noteworthy in the history of Islam, since the emergence of Islam there was no distinction between religion and politics. After the death of the Prophet, *Imams* became his successor and ruled over the Muslim community, but the death of the Eleventh *Imam* and mysterious disappearance of the Twelfth *Imam* created vacuum for the leadership of Muslim community. In the absence of *Imam*, the responsibility of leadership fell on the *ulema*, who became protector and defender of Muslim community until the reappearance of Mehdi. On the one hand, the *ulema*

---

1 *Umma:* the entire Islamic community without territorial or ethnic destination.

placed themselves the defender and protector of the Muslim community and they considered themselves the legitimate ruler of the community in the absence of the Twelfth *Imam,* on the other, monarchy claimed itself the legitimate ruler of the country. But the legitimacy of the monarchy was always in question because monarchy is incompatible with Islam as the Quran says that "affairs of the people should be conducted on the basis of mutual consultation." [2]

In the Safavid period, *Shiism*[3] became the state religion. It was the first time in the history of Iran that a ruling dynasty declared *Shiism* as a state religion. Despite declaring Shiism as a state religion, it did not precede over politics. During Safavids, relations between the state and *ulema* were cool but cooperative. But in the last days of the Safavids, relations began to deteriorate. Finally, during the Qajars, relations between the state and *ulema* deteriorated on both the internal or external issues, and the *ulema* fought against the state and questioned monarchy's legitimacy. In the 19th century, the *ulema* enjoyed power and influence derived mainly from their control over many functions, although they were not a formal part of executive as some of them had been under the Safavids. The semi-autonomous position of *Shii* administrative and judicial institutions may have been more favourable in acquiring social hegemony than their official status under the Safavids. Whenever the *ulema* perceived fear of foreign domination over Iran either political or economic and erosion of their position in society, they used their social status in the form of protest and demonstration against the state as the Reuter Concession in 1872 and Tobacco Concession 1892.

In the late 19th and the early 20th century, the *ulema* claimed greater power and influence in society. They protested against the despotic rule of the Shah and the growing foreign presence. The demonstrations and protests culminated into the Constitutional Revolution in the early 20th century. In the beginning of the 20th century, Iran passed through turmoil and confusion. Reza Khan, Commander of the Cossek Brigade, exploited the situation; and cleverly overthrew the Qajar dynasty. In the early days of his reign, he maintained friendly relations with the *ulema*. But Reza Shah's relations with the *ulema* strained and even after his forced abdication in

---

2   *Al-Quran,* 42:38.

3   The term "*Shiism*" will be used to denoted *Ithna Ashari* "Twelver" or Jafari branch of *Shiism* unless otherwise noted.

1941 and accession his son to the throne did not improve relations between them.

The decades of 1960s and 1970s witnessed the growing assertion of the clergy. The Shah sought to undermine the social position of the *ulema* through the White Revolution and various other reforms. Imam Khomeini mobilized masses against the despotic rule of the Shah and denigration of Islam. Ali Shariati and Murtada Mutahhari played major role in organizing protests against the Shah. The Shah's despotic rule and his repressive policy brought diverse sections of society at one platform and challenged the Shah's rule. Finally, the people overthrew monarchy in 1979 and Iran entered into a new era.

The redefinition of Islam from a religion promising other-worldly salvation to an ideology harbouring this-worldly is the most important feature of Muslim collective consciousness in modern times. The term ideology represents a revolution in both Islamic thought and action. Virtually, it is non-existent in any classical Islamic text or context.

Islam and all its derivatives refer to the body of doctrinal beliefs that emanate from the *Quran* and *Sunna*. This doctrinal apparatus constitutes the foundations of both the Islamic culture and civilization. Ideology and all its derivations refer to a set of interrelated conceptions and notions of political commitment and mobilizations that seek to (a) provide an interpretation of the existing relations of power and (b) chart the course of actions to alter them. At this conceptual level, the term ideology also encompasses utopia, defined by Karl Manheim an intellectual commitment to negate and alter existing conditions.[4]

Ideologisation of religion refers to the act or process of deriving normative statements about social, political, and economic relationships among the people from the ethical or metaphysical commandments of religion, or, in Ali Merad's words, "to formulate the content of Islam in terms of norms and values of social-political order."[5]

---

[4] Karl Manheim, *Ideology and Utopia: An Introduction to the Sociology of Knowledge* (New York: Routledge, 1936), P. 40.

[5] Ali Merad, "The Ideologization of Islam in the Contemporary Muslim World," in Alexander S. Cudsi and Ali E. Hillal Dassouki, eds; *Islam and Power* (London: Croom Helm, 1981), P. 37

There are manifold meanings of the term ideology. According to Geirger, ideology:

> as system of ideas about social reality that is articulated with internal consistency and elaborated logically on the basis of initial assumptions, and that forms a well-defined written corpus, independent of people's minds to which one refer and that can form the basis of exegesis, comment and indoctrination.[6]

The term ideology is an elusive, impalpable and abstract concept. It is a rational statement of ideas about society and politics. This rational statement of ideas about society and politics is used in day-to-day society's conduct. Thus, ideology is needed for each and every social and political system to govern and regulate the relations of its members with/between one another. Rules of this kind are expressed in the pattern of every day conduct. These rules are manifested in the formal ways like myth, ritual, ceremony and institutional functions. As long as these are expressed implicitly and are not spelt out in formal ways, this can not be called ideology in the full sense of term.

It can be called ideology in the full sense of term, when myth, ritual, and ceremony are expressed in the formal ways and come into action after interacting with social and political system. Then it becomes ideology. In this perspective, a person may ask certain type of questions about the cultural patterns, in terms of which he thinks and acts. Why do we perform this ritual? What is the purpose of this ritual and ceremony? What does it mean to the life of our society? What aspects of our life doe it symbolise? These typical questions are raised only when the existing socio-political order is not satisfying their needs and aspirations, then people search for an alternative.

In a nutshell, ideology is a form of thought and expression that usually arises in socio-political environment that are discerned to be changing. In such situation, supporters of the existing order put forward their arguments in its support and try to explain why it is right and legitimate. In contrast,

---

6   Theodor Gaiger, *Die Soziala Schichtung des deutschen volks* (Stuttgart: Ferdinan Euke, 1932) pp. 77-78, quoted in H.F. Chehabi, *Iranian Politics and Religiuios Modernism: The Liberation Movement of Iran Under the Shah and Khomeini* (London: I.B. Tauris, 1990), p. 67.

opponents explain how the current order and system of things is wrong and how it must be transformed so as to create a rightful society and polity.

Every ideology arises within a specific cultural setting and is intended to address the grievances of that cultural setting. Its proponents use the most powerful symbols available to that culture. These symbols are quite consciously chosen as symbols to represent the whole body of ideas which has been worked out in general language. Like ideology, Islam can also be understood in terms of language. Islam is a language defined by its subject matter while ideology is language defined by its structure and function.

The believers of Islam lead their life according to the Quran and the sayings and doings of Prophet Mohammad. The *Holy Quran* touches all aspects of life: theological, ethical, legal, social, political and so on. This discourse often takes place in the sphere of social and political action and then it converts into ideology. Islamic axioms only after coming into social and political action become ideology.

> The ideologisation of religion is a reaction to the secularization of society, but ironically it is also an expression of that very process. It represents a very deliberate downplaying of the sacred, metaphysical aspect of religion in favour of a this-worldly set of a prior solutions to socio-economic problems.[7]

The relationship between religious symbols and socio-economic factors is one of the perennial inter-action. It is fact that "the religion can provide substance to an ideology as well as a metaphysical catalyst to its legitimacy."[8] What is necessary in a theoretical perspective which manages to incorporate both elements. Just as religious ideology does not merely reflect social and economic pressures, in the same way, it does not in a vacuum separate social and economic realities. It is in a creative back and forth dialogue between material and ideological factors that one can search for the reasons behind the Iranian Revolution.[9]

In the course of Iranian Revolution 1979, Islamic ideology was an utopia in the revolutionary posture. With the passage of time, it emerged

---

7   Ibid, p. 73

8   Anthony Chase, "Comparative Religious Politics: Iran and India," *Journal of south Asian and Middle Eastern Studies,* Vol. XIX, no. 4, Summer, p.33.

9   Ibid, p. 33.

as a dominant ideology. Islamic ideology got momentum bit by bit through the use of religious symbols that were used in transmutation of the *status quo*. The Islamic aspect of uprising took upper hand during the Revolution, and later it became a vital political force, and began to shape the social and political system of Iran in the aftermath (1979).

Specifically, ideological unity is central in the struggle against the regime and should be regarded a forceful ideology against the regime that is built upon a set of images, symbols, and concepts. These symbols, images and concept are used to appeal and mobilize effectively the masses in struggle against the old regime. But it is possible that the ultimate meaning and interpretation can vary widely from revolutionary faction to revolutionary faction. According to definition, the set of images, concepts and symbols that is identify as "revolutionary ideology"; the definition of the ideology as programmes as such leads to misleading interpretations of the symbolic dynamics of revolutionary struggle because it varies from faction to faction. Factional struggle over programmes is important in determining the outcome of a revolution, but the battle over programmes cannot be fully comprehended without an adequate conceptualization of the role of ideology in uniting the revolutionary coalition that oppose the old regime. Despite their diversity, the revolutionary factions use these set of images, and concepts where all factions treat as legitimate. These images, signs, and precepts depict the weakness of the old regime (outdated, oppressive, and beyond hope) and appeal to generalized cultural images and symbols, those are not controversial within society. The unifying ideology might also identify some consensual views of the central aspects or origins of the problems of the old regime. In the Iranian Revolution 1979, the central points of agreement of unifying the opposition to the regime were anti-imperialism, anti-monarchy and the underspecified that the shah's regime was an evil and beyond redemption and Islam can provide an indigenous alternative.

All diverse sections of society shared the basic tenets of *shii* Islam, and derived their ideal models implicitly or explicitly from the same source of jurisprudence, namely the *Quran, Sunna*, reason through *ijtehad,* and consensus. However, each adopted different option on issue relating to political philosophy, sociology, economics, and civil law. So, each appealed to one or more social groups by presenting a different kind of ideal life and society. These diverse groups repelled by one segment of society were attracted by another. Consequently, a very large majority of Iranians were attracted to one or another segment of society, all united under the umbrella of Islam.[10]

After collapse of the old regime, in building the revolutionary state, the main ideological battle is an effort to specify the meaning of symbols, images, and concepts that is to translate an underspecified ideology into specific revolutionary state programmes. Revolutionary crises typically manifests a legacy of ideological unity organized primarily opposition to the old regime and symbols that draw upon shared cultural symbols, it looks to the past and the present both and employees these symbols and images against the existing regime for future course of action.

The revolutionary ideology draws upon a large cultural heritage, but invoking that heritage alone, is quite inadequate in explaining the pictures of revolutionary process and the dynamics of revolutionary ideology. The cultural symbols and concepts are quite flexible in practice, thus, such cultural heritages determine the range of possibilities that can be acceptable to a given revolutionary coalition but only broadly inform actual revolutionary ideology.

Conceptualizing Ideology as Programmes or "culture"

Ideology has been defined through many approaches. Whether, ideology should be considered the specific political programmes of particular groups or should be conceptualized as a pre-existing, overarching system of meaning that incorporates all significant revolutionary factions. Voluntarist approach developed in response to the Iranian Revolution emphasis conscious programmes.[11]

Theda Skocpol's original approach to revolution in states and social revolutions encourage a voluntarist's conceptualization of ideology as the conscious programmes of different factions. She rejects her previous view that ideology is irrelevant to revolutionary dynamics, but now she defines ideology as a conscious programme by which activist construct a

---

10   Ali Rahnema and Farhad Nomani, eds., *The Secular Miracle: Religion, Politics and Economic Policy in Iran* (London: Zed Books, 1990), pp. 19-36.

11   See Theda Skocpol, "Rentier State and Shia Islam in the Iranian Revolution", *Theory and Society: Renewal and Critique in Social Theory*, Vol. II, 1982, pp. 262-283; Shahrough Akhavi, "Ideology and Praxi of Shiism in the Iranian Revolution," *Comparative Studies in Society and History*, Vol. 25, 1983, pp. 195-221

revolution in voluntarist fashion.[12]

However, it has not been always seen that an entire revolution is guided by some conscious programmes as we had seen in the Iranian Revolution. The entire revolutionary factions came together under the banner of Islam but were typically very diverse.

There is a difference between "ideology", defined as a self-conscious articulated political and social programme and "culture", referring to the background assumptions, values etc; that inform social action but are broad enough to serve as a repertoire permitting for various applications. According to Swidler, ideologies are innovative strategies of action that are distinct from, and in competition with, existing cultural frameworks. Revolutions might include a number of ideologies, but ultimately must become part of the larger, more durable "culture" to have lasting influence.

It has also been seen that not only one programme guides a revolution from beginning to end, some approaches that define ideology as a conscious, factional programmes have also seen that ideologies draw upon larger cultural frameworks and change in the course of revolution.[13] Goldstone's approach is one of the most important among these approaches, draws from Ann Swidler's view of culture as strategies of action that actors shape by drawing upon a large and diverse cultural "tool-kit".[14]

According to Mansoor Moaddel, ideology influences revolutionary dynamics in the form of episodic discourses. His definition of "deology" as "episodic discourse" is actually what the "tool-kit" approach calls "culture". He refers the episodes are somewhat large historical period, as he means to refer to transnational discourses that develop and hold sway over the course of decades.[15] Ideology as an episodic discourse refers to "a set of

---

12 See Shahrough Akhavi, "Ideology and Praxis of Shiism in the Iranian Revolution", *Comparative Studies in Society and History,* Vol. 25, 1983.

13 See for instance, Eqbal Ahamd, "Comments on Skocpol", *Theory and Society: Renewal and Critique in Social Theory,* vol. II, 1982, pp. 293-300; Walter, L. Goldfrank, "*Commentary on Skocpol,"* Theory and Society, Vol. II 1982, pp. 301-304.

14 Goldston, "Ideology, Cultural Frameworks, and the Process of Revolution" *Theory and Society: Renewal and Critique in Social Theory,* Vol. 20, 1991, 405-453; Ann Swidler, "Culture in Action: Symbols and Strategies", *American Sociological Review,* vol. 51, 1986, pp. 273-286.

15 Mansoor Moaddel, "Ideology as Episodic Discourse: The Case of he Iranian Revolution", *American Sociological Review, 16 Ibid; p. 359.*

general principles, concept, symbols and rituals used by actors to address problems in a particular historical episode.[16] Thus, Moaddel seeks to explain revolutionary change by resorting to what tool-kit theorists call culture.

Farhi has been considered a functionalist, whose depiction of the working of the *Shiite* ideology in the process of the Iranian Revolution is different from other approaches. For functionalist, *Shiite* ideology guided the revolution from beginning to end, that ideology is defined as a worldview, which includes orienting frames and value system.[17] For example, Arjomand argues that evolving Islamic political culture overwhelmed Iranian society.[18] The unique problems with the functionalism emerge and it is not clear exactly how this ideology overwhelmed Iranian society. The theoretical explanation largely ignored the historical reality of important factions that did not share in the theocratic vision that ultimately dominated the revolution. It is difficult to trace any revolution where the ideology of the post-Revolutionary state had been shared by all significant revolutionary factions of the country.

Architects of Islamic Ideology in Iran

Jalal Al-e Ahmad

In the Iranian modern history, one of the principal figures who articulated the shift from the secular to the Islamic symbolic context is Jalal Al-e Ahmad. He started his political activity as a deeply religious man. His religious commitment had a lasting effect on his entire life, especially in his early political consciousness. In the early days of his life, he was attracted to two major ideas: nationalism and socialism. The first attraction was reflected both in Jalal Al-e Ahmad's interest in the ideas of Ahmed Kasravi and his deeply nationalist orientation. Al-e Ahmad's political engagement, namely socialism, was institutionalized in the Tudeh party,

---

16 Ibid; p. 359

17 Faideh Farhi, "State Disintegration and Urban-based Revolutionary Crisis: A Comparative Analysis of Iran and Nicaragua," *Comparative Political Studies*, vol. 21, 1988, PP. 231-256; Farhi in this article is only mildly functionalist, her view of ideology is somewhat developed. Despite explicity conceptualizing ideology as a general world view, she also implicitly treats, ideology as purposive revolutionary plans.

18 See Said Amir Arjomand" Iran's Islamic Revolution in Comperative Perspective" *World* Politics, Vol. 38, 1986, PP. 383-414; Arjomand, *The Tuban for the Crown: Islamic Revolution in Iran* (Oxford and New York: Oxford Univ. Press, 1988).

under the ideological banner of which al-e Ahmad pursued his political concerns. Later he became disenchanted with the Tudeh party and quit. Gharb-Zadigi (Westoxication), a product of this period, was the most articulate foundation of the Islamic ideology.[19]

There was fundamental problem of western secular ideologies in mobilizing a Muslim nation of political purposes. Al-e Ahmad tried to demonstrate how the same political ends could be formulated and achieved by utilizing the Islamic source of revolutionary symbols. He recognized that primary task of a revolutionary ideology was to communicate its political concerns to its constituency. To accomplish this end, the most important element is the orchestration of a set of common symbols (i.e., indications of collective mythologies), that cover the messenger, the message, and those who are addressed. However, the European ideologies were an alien ideologies for Muslims and incapable of striking in the minds and souls of their recipient. The *Shiite* collective memory played major role in bringing the revolution. In this connection, the supreme symbols of suffering, injustice, perseverance, rebellion and the final establishment of the peace of rightly guided, constituted the marrow of public piety.

Gharb-Zadigi represented a turning point in the Iranian political culture. Though primarily a seething attack against the westernisation of Iranian culture, the book has also a cryptic agenda: return to common (i.e. Islamic) thought. It begins with a diagnosis of a "disease" called "Westoxication" and concludes with returning to the *Quran*. But this return was intended for a specific purpose politics. As "westoxication" was a byproduct of political hegemony, its rejection was the manifesto of a political programme - the Islamic ideology.

Ali Shariati

Ali Shariati is the most articulate proponent of the Islamic ideology. He sought to equate specific *Quranic* terms with "ideology". The *Quranic* term *Al-millah*, is used for "people" or "nation" is closet in meaning to "ideology" he believed; it expressed the same "common school of all

---

19   Jalal Al-e Ahmad, *Gharb-Zadigi (Westoxication)* (Tehran, 1341 [1962])

prophets."[20] The *Quran* could also be taken for the Islamic ideology.[21] But equally applicable are the highest symbols of authority in Islam: faith (*al-din*), Prophethood (*nubuwah*) and messengership (*risaleh*).[22]

Shariati sought to make distinction between *maktab* (school) and ideology. The *maktab* refers to the school of philosophy articulated by al-Farabi or ibn Sina, and ideology represents a doctrinal movement. Ali Shariati claimed that Prophet Mohammad established an ideology. If this ideology propagated, would bring forth the revolutionary figures such as Ali and Hussein. The *maktab* engages the mind, whereas ideology directs the action.[23]

Through comparing and contrasting "science and philosophy" with "ideology" Shariati put forth what is meant by the Islamic ideology. Philosophy and science are concerned with "phenomenology", whereas ideology evaluates what is right and wrong. Philosophy and science do not go further than "understanding"; ideology "leads". Philosophy and science justify "the values"; ideology annihilates or creates values. Philosophy and science bring forth philosophers and scientists, ideology brings forth revolutionary intellectuals.[24]

After contrasting the active ideology with the passive knowledge, Shariati articulated a series of conceptual categories that constitute the "common language" (*zaban-e mushtaraka*) of Islam and ideology. "Armed struggle" is *Jehad*; "the people" are *nas*; "collective ownership" is divine ownership; leadership is *imamah*; the demeaning life of the bourgeoisie is this worldliness; and "the government of the people" is *ijma*.[25]

Shariati contended that without rooting their identity within their religion and culture, non-western peoples could not fight western imperialism; it is a prerequisite for Islamic struggle.[26] For Shariati, the term

---

20   Ali Shariati, *Shia (Shiism)* (Tehran: Husayniyah-I Irshad, 1357 [1978]), P. 91
21   Ibid.
22   Ibid.
23   Ibid.
24   Ibid; pp. 93-94
25   Ibid; pp. 95-97
26   Ali Shariati, *Islam Shenasi* (Tehran, 1972) pp. 15-17

returning to "one's roots" did not mean returning to the Aryan (racial) roots of Iranians but to their cultural roots. Islamic culture had completely cut Iran off from its pre-Islamic culture and as such, return to our roots means not a discovery of pre-Islamic Iran, but a return to our Islamic... roots.[27]

Shariati provided a dynamic interpretation of Islamic concepts. Such elements as *umma, imamate, adle, shahadat, hijira, entezar, shirk* and *nezam-e tawhidi* became action-oriented concept. The methodology which Shariati employed in transforming Islamic concepts into a dynamic ideology was uniquely Islamic.

Shariati stressed that Islam is an ideology capable of providing solutions to all problems. The centerpiece of his ideologisation of *Shiism* in his formulation of an idea "*Alavi*" *Shiism*, which he contrast with the actual "Safavid" *Shiism*. The former is dynamic, liberation, and embodied by Imam Ali, where as the latter is sterile, exploitative and represented by the *ulema* ever since *Shiism* became Iran's state religion under the Safavids.[28] The most important point was his rejection of the traditional view that ordinary Muslims should be passive politically as they waited for the Hidden Imam; instead they should be ready to follow the guidance of conscientious, responsible, pure men representing the leadership of the *Imam*, and to work for an attainment of social justice and other reforms. No was merely the Intercessor, who could help one to endure suffering, he was the great exemplar, fighting and sacrificing his life not merely for the restoration of the rule of the Prophets, but for cause of social justice to oppressed peoples throughout the world.[29]

According to Shariati, Safavid *Shiism* is polytheistic Islam. This brand of *Shiism* claims the mantle of Islam since it invites the people to engage in individual religious practices (*ebadat*), and invoking the cause of Islam, it undermined the essential social, political and economic message of the faith. Reducing Islam to the practice of prayers, fasting, going on pilgrimage, and even waging holy war, depoliticized the people and diverted their energy

---

27 Ali Shariati, *Bazghashti* (Tehran, 1978), pp. 11-30

28 For a summay of Ali Shariati's formulations. See Shahrough Akhavi, *Religion and Politics in Contemporary Iran: Clergy State Relations in the Pahlavi Period* (Albany: State Univ. of New York Press, 1980), pp. 143-50 and 231- 33.

29 N. R. Kiddie, ed. *Religion and Politics in Iran: Shiism for Quietism to Revolution* (London and New Haven: Yale Univ. Press, 1983), p. 140.

from establishing the new Islamic social order.³⁰

Shariati, thus, self-consciously set out to create an ideology, which he regarded an indispensable for struggle. Amir Arjomand has argued that he was above all influenced by Durkheim, and that what he called "ideology" corresponded to Durkheim's collective consciousness.

The ideal leader is the *Imam*, whose intrinsic qualities distinguish him from the masses and who has to lead them not necessarily in a manner that would maximize their happiness, but rather with their reform and improvement in mind. It is the *Imam's* task to lead people from "what they are" to "what they should be".³¹

After the Islamic Republic's repression of Islamic opposition, parties and groups that looked up to Shariati as their spiritual ideology become suspect. In 1983, the Association of the Instructors of the Qum seminary schools, which is a powerful religio-political organization, published a book on Mutahhari's defence of Islam against Shariati's conspiracy against the faith. Shariati was portrayed as "a poisonous deviationist whose ideas, according to Mutahhari, were based more on socialism, communism, historical materialism and existentialism than Islam."³² The condemnation of Shariati's view through the words of no less than Mutahhari came to be considered the Islamic Republic's official line on Shariati.

Khomeini had referred to Ali Shariati as a divisive phenomenon, the introduction of whose ideas is alluded to as a pre-planned satanic plot aimed at breaking up the unity and common cause of the Muslims, thus sapping their energy.³³

Murtada Mutahhari

Jalal Al-e Ahmad envisioned the Islamic ideology as a rebellion against the west and Shariati articulated it in comprehensive political terms, Mutahhari tried to extend it to the very heart of Islamic jurisprudence and

---

30 Ali Shariati, *Mazheb Aleye-e Mazhab* (n.p., n.d.), p. 42.

31 Ali Shartiati, *Emmat Va Imamate* (The Umma and Imamhood) (Tehran 1977), pp. 62-63.

32 Ali Abulhasan, Shahid Mutahhari: Efshagar-e Towte'eh (Tehran: Dafter-e Entesharat-e Eslami, 1984), pp. 236, 417.

33 Ruhollah Khomeini, Sahifeh-e Nur, vol. 2 (Tehran: Markaz-e Madarek-e Farhanghi-e Enqelab-e Eslami, 1983), p. 250.

philosophy so as to give it an intellectual legitimacy. Mutahhari argued the Islamic ideology, nothing less than *sharia*.

Mutahhari's definition of ideology reflects his effort to mobilize public pieties:

> What will give unity, direction, and shared aspirations to the man of today, and a fortiori to the man of tomorrow, what will serve as touchstone of good and evil, of musts and must nots, is an elective conscious, inspirational philosophy of life armed with logic-in other words a comprehensive, perfect ideology.[34]

Mutahhari's binary purpose was to attack and restrict the manifestations of the secular ideology. His *Lial-i Girayish bi Maddigari* (the Cause of Attraction to Materialism) as well as his substantive notions to Allamah Sayyid Mohammad Hussein Tabatabai's *Usul-i Falsafah va Ravish-e Realism* (The principle of philosophy and the Realistic Method) were directed specifically against the total secular ideology at both its political and philosophical levels.[35] The formulation of Islamic ideology was concomitant with Mutahhari's rejection of any mode of secular ideology.

Mutahhari's gist was to give the Islamic ideology a philosophical (i.e. rational) grounding, but it is absolutely in this respect he differed from Shariati. By categorizing human actions as "pleasure oriented" and goal oriented, Mutahhari agued that insufficiency of reason directs the course of human conduct.[36] He argued that the ideology is the supranational legitimacy of "a comprehensive, harmonious, and concrete design whose central objective is to perfect man and secure universal happiness".[37] This grand design is ideology. There are two types of ideologies:

> Human and corporate: human ideologies are addressed to the human species, not to some special nationality, race or class, and have for their motive the salvation of the whole human species. Corporate ideologies

---

34 Murtada Mutahhari, Fundamental of Islamic Thought (Berkely and California: Mizan Press, 1982), p. 51

35 See A. S. M. H. Tabatabai, *Usul-i Falsafa Va Rawish-i Realism (The Principles of Philosophy and the Realistics Method)* Qum: 1332 [1953]).

36 Mutahhari, n. 34 pp. 46-50

37 Ibid; p. 50.

are addressed to a certain group, class or stratum and have for their motive the liberation, or the hegemony of that group.[38] Beyond all doubts, Islamic ideology is human and arises from the primordial nature of man.[39]

Mutahhari has laid down the theoretical and philosophical aspects of the Islamic ideology which arises from the primordial nature of man.

Mutahhari's juristic notion of Islam is an attempt to revive Islam as a potent ideology capable of redressing the social, political, economic and cultural ills of Iran. To attract youth, Mutahhari's approach was through invitation and intellectual persuasion. As such, his thought was reformist rather than evolutionary. He did not accept the notion of radical Muslims that piety and righteousness were the monopoly of the oppressed and the disinherited.[40] He thought that believers and the pious could be found among all classes. Thus, Mutahhari sought to demonstrate that the essentially Marxist notion of social polarization of the basis of the exploited and the exploiters was alien to Islam. Mutahhari thought that Islam did not conceive of the disinherited as the sole class of the believer and pious that actively participated in social movements, and their condition did not constitute the only concern of the revolution as Shariati thought.

Mutahhari rejects the radical position of Shariati that Islamic social justice expresses equality in income or wealth. In his view, Islam assured equal opportunity for all, but differences in human capability, effort, aptitude, dexterity, and work habit should be rewarded accordingly and consequently they should be different. While Shariati expressed that there should be equality in income or wealth since a large portion of society should not be deprived.

Mutahhari was very much close to the modern notions of freedom of thought and expression. Mutahhari stressed that freedom of thought and expression are pre-requisite for the development and evolution of mankind. He persistently reminded that "in the Islamic Republic there will be no limitation on the freedom of thought and all should be free to present

---

38   Ibid; p. 52
39   Ibid; p. 53.
40   Murtada Mutahhari, *Naqdi bar Marxism* (Tehran: Entesharate-e Sadra, 1984), p. 124.

their authentic ideas."⁴¹ At the same time, he warned against conspiracy, wrong ideas and opinions harmful to both the individual and society, but he was not in favour of as Khomeini restricted the flow of right ideas and opinions.⁴²

Mutahhari was critical of political democracy, since it elevated the will of the majority to a position above that of God. He argued the replacement of divine law by man-made laws as a modern-day aberration which he believed to have disastrous consequences for the Islamic community. According to Mutahhari, the position of leadership and decision-making is reserved for the clergy. He argues that only those who are thoroughly familiar with the *Quran*, the *Sunna*, the Islamic Jurisprudence and Islamic epistemology can occupy position of leadership. Mutahhari's emphasis on the role and significance of the clergy is a response to Shariati's anti-clerical notion.

S. Hassan Modarres

Modarres provided an exemplary model for religious inspired political action. As a young cleric, he had been a leading constitutionalist activist during the revolution of 1906 in his native town of Isfahan. Modarres constantly opposed foreign intervention in Iranian affairs. He used Islam as an instrument against the foreign penetration in Iran. During World War-I, he became a member of the nationalist and pro-central powers provisional government. After the war, his house became one of the main meeting places for opponents of the 1919 treaty.

At the domestic level, he opposed Reza Shah's nomination as Prime Minister, the abolition of the monarchy, and Reza Shah's accession to the throne because he did not see Islam's compatibility with monarchy. Modarres's opposition to Reza Shah proved costly. Reza Shah arrested him in 1929, then assassinated in 1938.

He was a devoted religious person who took political action in defence of Iran and Islam. He stated, "our religion is the same as our politics, and our politics is the same as our religion..."⁴³ The source of our politics is our

---

41   Murtada Mutahhari, *Piramun-e Enqulab-e Eslami* (Tehran: Entesharate-e Sadra, n.d.) p. 11.

42   Rahnema and Nomani, n. 10, p. 43.

43   Quoted in Abul Hasan Bani Sadre, *Vaziat-e Iran Va Naqsh-I Modarres (Iran's*

religion. He put forward Islam as an ideology by combining religion with politics.

Mehdi Bazargan

Bazargan was one of the leading revolutionary leaders during the Revolution 1979, who headed the first provisional government after dethroning the Shah. He was a religious scholar and a nationalist. According to Bazargan, "Islam is insolubly linked with Iran, and is the major, albeit not the only ingredient of Iranian society."[44] For Bazargan, the main source of Muslim plight is the early history of Islam when religion withdrew from public affairs; pious people concentrated on practicing their religion and left the conduct of social and political affairs to those not committed to Islamic values. The result of this divorce was the emergence of a class of religious men totally oblivious to practical concerns. So, religion should not be withdrawn from public spheres because it is the religion which provides correct direction.

The combination of religious modernisation and moderate nationalism is not peculiar to Iran, as earlier Arab Islamic modernist such as Mohammad Abduh in Egypt and al-Kawakibi in Syria also combine both elements.[45] In all cases, this nationalism is justified by the *hadith* "*hub al-vatan min al-iman*" (the love of the motherland is part of religion).

Bazargan points out, if Muslims want to improve their lot, they must take their destiny in their own hands. At this juncture, he calls for the revolutionary action to accomplish goals. He repeatedly quoted a *Quranic* verse dear to all Islamic activists: "God changes not what is in a people, until the change what is in themselves".[46]

He also called for less quietism on the part of the *ulema*. He repeatedly urged the *ulema* to lend their support to the nationalists and become politically active. Ultimately, the necessity of a Muslim presence in politics led to the founding of the Liberation Movement in Iran, until its opposition to the Shah.

Situation and the Role of Modarres) (Tehran, 1977), pp. 124-25.

44 Chehabi, n. 6, p. 53

45 See Albert Hourani, *Arabic Thought in the Liberal Age* (Cambridge: Cambridge Univ. Press, 1968), pp. 156-60 and 271-73.

46 *Al-Quran*, 13:12.

According to Bazargan, religious affairs and socio-political matters are separate, but that their separation is asymmetrical, while politics must never interfere with religion, religion should inspire and inform all acts – social and political.

Bazargan's notion of Islam is unique in the sense that it tries to present Islam as a non-coercive and tolerant religion compatible with liberalism and political democracy. It is non-coercive and accommodating in which the "other"-anti-clerical intellectuals, the capitalist or the unveiled women - are neither castigated nor viewed as "corrupters on earth". By including the "other" in God's family, Bazargan singles out tolerance as the cornerstone of Islam.[47]

Bazargan argues that the observation and implementation of Islamic ordinances are considered to be private mattes left to the discretion of individuals. God desired individual to be free in their judgments and decisions. Once God has given individuals the freedom of choice, forced compliance with Islamic edicts becomes meaningless. The *Sharia* constitutes the main objective for Islamic society. According to Bazargan's notion of Islam, God does not wish to impose his view of what is good on individual, since coercion would negate their God-given freedom of chose. Even individuals do not perform their obligatory religious duties, such as fasting and prayers, they may still be considered as Muslims. As long as monotheism is not negated, individuals can not be branded as apostates since the *Quran* says that "there can be no coercions in religion."[48]

Bazargan says that as soon as Prophet was appointed to govern society, God ordered him to "consult with the people on illness and policies"[49] that concerned their lives. Islamic government necessitates consultation with the people, and political democracy is organized to constitute the cornerstone of Islamic political thought. By using the practice of the Prophet as his model of Islamic government, Bazargan argues that "one thousand years before the emergence of the concept of democracy in the West, the government of the people, by the people was practiced in the days of the Prophet."[50] For Bazargan, blind obedience and the imposition

---

47   Rehnema and Nomani, no. p. 105.

48   Mehdi Bazargan, *Bazyabi-e Arzesh-ha* (Tehran: n.p. 1983), vol. 1, p. 78.

49   Ibid, vol. 3, p. 12.

50   Ibid, vol. 1, p. 117.

of a religio-political monolith is a clear violation of Islamic precepts. He rejects the forced imposition of religious or political instructions, even by a *marja-e taqlid*, since it tampers with the principle of man's freedom and responsibility.

For Bazargan, there is no Islamic justification for the government of the Jurisconsult (*Velayat-e Faqih*) if it is understood as a position of unlimited power with unaccountability to the people. Khomeini's edict of 6 January, 1988, involved the absolutist government of the Jurisconsult (*Velayat-e Motlaq-e Faqib*) and gave an absolute legal power to the Jurisconsult. Bazargan's political organization, Freedom Movement of Iran (FMT), reacted sharply on this edict which declared, "from a socio-political point of view, the absolutist government of the Jurisconsult is nothing other than religious and state despotism and dictatorship, resulting in the disappearance of freedom, independence and identity."[51] Khomeini's thesis is entirely different from Bazargan, where Khomeini assigns an absolute power to the *Velayat-e Faqih*.

Ayatollah Khomeini

Khomeini was a religious man and he sought that Iran should be governed under the Islamic *sharia*. In the early stage of his life, he did not overtly oppose the Shah and monarchical system but only covertly and subtly attacked the monarchy. Khomeini work's central theme was the urgency of reestablishing Islam as a way of life and a method of government, the illegitimacy of the monarchy, and the *ulema's* proper role in the politics. These three interrelated issues underwent major transformations. He began as a reformer, operating within the parameters of orthodox *Shiism* and went on to become a revolutionary interpreter of Islam, and the founder of a new form of Islamic government. He employed Islam as ideology for overthrowing the monarchy.

Khomeini's first major overtly political treaty was *Kashful Asrar* (Secrets Unraveled) was published in 1941 immediately after Reza Shah's forced abdication. In *Kashful Asrar*, he looked as a reformer, the defender of the Persian constitution and the monarchy, who was mainly concerned about Iranian politics. The book was a straight attack on Reza Shah's policies and a response to *Secrets of a Thousand Years*, a book written by

---

51 Nehzat-e Azadi-ye Iran, *Tafsil va Tahilil-e Velayat-e Motlaqeh –ye Faqih* (Tehran: Nehzat-e Azadi Iran, 1988), p. 150

a member of Ahmad Kasravi's Pak Dini Movement, which denigrated the *ulema* as champions of superstition, and main cause of Iran's backwardness. Khomeini lambasted the propagation of Pak Dini Movement, and praised the *ulema* as defenders of Iran's national identity and independence. The first half of the book is devoted to theological exegesis but the second half presents the first programmatic assertion of the clergy's political role advance since the days of the Constitutional Movement.

According to Khomeini, the first principle of the Islamic government is that only God is legislator. "No one but God has the right to govern over any one or to legislate, and reason suggests that God himself must form a Government for people and must legislate. The laws are but the laws of Islam."[52] His second principle is that a Muslim should only "obey God, His Prophet and those in authority among you."[53] He stressed that Islam is a religion which should be a total way of life, and society must be governed according to *Sharia*.

After explaining the orthodox *Shii* doctrine that *Imams* were the legitimate authorities form Prophet Mohammad to 874. He stated that in the contemporary world, the most legitimate authority should be that of the *mujtahids*, the *fuqaha* and those most knowledgeable in the laws of Islam.

Khomeini's political activity expanded due to deep and widespread moral corruption and cultural decadence that

> the clergy insist that this shameful unveiling (of women), this "Movement of Bayonets",[54] has wracked both spiritual and material damage upon our country in gross violation of the laws of God and his Prophet. The clergy insist that this melon-shaped (men's) hat, a foreign left over, is a disgrace to the notion of Islam, forbidden by God and damaging to our independence. The clergy insist that theses co-educational schools, mixing young Girls and lustful young boys, destroy chastity and manliness... They insist that these shops selling wines and these factories making alcoholic drinks erode the minds of our youth, debasing reason,

---

52 Ruhollah al-Mussavi Khomeini, Kashful Asrar (Secrets Discovered) (Tehran, 1941), p. 184.

53 *Al-Quran*, 4:62.

54 The Shah's policies regarding dress was so that the soldiers were ordered to tear apart women's veils on the street with their bayontes.

health, chastity and courage amongst the people, by God's decree the drinking and selling of wine are forbidden, and these places should be shutdown. They also insist that music creates a mood of fornication and lust, undermining chastity, manliness, and courage, it is forbidden by religious law and should not be taught in schools lest it promote vice.[55]

He stressed for the mobilization of the people for the religions causes and approved the establishment of a special ministry for this specific purpose. It would seek not only to inspire each citizen, but also to train him to proselytize others.[56]

He opposed the existing Ministry of Justice and its judicial procedures. He thought that Islamic law would simplify trail procedures and eliminate costly lawyer's fees and parasitic judicial personnel.[57] He claimed that full implementation of Islamic panel code would eliminate injustice, theft and corruption within a year.

> If you want to eradicate theft from the world, you must cut the hands off thieves, otherwise your prison sentences will only help thieves and perpetuate theft. Human life can only be made secure through the guarantee of punishment, and only the death penalty ensures society's survival. Since prison sentences do not solve any problem. If adulterous men and women were promptly given a hundred lashes each, venereal disease would disappear in this county.[58]

In the later stage, he became politically active and started to mobilize the people against the Shah. When the Shah saw Khomeini's active participation in politics, the Shah forced him to be exiled in 1963. First he went to Turkey and then Iraq. He openly opposed monarchy and declared, "Islam is fundamentally opposed to the pillar of monarchy..."[59]

In the early spring of 1972, he issued a *fatawa*, requiring that financial assistance be extended to the families of political prisoners. He argued on

---

55 Khomeini, n. 35, pp. 213-14
56 Ibid; pp. 246-48.
57 Ibid; pp. 296-301.
58 Ibid; pp. 274-75.
59 Khomeini's Statement of 28 Rabi al – Thani 1391 H.Q./1971. He states furthermore, any one who looks at the biography of the Prophet in the matter of government will see that Islam has come to destroy all these places of monarchical oppression.

the basis of two *furu* of the faith: *Jehad,* and *al-amr bi al-maruf.*[60] He argued that these tow principles had provided the justification that "from the beginning of the mankind, Prophets and the clergy were charged... with rebelling against despotic government..."[61] This view is forcefully argued in his book *Hukumat-e Islami (Islamic Government)* which was published in 1971, was actually his various lectures in Najaf. During the course of lectures, he boldly attacked both monarchy and dynastic succession as alien to Islam. The *ulema* must not confine themselves to the routine of churning out regulations for the faith. Having an obligation to tend to political issues, they consequently omit themselves to oust corrupt officials and overthrow tyrannical regimes.[62]

The Islamic government will differ from representative and/ constitutional monarchies because all necessary laws have already been promulgated and revealed by the Prophet and *Imams*. Certainly there will be parliament but it will not engage in enactment of laws, instead it will be an "agenda setting" institution to clarify for the ministries the best means for administrating social services throughout the country. Furthermore, sovereignty shall repose in God alone. There is no question of royal rule in Islamic government, much less a government that is based on Kingship or Empire.[63] He argued that the government must be Islamic government and such a government would be governed by the *Velayat-e Faqih* (Guardianship of Jurisconsult).

Khomeini stated, "Islam is the religion of militant individuals who are committed to truth and justice. It is the religion of those who desire independence. It is the school of those who struggle against imperialism."[64] At length, Khomeini became rebellious against the monarchy and aroused anti-Shah feelings in the name of Islam to overthrow the monarchy. He used Islam very cleverly by denoting the Shah Anti-Iran and anti-Islam. So, people should actively involve in politics since Islam is a political religion. For Khomeini, even such rituals as the Friday prayers, festival prayers, the *hajj* (Pilgrimage) and "demonstrations of solidarity at Mecca, Arafat and

---

60   *Khabarnameh, Farvardin* 1351 H. Sh/1972 Quoted in Akhavi, n. 28, p. 164.

61   *Iran –I Azadi, Tir-Murdad* 1350 H. Sh./1971, quoted in S. Akhavi, no. 28, p. 164.

62   Imam Khomeini, *Hukumat-e Islami (Islamic Government)* (Tehran, 1971) P. 39.

63   Ibid, P. 55-56.

64   William Montgomery Watt, *Islamic Fundamentalism and Modernity* (London and New York Routledge, 1988), p. 135.

Mina are all of great political significance."⁶⁵

He stressed resistance to a despotic regime must be of all kinds, the *ulema* must use the mosques and religious occasions to mobilize the people; there must be unity between the people and the leaders. The people must be aware of the legal and political-economic solutions that Islam offers to their problems. Propaganda must be widespread and must reach the university students because they are the "staunchest opponents of repression, despotism, treachery, agents of imperialism and plunders of national wealth."⁶⁶

Struggle against imperialism can be of both types, violent and non-violent. Violence is essential because "life is a lesson and struggle... death is better than a life of humiliation; no other way out but continuation of the war by every means... to achieve honour and glory."⁶⁷ On the other hand, there must be passive resistance in the form of boycotts, non-cooperation with government institutions, and avoidance of any activity that would help the government. And at the same time, there should be established alternative structures to govern society.

Ali Shariati's notion of Islam was very much different form Khomeini's notion of Islam. He believed that the Islamic rule would be representative, democratic and welfare oriented and was against the religions despotism since he was attracted to the Western ideas such as anti-imperialism, anti-capitalism, anti-despotism, humanism, social democracy and socials justice. Basically, his concept of the government was non-clerical and non-theocratic concept which was entirely contrary to Khomeini's concept of the Islamic government.

Mehdi Bazargan was critical of the notion of the government of Khomeini, and he projected the liberal face of Islam as accommodating, tolerant and non-coercive. He did not justify Khomeini's concept of the *Velayat-e Faqih* in any way as Khomeini projected his Islamic form of government. He castigated the religious despotism of Khomeini, who monopolized the state power in the name of Islam.

---

65 A. Ezzati, *The Revolutionary Islam and Islamic Revolution* (Tehran: Ministry of Islamic Guidance, 1981), P. 96

66 J. S. Ismail, "Social Change in Islamic Society: The Political Thought of Ayatollah Khomeini," *Social Problems*, Vol. 27, no. 5, 1980, P.613.

67 Ibid; P. 614.

Institutionalization of Islamic Ideology and Use of Symbols

The conceptual elaboration and institutional propagation of the Islamic ideology were influenced by a number of organizations. The *Anjuman-e Mahanay-yi Dini* (Monthly Religious Society) was led by Mutahhari, was one of the most influential among the organizations. This organization held series of lectures. From 1960 to 1963, the society disseminated its ideas through its organ, *Guftar-e Mah* (Monthly Lectures). These lectures excited the minds of the clerics and students and created troubles for the regime. The Shah shut down the organization and its lecture series in the mid-March 1963. Other eminent personalities who associated with the Islamic Revolution, such as Mohammed Ibrahim Ayati and Sayiad Mohammad Beheshti were also active in the organization.

The most successful institutional expression of the Islamic ideology was the *Husayniyah Irshad*. It started in 1965 as the institutional expression and elaboration of the Monthly Religious Society. It had the nation-wide impact that the lectures and deliberations of the antecedent Monthly Religious Society never enjoyed. The Organization apparently revolved around *Husayniah* (in that sense the war devoted to the commemoration of Husein, the martyr third Imam of *Shii*), the adjective *Irshad* (guidance) reflected its pragmatists purpose. Among original members of the managing board of the *Husayniyah Irshad* were Ayatollah Mutahhari, Sayyed Hussein Nasr Sahabi, Husein Mazini, and Ali Shariati. Shariati's lectures made the organization much more famous and attracted the students from every corner of the country. Shariati's message was that the *Husayniyah Irshad* ought to be a model for the *hawzahs* (seminaries) of Iran. Mutahhari articulated the purpose of this organization.

> The *Husayniyah Irshad* knows it task to be to introduce Islamic ideology (to the youth) such as it is. This institution deems it sufficient to unveil the beautiful face of the beloved martyr of Islam (Imam Husein) in order to transform the love-seekers into restless lovers.[68]

The militant organization proclaimed the institutional legitimacy of the Islamic ideology, was the guerilla movement of the *Mujahidin-e Khalq Organization*. Its militancy demonstrated the most essential component of the Islamic ideology - physical force. The force took the form of massive mobilization, along with legitimate use of violence.

---

68 Akhavi, no. 28, p. 183.

In addition to these organizations, mosques (the established institutions of public sermons for religious ceremonies, especially in the month of *Muharram, Safar,* and *Ramadan*) provided momentum to the revolutionary appeal of the Islamic ideology. The prestige and fame of the organizers of these institutions encouraged the religious community to respond favourably to the call for an Islamic ideology. The intellectual dimensions of this ideology were elaborate in other intuitional setting, including the department of theology at Tehran University (where Mutahhari taught) and the *Madarssa-e Fayziah* (theological school) at Qum.

From ideal to the real, the Islamic Republic, and the Islamic Republican Party were the highest institutional achievement of the Islamic ideology in the post-Revolutionary Iran. But, the Islamic Republican Party was dissolved in the mid-1980s on the instruction of Imam Khomeini.

Martyrdom in Iranian Political Culture and its Significance

Throughout the history of Iran, martyrdom has been a recurring phenomenon to celebrate and safeguard the sacred boundaries. The martyrdom in the *Shiite* culture of Iran is a socio-historical one. Martyrdom is the struggle against social justice and oppression, is called to be the noblest of all cause. A Muslim's sincerity and devotion to the faith are measured by his/her readiness to sacrifice his/her life for it. Throughout the Iranian history, martyrdom has played crucial role in the fighting against the state oppression.

The never-ending impact of Imam Husein's martyrdom on the *Shiite* psyche and his exaltation as the lord of martyrs has a great significance. The martyrdom of Imam Husein and the events associated with it have a significant place in the consciousness of the *Shiite* Muslims. The martyrdom of Imam Husein is perceived as an event to restore the truth against the falsehood and justice against oppression. Imam Husein became a role model for political action and militancy for all suffering souls.

The martyrdom of Imam Husein and the popular reference to him as a *mazlum* (oppressed) has two connotation. First, it characterizes as an individual who has been oppressed or sinned against. Second, it signifies unwillingness, derived from a sense of noble generosity and forbearance to act against others. The glorification of noble suffering and the defiant embracing of death, the deliberate and conscious approbation of martyrdom have profoundly influenced the *Shiite* collective consciousness throughout history.

The festival of *Ashura rituals* of lamentation and self-flagellation increasingly became an outlet for the expression of the pervading oppression in their own lives. Identification with Imam Husein and his tragic fate enabled the *Shiites* to withstand their own suffering. The *Ashura rituals* were also used throughout history as instrument of cultural assimilation and mass mobilization. It is not new phenomena the rituals of *Ashura* were present in Iran as early as the tenth century under the *Shiite* Buiyd dynasty. The ritual of *Ashura* has also a functional value: to infuse a deeper *Shiite* identity among Iranians and to strengthen the communal bonds of solidarity and cultural loyalty.

Shah Ismail (1501-1524), the Safavid King, effectively used the incident of the martyrdom of Imam Husein, the Lord of martyrds to incite his soldiers against the Ottoman Turks in the sixteenth century, "we are Husein's men, and this is our epoch, in devotion, we are the slaves of the *Imam*, or name is zealot and our title martyr."[69] The introduction of the *Taziyyah* (a passion play) by the *Shiite* Safavid dynasty in the 16th century combined with *Rawzeh Khani* (recitation of the suffering of holy martyrs) throughout history symbolized a "submissive observance of pain and suffering as the hallmark of all worthy souls."[70] The significance of Martyrdom was not only confined to the Safavid dynasty but it was also used by the later dynasties who ruled over Iran. *Taziyyah* gave wide popularity during the reign of Nasir ud-Din Shah. It was the powerful instrument for arousing of religious emotions at the hand of clerics. The people had deep and widespread attachment to *Taziyyah*, it was a means to express loyalty to *Shiism*. The ritual of *Taziyyah* was used by both the Safavid and Qajar dynasties to ensure their hold over the masses.[71]

Historically, martyrs have been sacred symbols, confronting the sorrow and pains of the community. With the increasing politicization of Iranian polity after World War II, martyrdom assumed a political

---

69 Roy Mottahedeh, *The Mantle of the Prophet: Religion and Politics in Iran* (New York: Simon and Schuster, 1985), p. 173.

70 Hamid Ehayat, *Modern Islamic Political Thougth* (Austin: Univ, Press Texas Press, 1982), p. 183

71 Ibid., pp. 183 – 184.

significance calling on the faithful to sacrifice themselves for the cause. In the fast changing political culture of Iran, the term was used in new and highly politicized way.

In the later half of the twentieth century, it became popular conviction among Iranian intelligentsia that the ineffable felicity of the future is possible only through the massive self-sacrifice of the present. The political eschatology portrayed martyrdom as a small but necessary step on the path to the realization of the grand ideal of liberating humanity. Since autocracy was the symbol of inequality and oppression, it was intrinsically evil and had to be destroyed. The reformist and gradualist tactics were a deliberate treacherous betrayal and deception of the masses. Only a full-fledge social revolution could provide a viable remedy to the misery of the masses. In realizing this goal, the intelligentsia has to self-efface. Their faith in revolutionary change became the basis of their new political religion.

Ali and Husein, two paradigmatic figures of authority in *Shiite* Islam to accept and even glorify death, has a direct influence on the *Shiite* attitude toward death in general and martyrdom in particular. To fight against autocracy and for social justice, the populist intelligentsia sought to regenerate the society morally and to create a new social order. They must awake the people.

The Iranian political culture of the 1960s and 1970s provided the fertile ground for the use of religious symbols. Self-denial and an austere life style, forbearance and self-sacrifice were among the constituent elements of this political culture. The Shah's autocracy created opposition which was unified in the name of religion. Martyrdom became a political symbol. In this context, the politicization and exaltation of martyrdom permeated in the political sphere of Iran.

While rituals, rites, and symbols have social function, once practiced they develop dynamism and a life of their own which binds the continued existence of the community to the vitality of traditions. Commenting on the political significance of the rituals of *Ashura* in Iran, Sheikholeslami asserts,

> The commemoration of the deceased emphasized the historical continuity of the community, and the social sentiment which the rituals arouse in more than sufficient to compensate for the death, i.e. the

breach of solidarity. All these mourning rituals are associated with the commensolity which brings the community together and the partaking of the food in particular bring life, contrasted with death, into a clearer focus.[72]

The martyr may die, but martyrdom is eternal.

Martyrdom has been used not only to sanction certain political ends but also to maintain communal solidarity and loyalty. Historically, the integrative power of such symbols and signs had been significant in inculcating a sense of identity and culturally assimilating and politically mobilizing the populace. The remarkable resonance of this tradition in secular political culture is indicative of the vitality of religious symbols in post-traditional society.

According to Ayatollah Murtada Mutahhari,

> The blood of a martyr is not wasted. It does not flow into the ground.... And is transfused into the body of his society.... *Shahadat* means the transfusion of blood into a society.... It is the *Shahid* who infuses fresh blood into the veins of the society.[73]

These two references of grand *Shiite* martyrs, Ali, and Husein, are made to legitimise their call on martyrdom. He asserted, "the sacred cause that leads to *Shahadat* or the giving of one's life has become a law in Islam. It is called *Jehad*."[74]

In the same way, Khomeini asserted that "the martyr is the heart of history and the blood of each martyr is like a bell which awakens the thousand."[75] Through martyrdom a society strengthen its ties and revive itself spiritually.

The most politicized and systematic exposition of martyrdom was

---

72 Ali Reza Sheikoleslami, "From Religious Accommodation to Religious Revolution: The Transformation of Shiism in Iran," in Ali Banuazizi and Myron Winer, eds., *The State, Religion, and Ethnic Politics: Afghanistan, Iran and Pakistan* (Syracuse and New Yrok: Syracuse Univ. Press, 1986), p. 229.

73 Mehdi Abedi and Gary Legenhausen, eds., *Jehad and Shahadat: Struggle and Martyrdom in Islam* (Houston: Institute of Research and Islamic Studies, 1986), P. 136.

74 Ibid., P. 129

75 *Tehran Times*, 16 November, 1982.

articulated by Ali Shariati, the intellectual forerunner of the Revolution 1979 and the hero of Muslim youth. For Shariati, one of the greatest and most revolutionary contributions of Islam to society has been to infuse a sense of devotion and sacrifice in the pursuit of justice.[76] Through martyrdom a society refines itself. Shariati utilized the deep tradition of martyrdom in the Iranian culture to evaluate the level of commitment and generate the spirit of militancy and self-sacrifice necessary in any successful political struggle.

Martyrdom is a recalcitrant gesture renouncing the present order. It is a self actualization through negations. It is an act of self-aggrandisement that enables individuals to transcend time and be placed on the highest summit of history. Since political sincerity is measured by the degree of self-sacrifice, martyrs become political capital and an asset for legitimacy and credibility. No organization can grow substantially without any previous accumulation of martyrs.

Throughout the Revolution 1979, the *ulema* as custodians of the *Shiite* faith used the tradition of martyrdom to mobilize millions against the Shah's regime. When some demonstrators were shot by the security forces, the clerics effectively employed the tradition of commemorating the deceased on the seventh and the fortieth days after their death to mobilize even larger members of people. Thus, as the number of martyrs rose, so did the number of anti-Shah demonstrators.[77] Since its ascendance, the Islamic Republic has used the post-Revolutionary martyrdom that occurred during its eight years war with Iraq to maintain a permanent state of mass mobilization and to ward off criticism by presenting itself as the guardian of the honour and blood of martyrs.

In the aftermath of the Revolution, a Foundation of Martyrs was established. The families of martyrs were given preferential treatment in receiving coupons for food subsidies, entrance to universities and job placement in governmental bureaucracies. Large number of urban poor, peasantry, and lower middle classes volunteered for the war with Iraq,

---

76 Ali Shariati, *Eqbal Mamar, Tajdid Bana-ye Tafakkur-e Islami (Iqbal, the Architect of the Renewal of Islamic Thought)* (Tehran: Forough Publications, 1973), p. 29.

77 It is parallel here with Lebanese Shiite increasing bid for political power in the country. As the Israeli invasion of Lebanon led to their concomitant confrontation with the hitherto subdued and submissive Shiite community in the south and as the number of *Shiite* grew, so did their involvement in politics and their political power.

thinking if they died, heaven awaited them and financial security and honour awaited the family members they had left behind. The worldly inducement was so prevalent during the war years that the government on its part made an attempt to maintain religious sanctity historically associated with the aura of martyrs and martyrdom.

Islam in Historical Perspective and its Fusion with Politics

The founder of the Islamic state Prophet Mohammad was both the spiritual and temporal ruler of the Muslim community in Mecca and Medina. Upon his death, the community gathered to choose a successor, and in this choice the learned men played a decisive role. The sources of the knowledge were *Quran*, *Sunna* and *Hadith*. These three elements were compiled, aggregated and codified in Arabic language in years of following Mohammad's death. The early days of Islam had been reflecting that the *ulema* had played major role in determining society. They derived their status in the early Islamic community from their participation in the selection of the caliph and from their codification and interpretation of the religious law. The *Quran* explicitly refers to the *ula al-amr* (those who are in authority), meaning spiritual leaders of the community.

From the time of the *hijra*,[78] the Muslims constituted not merely a religious community but also a body politics. Muslims consider the state and community formed by Prophet Mohammad as distinctively Islamic. So, in the early days of Islam the religion and politics was not separated but amalgamated and Prophet Mohammad had both the spiritual and temporal powers. Even after his death, the Caliphs and *Imams* enjoyed the same power and authority as the Prophet Mohammad had. But the difference between Prophet Mohammad and the caliphs and *Imams* was only in the enjoyment of the spiritual status and rank, and not in the enjoyment of power and authority. Thus, religion and politics was not separated in two different compartment but coalesced.

In *Shii* Islam, there were two conditions existed. First, the situation existed before 874 a period when *Imams* were visibly present on earth, so, the question of delegation of authority did not arise; second, the period after 874 in which *Imam* went into hiding, the question of delegation authority became problematic.

---

78 *Hijra*: the emigration of Prophet Mohammad from Mecca to Median in 622 AD.

It was the period between 874 and 920 when *Imami Shiism* took definite shape. The notion of *Shiism* which developed during this period cannot be called an *Imami* or "twelver" form of *Shiism* before the death of the Eleventh *Imam* and the disappearance of the *Twelfth Imam*. The "twelver" or *Imami* form of *Shiism* can be called only after the mysterious disappearance of the *Twelfth Imam*. The early development of the *Shiism* was at the two levels: *proto-Shiism* under the Umayyad; and *proto-Shiism* under the Abbasids.

During Abbasid, *Imami Shiism* had an ambivalent attitude to *de facto* authority. The Abbasid ruled and derived its legitimacy on the basis of the assertion that Mohammad transferred the *Imamate* to his uncle al-Abbas, who had handed it on to his descendents the Abbasids. On the other hand, those who were sympathisers of the *proto-Shii* came to be more and more exclusively concerned with the descendants of Ali. It is well known that the Abbasid heavily invoked *Imami* themes in their movement to overthrow the Umayyads, and many of the latter Abbasids also harboured certain sympathy toward *Imami Shiism*.

Shiism is based on the concept of *Imamate*. It is an institution of a succession of a charismatic figure who dispensed true guidance in comprehending the esoteric sense of prophetic revelation. The *Shii* notion of *Imami* theory is based on fundamentally three things. First, the most important and distinctive feature of *Shiism* in general, is the cult of the charismatic leader; second, the notion of the Mehdi; third, is the conception of the transmission of authority by designation.

The Twelver *Imami Shii* theory of the *Imamate* has made the *Imam* practically equal to the Prophet, even though *Shiism* accepts that theoretically, the holy law forbade the status of prophecy to the *Imam*. The *Shia* insists that the *Imams* are the replacement (*quim maqam*) of the Prophet and vested the temporal power with divine sanction. *Imam* is the infallible, omniscient agent of God who carries the news of his commandments to men. Without the *Imam* men could not know what God wants of them.

Abu Sahl Ali bin Ismail, played an important role in theorizing the doctrine of *ghaybat*, the occultation of the *Imam*.[79] The rotation of the Twelve *Imam* came to an end in 874 when the Eleventh *Imam*, Hasan

---

79 On the Naubakhti family, see Abbas Iqbal's *Khandan-I Naubakhti*, (Tehran, 1933)

al-Askari died in 874 and his infant son the twelfth *Imam* disappeared mysteriously probably in 878. After the mysterious disappearance of the son of the Eleventh *Imam*, a period of nearly seventy years was represented by a succession of four agents (*wakil*), which the Hidden *Imam* was visible only to a succession of four agents, which is known as "Lesser Occultation" (*Ghaybat-e Sughra*). The last agent in this succession, Ali bin Mohammed as-Samarri died in 940 that ended the communication with the Hidden *Imam*. After his death, the period is known as "Greater Occultation" (*Ghaybat-e Kubra*). The absence of a human intermediately shall continue until the *Imam's* return on earth as the Mehdi.

The concept of the occultation of *Imam* has attributed a distinct character to the *Ithna Ashari Shiism*. The elaboration of concept has been a constant preoccupation of *Shii* philosophers, particularly in the Safavid and post-Safavid Iran. The concept of *taqiyah*[80] is itself combined with the *Ithna Ashari Shiism* and it essentially projects, the quietist position of *Imami Shiism* in respect to worldly authority.

After the occultation of the Twelfth *Imam*, *Shiism* became even more quietist in its attitude toward worldly power. The passive, although denial of legitimacy and not excluding repeated clashes with regimes and dynasties prohibited the advocacy of total overthrow of the existing order, in the name of legitimate alternative. While the *Imam* remained in occultation, and shadow of illegitimacy was bound to cover all worldly activities above all those related to government.

The conceptualization of the *Shii* theory began soon after the beginning of the Greater Occultation when the Buwayhids, a dynasty with *Shia* loyalties, gained control of the center of the Abbasid caliphate. But in fact, the Buwayhids did not replace it with an *Imami* caliphate. Like the Buwayhids, the Hamdanids, another dynasty of *Shii* affiliation gave formal allegiance to the Abbasid caliphate. This dynasty did not pay much attention to the *Shii* theme.

With the establishment of the Safavid dynasty in 1501, the first Safavid ruler Shah Ismail, elevated *Shiism* to the status of state religion. The event was a turning point in Iran's history and finally associated an

---

80 *Taqiyah*: The Principle of prudential dissimulation of belief for the purpose of safeguarding the *Shii* community, particularly in time of danger. This concept was used by the *Shii* ledaders at various occasions.

inalienably with Iran. The creation of an elaborate *Shii* clerical apparatus with a differentiated hierarchy and specific judicial and administrative strata was an integral part of the construction of a centralized Safavid state. During the Safavid period, "clerical and state power had become so intertwined that it was customary for Safavid Shahs to marry the daughters of the supreme *Shii* clergy."[81]

Under the Safavids, "the ruler was assumed to be the representative of the Hidden *Imam* and even attributes to the *Imams* tended to be transferred to him."[82] The rulers also assumed themselves the "Shadow of God". They regarded as the representative of God and they acknowledged themselves as descendants of Musa al-Kazim, the Seventh *Imam*. Thus, there was no separation of religious and temporal body rather they commingled.

With the development of the Safavid state, the close relationship between the state and its established religion implied a domination of the *ulema* by the kingly power. "The ascendancy of the political power of the Safavid state over religion was typified in the position of *Sadr*, the official who controlled religious affairs and institutions on behalf of the state appointed the *Shaykhul Islam*, the chief dignitary of the religions classes."[83] The *Shar* courts and their judges were subordinate to *Urf* courts and to the *divanbigi* (the supreme official in secular jurisdiction).

Henri Corbin, an eminent scholar of *Shiism*, has indicated the significant consequences of the establishment of *Shiism* as the state religion by the Safavids. *Shiism* gave birth "to something like an official clergy, extensively concerned with legality and jurisprudence, to such a point that original *Shiism* in its essence Gnostic and theosophic, has so to speak, to hide itself."[84] The *ulema* emerged dominant player in the Safavid period and played role as the *Imams*. But *Shiism* denied legitimate authority to worldly power, thus, too, no authority in the strict sense of the term resided in the *ulema*. Rather they fulfilled a practical function of considerable importance to the community as a result of which they have

---

81　M. Ravands, *Tarikh-I Ijtama-e Iran* (A Social History of Iran). Vol. 3, (Tehran, 1978), p. 481

82　Hamid Algar, *Religion and State in Iran 1785 – 1906: The Role of the Ulama in the Qajar Period* (Berkeley and Los Angeles: Univ. of California press, 1969), p. 27.

83　Ibid; p. 27.

84　Ibid; p. 5.

had *de facto* authority. In narrow sense, the *ulema* were intermediaries between the community and the *Imams*, which some of the authorities of *Imams* reflected upon them: they are "proofs" of the *Imams*. Similarly, the *Imams* were intermediaries between the source of divine guidance and the community. But this can not be concluded from this comparison that the *ulema* have had any authority similar to that of the *Imams,* or that they could legitimately lay claim to infallibility. The *mujtahids* came to personify the leadership of the community, and this was one of the chief sources of their political and social influence in Qajar Iran.

The effective end of the Safavid dynasty at the hands of the Afghans marked the beginning of a period of danger for *Shiism* in Iran. In this period, learning declined, its shrines were treated with disrespect, its *ulema* neglected and oppressed, and it was almost reduced from that position of pre-eminence in Islam and it regarded as a mere equal of the four *Sunni's* schools. However, ultimately *Shiism* emerged from the interregnum between Safavid and Qajar rule with increased strength, and with the role of its guardians, the *ulema*.

Afghan invaders entirely disrupted the cultural and religious life of Iran. Isfahan, the Safavid capital was completely devastated and plundered. While political unity of Iran was temporarily re-established by Nadir Shah in 1736, was no longer on the basis of *Shiism*. In fact, he considered the religion of Shah Ismail (founder of the Safavid dynasty) to be *bid' at* (reprehensible innovation), and himself called upon to remove it. His actions against the *ulema* were well known: the confiscation of *waqf* property, the abolition of the post of *Sadr*, the restriction of all jurisdiction to *Urf* courts, and the strangling of the *Shaykhul Islam*.

The Afghan invasion in the early 1720s brought about the collapse of Safavid power. The next seventy years or so witnessed a time of trouble. With the advent of the Qajar dynasty (1779-1925), the *ulema* began in practical terms to reassert their independence form the state. Lambton argues that the Qajar Shah continued to be called "the shadow of God on earth", but they did not pretend to be the descendants of the Prophet and the *Imams.* She says that the *Imam's* "mantle... developed upon the mujtahids".[85]

---

85   Ann K. S. Lambton, "Quis Custodiet Custodes? II, *Studia Islamic VI,* 1956, as cited in Akhavi, no. 28, p. 15.

In *Shiism*, fundamental duty of the believer, after belief in God and the Prophet is *velayat* (the supervisionship of the *ulema*), complete loyalty and obedience to the Hidden *Imam*. "He who dies without, recognizing the *Imam* dies an unbeliever."[86] Since the withdrawal of the *Imam* from the control and guidance of the community is only apparent, and not actual, this primary duty remains intact. At the same time, the *mujtahid* is needed to provide immediate guidance in matters of practice. *Mujtahids* are those whose judgments are accepted, the most important *Shia ulema*. Their eminence depends essentially on the acquisition of the rank of *ijtihad*. Literally, *mujtahid* is one who exercises *ijtihad*, that is, searching for a correct opinion (*ray-i savab*) particularly in "the deducing of the specific provision of the religious law (*furu*) from its principles (*usul*) and ordinances"[87] The principles upon which *ijtihad* may be exercised are the Quran, the *Sunnat* (practice) of the Prophet, the traditions of the *Imams*, and the consensus, *ijma* of the learned science the beginning of the Greater occultation.[88] In a society, there may be many *mujtahids*. Thus, to accept pronouncement of any one *mujtahid* is not, per se, obligatory, for the *mujtahid* may claim no infallibility and *mujtahids* will vary in their opinion and rulings. Moreover, the institution of *mujtahid* has had an important merit of ensuring a continuous leadership of the community and providing a source of immediate authority. The prime task of the *mujtahid* is providing leadership and guidance to the community.

One of the most important functions of the *ulema* is the dispensation of justice. The dual nature of the judicial system was not amended until the introduction of the first civil code in 1911. The courts presided over by the *ulema* were known as the *Shar* courts, and the system of laws controlled by the state was called *Urf* courts. *Urf* had been called common law or law of precedent, but no records of proceedings were kept, and verdicts delivered were not necessarily committed to writing. *Urf* jurisdiction was dispensed by the state without reference to established principles, according to the needs of the state at a given time through the medium of the governs of towns.

---

86 Mohammad b. Yakub al-Kulyani, *al-Kafi fi Ilm ad-Din* (Tehran, 1379 Q/1959-1960, as cited in Algar, n. 82, p. 6.

87 Hujja ul-Islam Muhamad, *Sanlagi, Qadar dar Islam*, (Tehran, 1338, Sh/1959-60), p.14.

88 Ali Akbar Dihkhuda, *Lughatnameh*, (Tehran, 1326 Sh/1947), p. 1033.

The *Urf* courts dealt with primarily offences directed against the state or public security, such as rebellion, embezzlement, forgery of coins, spreading false rumor, theft, banditry and drunkenness, the *Shar* courts concerned more with disputes and litigation of a personal or commercial nature. The *Shar* courts were powerless in those matters because it did not have ability for the most part, to enforce their decision, the execution of verdicts was in the hands of the *darugh* or *kadkhuda* (the town or village head man), so the implementation of the decisions were not certain.

Throughout the 19th century, this interaction of the two types of courts, combined with the lack of any formal demarcation of their jurisdictions, was a major source of conflict between the state and the *ulema*. The state attempted to assert its judicial power. It meant restricting the prerogatives of *ulema* who on their part would not accept the validity of the *urf* jurisdiction.

By the end of the interregnum, relation between the *ulema* and the state had been changed. First, an evolution in *shii figh* took place that asserted the role of *mujtahid* in directing the community and even in ruling it. Second, with the establishment of the Qajar rule, the *ulema* expected the same position as had in the Safavids. The Qajar Shahs called themselves "shadow of God on earth", but their claim to divine appointment was only formal.

According to *Quran*, those in authority should command the good and forbid the bad (*al-amr bi-al- maruf va al nahi an al-munkar*) form the masterpiece of the *Shii* theory of government. It is asserted that "opposition to tyranny is a fundamental and pervasive characteristic of *Shii* Islam".[89] The religious system provided most of the formal legal structure it means the religious leaders, with their broad legal. Social and educational functions influenced the limits of powers of the ruling class. Judicial functions were dominated and education was monopolized by the religious class.

The state was opposed by the clergy in the nineteenth century on two grounds, anti-imperialist and the anti-Qajar. The anti-imperialist opposition resulted from encroachment of foreign, non-Muslim states upon Iran, Muslim territory. Basically, this opposition was intended

---

89 Hamid Algar, "The Oppositional Role of the *ulema* in Twentieth Century Iran" in Nikki R. Keddie, ed., *Scholars, Saints and Sufis: Muslim Religious Institutions Since 1500* (Berkeley and Los Angeles: Univ. of California Press, 1972), P. 231.

against "infidel" foreign political and economic penetration in Iran. Iran's government increasingly came under the influence of infidel foreign power, Russian and Great Britain. The *ulema* acted as upholders of the traditional values, promoting territorial integrity of the *Dar al-Islam* against the *Dar al-Harb*.[90]

The second ground of opposition, the ulema opposed to tyrannical nature of the state. This type of opposition surfaced at the minor level in the late Safavid period. The anti-government opposition by the *ulema* during the Qajar period was opposed by two factors. First, this opposition was usually local (but not always local as Reuter concession in 1872 and Tobacco Concession in 1891-92), aimed at acquiring more political influence or political control on the local scene (but not always local scene they represented national feeling at national level). Second, the *ulema* opposed the state in the 19th century because it encroached upon the *ulema's* socio-economic and political positions. The state tried to restrict the role of the religious community and to cut down state pensions to the *ulema*.

In the Qajar period, relationship between the state and the *ulema* was uneasy because the state did not want interference of religion in the administration. The *ulema* sought that the state should not pursue its policy against them because they are the custodians of religion and their service was the service of Islam. But the state had its own difficulties. There was uneasy relationship between the state and the *ulema* during the Qajar period. Particularly, during reign of Nasir ud-Din Shah, the relation between the *ulema* and the state deteriorated rapidly and culminated in the Constitutional Revolution at the dawn of the twentieth century.

There were several reasons for deteriorating between *ulema* and state relationship. The state encouraged presence of foreign powers and individuals for securing ready cash. Their presence was secured in the form of economic and commercial activity unfamiliar to the Perso-Muslim mind. Thus, the *ulema* led the second Perso-Russian war and undertook themselves the duty of defending the national honour against infidel aggression. The internal and external enemy represented two aspects of the same danger, namely the disappearance of Iran as a Muslim country.[91]

---

90 For an analysis of this conflict in the nineteenth century see Algar, no. 83.
91 Iran adopted its cultural and religious traditions overwhelming the Islamic traditions.

The *ulema* considered that their prime is to deter this danger. The throughout the reign of Nasir ud-Din Shah direct clashes between the *ulema* and the Shah, primarily in Tehran but also in provinces increased frequently. As the scope and importance of the *ulema* increased, so was their involvement in affairs. The power they enjoyed, political and economic, despite the tyranny of Nasir ud-Din Shah, increased rather than decreased.

While Muzaffar ud-Din Shah enthroned in June 1896, the state was in much confusion due to many factors. The relation between the *ulema* and the state was in uneasy state and the *ulema* had placed themselves as national leaders. The state was in acute financial crises. The main source of unrest and discontent in the reign of Muzaffar ud-Din Shah was the financial problem that resulted from the extravagance of Nasir ud-Din Shah and the mismanagement of Aminus Sultan. It derived toward the necessity of foreign loans and then in turn to the encroachment of Russian economic influence. On the issue of foreign influence in Iran, the ulema every time opposed any type of foreign activity on the territory of Iran. Iran plunged into crisis on Russian Concession to Iran, was primarily led by the *ulema*. The *ulema* represented the national feeling and finally culminated into the Constitutional Revolution (1905-1906).

The *Ulema's* Opposition against the Foreign Encroachment

The Treaty of Gulistan (1813) was concluded after the first Perso-Russian war that left certain areas ill-defined. The Russian occupation of Gokcha in the Khenate of Erivan and refusal for withdrawal gave birth to the hostilities. The Perso-Russian hostility caused the second Perso-Russian war. The second Perso-Russian war was not started by the state since it knew its constraints, but was the product of the *ulema*. The *ulema* led the war against the Russian occupation. Main leader of the war was Abbas Mirza. The clergy declared war against Russia in the religious context because it occupied a Muslim territory. So, they declared war against the Russians as a holy war (*Jehad*). The Shah, Fatah Ali Shah, was reluctant to declare war on the Russia as a *Jehad* because he was very much aware of his county's constrains but was forced to do so since national feelings were in favour of war with the Russia. The Shah was forced to declare war against Russia because he himself felt alienated from his own men.

Iran during Qajar times was never an Islamic State in any sense of the term, no consistent effort being made to enforce the *Sharia*.

The direct interference of the *ulema* brought the agitation to a new state of zeal. The *ulema* acted as the *de facto* leaders of the nation. The effective leadership of the people was still in the hands of the *ulema*. "Affairs reached such a point that the rulings of the *ulema* were given precedence over the commands of the king… Were he to have opposed their policy, the people of Iran would have destroyed the monarchy."[92] However, current of enthusiasm was temporary but significant. It was strong enough to determine state policy and portrayed explicitly the close alliance between religious and national feeling. It was conviction that the survival of Iran as a nation was similar to its survival as an Islamic nation. This conviction was voiced with great lucidity in the later part of the century. The agitation also reflected the primary alienation between the state and the nation, and the difference of interest between the two. In this alienation, the *ulema* embodied the aspirations of the people. Unfortunately, in the second Perso-Russian War 1827, Iran was defeated. Thus, the second Perso-Russian war ended disastrously. At the out set, the *ulema* had used religious symbols as an instrument for the arousing the people. The success in arousing these emotions revealed their political strength as leader of the nation. The contradiction between the state and the nation affected the course of war; the ever-increasing foreign influence gave a new dimension to *ulema*'s role of leading the nation against the state.

The events came to surface as a confrontation between the people and government, in which *ulema* acted as inspirers and leaders of popular feeling and defenders of the national honour. The mass was not following the government orders but they followed the orders of the clergy. The closing of the *bazaar*, the gathering in the *Masjid-i Shah*, the use of martyr's corpses to inspire violent anger – all these are elements of Iranian history which recur in later, more serious situations. The episode of Griboyedov's murder produced the first clear confrontation between the government and the people that confrontation was religiously motivated and centred on the person of a *mujtahid* was not coincidental. The government became increasingly suspected of treason and cooperation with foreign, non-Muslim powers; the *ulema* were the national leaders to oppose it. The events connected with the murder of Griboyedov did not have immediate consequences of any importance, but it had on many later developments.

---

92   Algar, n. 82, P. 90.

During Nasir ud-Din Shah, modernization and industrialization was introduced in Iran that brought contact with the Europeans. Mirza Husayn khan accompanied Nasir ud-Din shah on his first official trip to Europe in 1873. He intended to start administrative reforms in the course of modernizing Iran. This visit led indirectly to a strengthening of European influence, and became closely associated with the granting of the Reuter concession. The precedent established by this journey led to growing lavish expenses, necessitating in turn the negotiation of foreign loans, and the further penetration of the nation's economic life by foreigners.

The *ulema* protested against Mirza Husayn khan while the Shah and Mirza Husayn khan were in Europe. This protest centred on the granting of a concession, in 1872, to Julias Reuter, a British financier, for the exploitation of all minerals and forest in Iran, and for the construction of railways.[93] The surrender of a major chunk of the economic resources of the country into foreign hands was bound to be resisted by the *ulema*. The importance of the Reuter Concession was more than economic. Britain sought Iran as a buffer state against Russia's southward expansion, and was planning to strengthen it by economic regeneration like the Reuter Concession. The government hailed foreign entrenchment in the country for hastening reforms which was the most effective basis for any political influence. For the *ulema*, foreign influence was unpleasant because the close alliance with the state would have strengthen their traditional enemy thereby endangered their own influence and function. The construction of the railways was opposed by the *ulema*. For the people, railway was a symbol easily understood as an intrusion of the mechanized west and bringing about an undesired intimacy with the outside world.

When Nasir ud-Din Shah was on his return from Europe, the *ulema* placed him their demand for the dismissal of the Sipahsalar, Mirza Husayn khan and the cancellation of the Reuter concession.[94] The *ulema* projected themselves the protector and defender of the national interests against a treacherous government and foreign influence. Like the Tobacco Monopoly, the Reuter Concession was primarily a foal point for many elements of unrest and discontent. Sectional grievances subsumed under a single protest voiced in religious terms and led by the *ulema*. On this

---

93   For the text of the Concession see H. Rowlinson, *England and Russian in the East*, (London, 1875), PP. 373-376.

94   Abdullah Mustavfi, *Tarikh-i Idari, va Ijtima-i yi Daura- yi Qajariaya ya Sharh-i Zindagani- yi Man, Vol.I*, (Tehran, 1321 Sh/1942-43), pp – 127-129.

occasion, the few involved in number, with the Tobacco Monopoly the whole nation felt itself affronted, and the role of the *ulema* as national leaders received unequivocal expression.

Nasir ud-Din Shah left for Europe third time in 1889. This journey like the first one was associated with the grant of economic concession and monopolies in which Tobacco Concession was one of the important concessions to the British.

The protest against the Tobacco Concession represented on the one hand, an iteration of the *ulema's* traditional role in opposing the state, and on the other paved the way for the Constitutional Revolution. On numerous occasions, the *ulema* acted against the state in order to defend national interest. On the issue of Tobacco concession virtually the whole nation was united under the leadership of the *ulema*. The agitation was not merely a protest against a specific measure taken by the government rather centered on the question of the Tobacco Monopoly, which was essentially a direct confrontation between the people and the State, in which the leadership was exercised by the *ulema*. It clearly showed a new determination and sense of direction. Moreover, the agitation took place in the context of increasing foreign interference in Iran, an above all inspired it with a sense of urgency that concerned for the very survival of Iran. Thus, the traditional dual role of the *ulema* opposition to the state and resistance to foreign penetration found its greatest expression. This duality was passed on by the *ulema* to the Constitutional Movement.

The preliminary negotiations were completed in London during Nasir ud-din Shah's third visit to Europe in 1889. [95] In the spring 1891, the agents of British Company to which the monopoly had been granted, started to arrive in Iran. All rights regarding sale and distribution of tobacco inside Iran, and the export of all tobacco produced in Iran, were vested in the Imperial Tobacco corporation, "which in return was to pay the Iranian government 15 million a year."[96] Furthermore, the regulation of the early crop was the prerogative of the company. Under these circumstances, popular unrest and discontent was bound to arise as soon as the agents of the monopoly started their activities.

---

95   Ibid; P. 470.

96   Ahamd Kasravi, (*Tarikh-i Mashruta- yi Iran (History of Constitutional Movement in Iran). Tehran, 1340 Sh/1961), p. 15.

At the outset, disturbances began in the capital in March 1891, and very soon agitation extended to the other provincial cities. In May 1891, one of the leading tobacco merchants of Fars, Hajji Abbas Urdubadi, called the *bazaar* of Shiraz to be closed in protest against the monopoly. Hajji Sayyid Ali Akbar Falsiri mounted the pulpit (minber) in the Masjid-i Vakil to preach against the government policy in general, and the granting of the Tobacco Monopoly in particular. He called for *Jehad*, if the agents of company did not deter from entering into Shiraz. Falsiri's expulsion order issued from Tehran, the governor of Shiraz expelled him form Shiraz. When Falsiri's expulsion order was known in Shiraz, the merchants of Shiraz gathered in the Shrine of Shah Chiragh, where they were fired upon by the Governor Qavam ul-Mulk's troops and compelled to disperse. The following day, the agents of the monopoly entered Shiraz.

It is noteworthy, cooperation between the merchants and the *ulema* took place from the beginning of the agitation. This cooperation was based not only on common interests in opposing the Tobacco monopoly, but also on the position of each group in Iranian society. They represented two powers largely independent of the state: that of the economic enterprises and that of religious direction. The influenced of the state either in the capital or large cities like, Tabriz, Isfahan, and Shiraz, was likely to be exercised at the expense of both ulema and merchants. The excessive taxation affected commercial interests while Urf jurisdiction meant a reduction of clerical power. The *ulema* called the closure of the *bazaar* that paralysed urban life. It provided the *ulema* a powerful instrument of pressure.

"Shaykh Murtada Ansari had declined to make political used of his power and initially Mirza Hasan Shirazi showed a similar reluctance."[97] Initially, Mirza Hasan Shirazi did not want to involve in the political matter but he was forced to intervene. His intervention began with a telegram to Nasir ud-Din Shah on 26 July 1891, protesting against the disrespect shown to Sayyid Aki Akbar, an also against the granting of the Tobacco Monopoly. The Shah did not reply to his first telegram and Mirza Hasan Shirazi wrote to him again in September 1891, setting forth in detail his objections to the Tobacco Concession. But he did not get satisfactory reply, then he empowered Mirza Hasan Ashtiani to act on his behalf in combating the monopoly.

---

97 Ibrahim Taymuri, *Tahrim-iu Tanbaku ya Avalin Muqavamat-I Manfi dar Iran*, (Tehran, 1328 Sh/ 1949), p. 87

Early in December 1891, there appeared a *fatawa* in Tehran declaring "the use of tobacco in any form to be a tantamount to war against the hidden *Imam*, i.e., *haram*".[98] Its effect was immediate and total, the use of tobacco was given up all over country.

The government decided to threaten Mirza Hasan Ashtiani with banishment from Tehran unless he contradicted the prohibiting *fatawa*. Nasir ud-Din Shah wrote a harsh letter to him. Mirza Hasan Ashtiani decided to leave Iran but his followers did not allow him to leave, and mob gathered around his house and were ready for *Jehad*. The troops fired upon the mob and demonstration called off. Finally, Nasir ud-Din Shah convinced that it is impossible for further upholding the Tobacco Monopoly. He communicated with Mirza Hasan Ashtiani on the issue of Tobacco Concession. After clear indication from the government, Mirza Hasan Shirazi issued a statement to end the boycott. Ultimately, the government rescinded the Tobacco Concession to the British Company.

The agitation against the Tobacco Concession, however, was far more than the expression of personal or sectional discontent in religious terms through the medium of the *ulema*. It surpassed, not only this, but all precedents of clerical intervention in national affairs. It was a watershed in Iranian history, the *ulema* mobilized the masses against the state in the name of Islam.

The alliance between the *ulema* and merchants became more pronounced and effective form the time of the agitation against the Tobacco Monopoly onward and found its greatest expression in the events of the Constitutional Revolution 1905-06. The main reason of the agitation was conceived of as the increasing foreign danger to Iranian independence. The tobacco merchants resented having to sell and buy at prices arbitrarily fixed by a foreign company. The foreigner issue caused economic and commercial problems for the *ulema*. The appearance of large number of non-Muslim foreigners, working to Tobacco Corporation was one of the most important reasons for the agitation, their presence was resented by the *ulema*. The foreign presence in the economic affairs of the country endangered Iran's existence was perceived by the *ulema*.

In the late nineteenth century, Iran was very much in acute financial crisis. To avert crisis, Amin-us Sultan negotiated a loan of 2.5 million

---

98 Mustavfi, n. 94, p. 12.

rubles from the Russian government in 1900, with interest at 5 percent, to be paid within seventy five years. Among the conditions attached to the loan was one that Iran should not contract debt to any other government until it was repaid. The threat of foreign financial domination came closer to Iran that aroused combined hostility of the *ulema* and the merchants again. A concession was to be granted to Russian company to construct a road form the border at Julfa to Tabriz, the *ulema* of Tabriz raised their voice in protest.

An agreement was signed between Iran and Russia on the exploitation of fishery in Gilan, in return Russia awarded loan to Iran. It established Russia's control over fisheries in Gilan. The act created opposition of the *ulema*, particularly Hajji Mohammad Rafi Shariatmadari, the Chief *mujtahid* of Gilan. The protest was directed against certain symbols of foreign influence in the town, schools, hostels, and wine shops which directly effected the Islamic culture and values.

The *ulema* were searching an opportunity to gather against the government and they got in the Russian concession. The traditional role of the *ulema* was again played by them. The *ulema* were aware of their power and influence. Amin-us Sultan's involvement with the Russians created discomfort in the religious community. The *ulema* did not follow the line of Murtada Ansari and Mirza Hasan Shirazi, and "were prepared to work for the overthrow of the monarchy".[99] The *ulema's* opposition to Russia led towards the Constitutional Revolution. The doctrinal based protest of the *ulema* to the monarchy was intensified as the danger of foreign dominance increased. The policies of Amin-us Sultan helped to increase that danger.

The Constitutional Revolution occurred as a result of all previous events. The ulema and merchants forged alliance against the state. Their demand was to restrict not only the unfettered tyranny of the monarchy and its agents, but also to ever-increasing entrenchment of the nation's economic life by foreigners. The existence of religio-national community was felt to be in danger, and as before, the *ulema* led and expressed the reaction to that danger.

The agitation began just before Muzzafar ud-Din Shah left on his third journey to Europe in June-July 1905. The merchants of Tehran closed down the *bazaar* and took refuge in the Shrine of Shah Abdul

---

99　Algar, n. 82, p. 234

Azim in protest against the Belgo-Russian economic influence. The Crown Prince, Mohammad Ali Mirza, who was assigned with the government of the capital during his father's journey to Europe, enabled to thwart the disturbances with the help of Sayyid Abdullah Bihbihani. The use of Bihbihani's influence made it clear that tacit cooperation existed between the *ulema* and the merchants in their opposition to the government.

The close relationship between Sayyid Abdullah Bihbihani and Sayyid Mohammad Tabatabai and a conscious alliance between the religious community and the merchants had far-reaching impact. The historian Kasravi considered as the prelude of the Constitutional Revolution. The leadership of the movement was provided by these two men outwardly.

During their protest, the *ulema* demanded for the foundation of a "house of justice" (*adalat Khaneh*). Initially, the government was not in mood in accept it, but when pressure was mounted, the government accepted it. Ayn-ud-Daula promised solemnly to Tabatabai that he would, as soon as possible, establish the *adalat Khaneh*, but when Tabatabai saw no sign of the pledge being kept, he started to demand the establishment of a *Majlis*, a Consultative Assembly. The *ulema* used Islamic idiom to arouse the popular feeling against the government whenever they found that people are being oppressed by the state apparatus. They assumed the legitimate enforcer of Islamic law, hence and expansion and penetration of their function.

The Constitutional Revolution (1905-1909) led to the enactment of the new constitution. The accomplishment of the constitution was a climax to a century of friction and conflict between the state and the *ulema*. The new constitution defined the clergy's power. The Article 1 of the constitution stated that *Imami Shiism* was the religion of the state. Moreover, the *ulema* prevailed in their wish to create a five-member board (Article 2) to review parliamentary legislation.[100] The membership of the board would compose of individuals appointed from among the top religious leaders themselves. This was never materialized even in the remaining Qajar period and throughout Pahlavi dynasty. But the constitution of the Islamic Republic has created such body, the Council of Guardians (Article 142-147).

---

100 Peter Avery, *Modern Iran* (London: Ernest Benn, 1965), pp. 130-131.

Pahlavi Dynasty and the Islamic Revolution

Reza khan sought to have close relationship with the *ulema*. He got their support from Najaf but not from Qum. In order to get their support, he played a significant role in facilitating their return although it is true that the British and the Iraqi government authorities were predisposed to their resumption of residence in the holy city. Naini sent a letter to the Prime Minister of Iran thanking him for the military escort he had provided the exiled *ulema* for their safe return journey. Reza khan strengthened his relationship with Naini by paying a visit to Najaf in January in 1925.

Reza khan began modernization. He started reform in administration on the European model, firstly started by Mirza Taqi Amir Kabir during the reign of Nasir-ud-Din Shah that was opposed by the ulema, and again reform was started by Mirza Husayn Khan Sipahsalar. In the process of modernization, the ulema's powers were striped off, so, they opposed it. Reza Shah followed the same line and curtailed the power of the clergy. He brought major changes in the educational and legal system of the country. *Urf* courts were guarded with heavy powers that were under the government control and *Shar* courts came under the control of the clergy, they had no much more functions. Those were appointed as judge who got degree in law from government colleges or universities as recognized the government. The regime curtailed the jurisdictions of the *Shar* courts in the law of 30 November 1931. This statute prescribed:

> Only the state courts and the office of the Attorney-General could approve the referral of a case to a religious tribunal. The latter could only take up matters related to marriage, divorce and the appointment of trustees and guardians. The activity of the *Shar* courts came under the supervision of the Attorney-General. Neither could the *Shar* courts pronounce sentence, being limited only to the determination of innocence and guilt in the narrow range of issues that served as their field of competence. Only state courts could pass sentences. Too, they were permitted the right of review of decisions made by *Shar* courts.[101]

The gradual encroachment upon the *ulema's* status and power continued, the government pursued the broad strategy and allowed the state administration to define the jurisdictions of the religious institution. Avery mentioned the position of the *ulema* that sharply changed from

---

101 Akhavi, n. 28, p. 40.

1925 to 1928:

> Early in that year the Queen, his consort and mother of the Crown prince, inadvertently let her veil slip to show part of her face during a ceremony in the Shrine Mosque at Qum. The officiating preacher denounced her for it. The Shah was in the Qum the next day with two armoured cars and a party of troops on call. He entered the mosque without taking his boots off and thrashed the *mullah*. He also ordered the arrest and removal of three criminals who in accordance with ancient procedure, had taken sanctuary in the mosque of precincts.[102]

The Uniformity Dress Law of December 1928 was considered as an attack on the religious institutions. Article 2 of this law specified the strata of society that were exempted. The traditional dress was ban for man and women had to remove their veil. Despite mandatory dress code to all, some people were exempted from the law.

The Shah brought many changes in the educational system of the country to lessen the religious hold over it. The schools and *madarssa* were run and administered by clergy on their own wishes. The government sought to make the educational system secular to maximize centralize authority. In January-February 1934, the Ministry of Education announced its permanent curriculum of studies for the intermediate and higher cycles in the theological colleges. The reforms in the educational system were brought not only at the lower level but at the higher level also. There was absence of various prayer and sermon books from the government curriculum.

The *ulema*-state relations were uneasy during Reza Shah because of his policies. He striped off their numerous powers consequently the influence of the *ulema* tended to decline. Their presence in the *Majlis* had been declined, "whereas the *ulema* constituted forty percent of deputies in the Sixth *Majlis* (1926-28), and around thirty percent in the Seventh (1930-32), the Eleventh *Majlis* which met in 1937 did not include even a single well-known and important figure from the *ulema*."[103]

---

102 Avery, n. 100, p. 288.

103 Donald Wiber, Reza Shah: The Resurrection and Reconstruction of Iran (New York, 1975), p. 263.

During Reza Shah, the *ulema* had been marginalized. The negative policies of the Shah towards the religious organizations resulted in marginalization of the *ulema*. With the abdication of Reza Shah in September 1941 in favour of his son, the political atmosphere of the country changed, and again the religious leaders began to assert themselves in the political domain. The ulema's involvement in this period derived from the ideas and actions of Sayyid Abu al-Qasim Kashani. This political activist and agitator, who had studied with the constitutionalist *ulema* of Najaf in the early part of the century- namely Mullah Mohammad Kazim Khurasani and Shaykh Husein Khalil Tehrani- saw his role as guardian of national and *Shii* interest against British imperialism. But his political maneuverings became politically significant only after the end of World War II. He played major role in the early 1950s.

The comeback of the *ulema* can be traced in the form of assertion of *Shii* public morality and culture. The religious leaders demanded to rescind the ban which was imposed by Reza Shah on public held passion plays (*Taziyah*) and narratives (*Rawzeh Khani*). This was accompanied by a return of the veil in city streets. Their agitation was success in causing the dismissal of the Governor of Khurasan province, who had been from the very beginning condemned by the *ulema* as the instigator of the 1935 Mashhad incidents.

The female enfranchisement issue united the *ulema*. The Shah sought to grant voting right to women in the way of process of modernization. When Musaddiq became Prime Minister in 1951 sought to grant voting right to women but in vain. Clergy pressure under the leadership of Burujirdi and Bihbihani, forced the Prime Minister Musaddiq to withdraw the bill on the women's vote which he had placed in the Assembly in late 1952.

The *ulema's* influence grew in this period because of rise of foreign influence in the forms of Western culture and communism. The Anglo-Iranian Oil Company (AIOC) was perceived by the *ulema* as the British imperialism over Iran which had been exploiting Iran for years. In 1951, the *ulema* intervened in politics and issued fatawa, the nationalization of Anglo-Iranian Oil Company. It is no doubt that this development marked the highest point of manifestation of politicization of the clergy's role in Iranian society since the Constitutional Revolution. *Fatawas* were issued from all sides including the *atabat*, Tehran, and the provinces. Ayatollah

Mohammad Taqi Musavi Khuansari, a *mujtahid*, who came out in favour of Ayatollah Kashani's idea of nationalisation and cited the *hadith* attributed to Mohammad, "he who, upon waking without concerning himself with the affairs of Muslims is not himself a Muslim. The faithful had no choice but to unite and cleave to the position advanced by Kashani as to nationalisation of the AIOC".[104] The *fatawas* of nationalisation of AIOC was issued from the various parts of the country.

The relationship between the clergy and the state deteriorated in the late 1950s and the early 1960s. The final expression of this fast deterioration came in the form of exile of Ayatollah Khomeini in 1963 to Turkey and later on he went to Iraq. The Shah's autocracy increased and determined to contain the influence of the *ulema* in society. He brought major structural changes in society that was called "White Revolution". The main purpose of this White Revolution was to contain and minimize the influence of the clergy in society. The Shah introduced the new Land Act which deprived the religious institutions and clergy to hold over their land which was the backbone of their financial sources. The *ulema* confronted with the regime on four main issues, (i) the growing autocracy of the Shah (2) the Land law; (3) Women's right; (4) the corruption of the regime.

Ayatollah Burujirdi, *marja-i taqlid*, wrote a letter to Jafar Bihbihani on 13 February 1960 complaining about the land reform bill drafted by the government in late 1959 and submitted it to the *Majlis* for its approval. Burujirdi declared that this bill was ill-advised against the *Sharia*. This land bill did not only contravene the holy law of Islam but constitution as well. Burujirdi asked Bihbihani to raise the matter in the *Majlis*, Bihbihani sent the Burujirdi directive to the speaker of the *Majlis* together with a covering letter stating his own objections to the bill.

Burujirdi-Bihbihani's reaction to the land reform bill marked a clear break in the cooperation between the *ulema* and state on public policy. It was the first public manifestation of clergy displeasure. The *ulema* were worried about the state's encroachment in their affairs. The *ulema* dominated the social spheres since it was a question of the structure of political power in society.[105] The unrest among the clerics was seen. The

---

104 Akhavi, n. 28, P.64.

105 The questions of social justice are addressed within the framework of the configuration and levels of power should be clear, given the fact that arrangements for the resolution of questions of social justice are formed by these possessing such power.

government did not want unrest among the *ulema* and conceded the their demand: religious instructions in the secular schools; closing down places of public entertainment on days of religious observances; reaffirming of the Shah's commitment to uphold the faith; assistance in the construction of new mosques; permitting greater numbers of pilgrims to participate in the annual pilgrimages to Mecca as organised by the Endowments Organisation etc.

The Land Bill of December 1959 ratified on 17 May 1960, was not in operation due to many internal loopholes. The death of Burujirdi, *marja-i taqlid* in March 1961, precipitated a new situation in the country. On 11 November 1961, the Shah promulgated an edict ordering the government to implement the May 1960 land laws.

The protest of the high ranking clergy to the land reform bill of December 1959 was natural. However, the bill endangered the vital interests of the *Shii* institutions and the requirements of the *ulema*. The *ulema* wanted to retain both religious and social roles and sought to establish the financial autonomy of the religious institutions. Historically, the sources of revenue of the *ulema* had consisted of, income from legal and clerical duties, such as registration of titles, noturisation of affidavits, court fees etc; annual revenues form endowed properties; contributions by the faithful in the form of religious taxes (*Khums*).

One of the unique features of the Iranian society was that the ulema were not dependent on the state assistance. There was an independent unique source of financial support for that stratum: voluntarily contributions by the people. Reliance on the people's largesse rendered the Iranian *ulema* independent of the state, a situation that was unique in the West Asia, over most of which the state had co-opted the clergy through its subsidization. The main contributor of the *ulema's* income was the masses. Therefore, any attempt to reform the structure of religious institution must receive their approval.

In addition to the financial dependence on the mass, another feature of the financial organization of the Iranian clergy was its extreme decentralization. As the system was constituted in 1962, the various *marja-i taqlid* sent their agents out to the provinces to collect the *Khums* form the faithful. Among all these sources, the land was the main source of income for the *ulema*.

The clergy opposed the land law on two grounds. First, the impact of the reform upon land held by the clergy as *waqf*, the revenues of which supported mosques, madarssa, ceremonials, and clergy/religious student salaries, stipends, emoluments and pensions; second, the *Sharia* laid stress on the sanctity of private property.[106] Thus, the *ulema's* opposition to the land reform bill was natural since it was the main source of their revenues.

Under White Revolution, the Shah started education in remote areas through the creation of Literacy Corps which was monopolised by the *ulema* since long time. The educational system of the country was basically run and administered by the *ulema* in which the religious educations were given to the students according to their own will. The head of the institutions determined that what should be taught to the students. The educational institution was an instrument through which they disseminated their ideas relating to religion and maintained their hold over society. So, the educational institution was the powerful means to inject the idea in the blood of the new generation for carrying out their ideas.

On the other side, the government was also determined to grant voting right to the women. In 1959, Burujirdi received Prime Minister, Iqbal, in Qum and effectively vetoed the regime's plan for a women's day parade in Tehran. The female enfranchisement was the long issue upon which the *ulema* reacted sharply.

The political reason for the opposition of the clergy was fundamental: arbitrary rule; the granting of the extraterritoriality, and more generally, foreign control of the certain aspects of the economy; the nation's policy in the Arab-Israel conflict, according to which oil was sold to Israel and cooperation between the two countries intelligence took place.

There was anxiety of the regime over the revival of deep-seated anti-foreign sentiment in religious circles. It had been Ayatollah Kashani who had successfully stoked the fires of anti-British emotions in the late forties and early fifties. Relations with Israel were later to become a powerful source of conflict between the Shah and Ayatollah Khomeini in mid-sixties. The conflict between religious section and Pahlavi dynasty began during the reign of Reza Shah. This conflict continued under Mohammad Reza

---

106 See Talqani, "Nazre Islam dar Barah-yi Malikiyat" *Guftar-I Mah dar Nameyandan-i Rafi Rasti Din,* Vol. III (Tehran: Kitabkhanah – yi Saduq, 1341 Sh/1962), in which he argued that principle of private property ownership is protected under Islamic law.

Shah and in 1963 erupted into the major religious opposition to his reign and policies. Khomeini first appeared on political scene, being arrested in 1963 and exiled first in Turkey and later to Iraq.

The government sought to penetrate in religious institutions. It established the Endowment Organisation in 1965, was supposed to play a key role. In the mid 1960s, the organisation began the publication of a journal which attempted to glorify the culture as mystical aspect of Islam. The image it wished to convey was of Islam as a state religion. With the creation of the Endowment Organisation, the government intended to take over madarssa administration.

The endowments organizations also provided financial support to students in *dabistan* (primary schools), *dabiristan* (secondary schools,) and *danishgah* (universities). These secondary schools included certain programmes for religious education in which some candidates could specialize. This was specially the case for the higher levels of learning.

In the 1960s and 1970s, the Pahlavi regime increased its pressure on the clergy. It continued its nationalization of religious institutions, took over mosques, shrines, religious schools, and transferred them to the State's Organisational endowments.[107] As the clergy's freedom of action was more and more restricted, increasing numbers of the *ulema* became hostile to the Shah.

The clergy-State relation was severely deteriorated in the 1970s. In 1972, the regime was increasingly seeking ways of actions against the ulema. The government sought to contain the spread of religion, so, it created a Religious Corps and shut down the Husayniyah Irshad which had become the threat of government. This was shortly after the commemoration of the 2500th year of monarchy in Iran. The celebration of the 2500th year of monarchy brought furore among the ulema, they thought that the shah is interested in exalting the monarchy which is incompatible with Islam.

By keeping the basic structure of policy, the Shah issued an imperial edict for the creation of the Religion Corps in August 1971. The reason for the creation of this *Sipah-e Din* was called for to propagate the ordinances of Islam and place spirituality at an equal level with desire for material progress under the banner of the White Revolution. Religion Corps fell

---

107 For detail see Akhavi, no. 28 P. 132.

under the state bureaucratic jurisdiction. The regime also created within the Endowment Organisation a Department for Religion Propaganda. The department was accountable for the training of religious propagandists. The Religious Corps and the Religious propagandists ostensibly constituted the regimes, vanguard of loyalists.

The modernization of the industry resulted increase in the higher number of jobs available in the urban areas that led to massive migration to the cities, especially Tehran. A city had no slums until the late 1960s suddenly had millions of recently migrated slum-dwellers who lived under extremely precarious condition.[108] The new religious organisations sprung up among the masses that strengthened the *ulema's* position. Most of these organizations were founded after 1965 and associated with the groupings of humbler occupations or of poor city quarters. Their names, such as Religious Association of Shoemakers, of Workers, of Public Baths, of the Guild of Fruit-Juicers, of Tailors and of the Desperate of (Imam) Husein. One must not forget that while these organizations were expanding, all forms of independent political activities were banned. Religion become the only out let for oppositional leaning in the country.

The complex structure of the organised opposition was not clearly defined of mass unprivileged and unsophisticated people, some educated for whom every thing about the Shah's political system and the Western culture introduced, was meaningless and oppressive. This category was consisted of newly urbanized but discontented persons who had been uprooted form the rural areas by the land reform programme of the White Revolution; some of the lower middle classes in the cities; and a large segment of the youth who had been divested of sense of cultural identity and alienated by the old socio-political structure. The opposition forces composed of a broad coalition of modern as well as of pre-capitalist or pre-industrial sectors, Islam had come to play a major and growing mobilisational role in the process. Islam was the only force within the civil society that the Shah could not manage to crush, and it was thus able to provide the organisation of ideology that all revolutions need.[109]

---

108 Farhad Kazemi, *Poverty and Revolution in Iran* (New York: New Yrok Univ. Press 1980), PP. 91-95.

109 Fred Halliday "The Iranian Revolution: Ulema, Development and Religioius Poulism," in F. Halliday and H Alavi, eds, *State and Ideology in the Middle East' and Pakistan* (London: Macmillan Education, 1988), PP. 39-49.

The causes of Revolution may be said that clergy rationalization, ideological statements, organizational activity and mobilization of resources proved absolutely critical in the unfolding development. The issues which the *ulema* had been responding were the issues which also affected other social forces in society. The intellectuals had long been sharply attacking censorship. The entrepreneurs and industrialists, who had entered into massive business from their former position as landowners faced a deteriorating credit and cash- flow problem in the year 1979-78 as the country found itself borrowing on the international financial markets. Agriculturists suffered from highly irrational and chaotic agrarian polices of the regime. The breakneck pace of industrialization had entirely destroyed the balance between the industrial and agricultural sectors. Peasants were becoming alienated because of the economic weakness. All these sectors had complaints about the phenomenal rise in the cost of living, the growth of a substantial middle-men stratum and by the purchase of high technologies in the west.

The shah's regime could be classified as a neopatrimonial dictatorship, a type of regime in which came to be focused on the person of the despot.[110] A great variety of discontents against the shah emerged in the 1970s. A troublesome world oil market led to domestic economic fluctuation, and the Shah responded with policies that often weakened his political support, for instance, an anti-profiteering campaign in which thousands of businessmen were arrested. Economic insecurity and the Shah's own policies helped to alienate sectors of society, such as middle-class, government workers and other well-off oil workers, who could not normally have been rebellious.[111]

The middle-class intellectuals suffered from the Shah's repression that already existed. The *bazaaris,* the traditional merchant class, and the *ulema,* resented the Shah's policies. The urban domination of West Asian societies confers great importance on the commercial hearts of the cities. Thus, a bazaar is not only a place where goods are bought and sold but, "a multifaceted entity comprising religious, commercial, political, and broadly social elements... and religion is the cement that binds this

---

110 Jack A. Goldstone, "Revolutions and Superpowers" in Jonathan R. Abdelman, eds., *Superpowers and Revolution (*New York: Praeger, 1986), PP. 38-48.

111 On the Shah's contributions to the crisis, see, Marvin Zonis, "Iran: A Theory of Revolution from Accounts of the Revoluition", *World Politics,* Vol. 35, 1983, pp. 595-606.

structure together".¹¹² The bazaar occupied the centers or cities, an area that also includes the mosques and *madarssa*. Thus, merchants and the *ulema* are in daily contact. Their close contact beneficial to each other: the *ulema* needed the *bazaaris* – as a mass basis to put pressure on the government, while the *bazaaris* needed the *ulema's* support and their protection against the arbitrary government. Moreover, merchants were also a prominent source of financial support for the religious institution and their activities.

As the movement to remove the Shah gathered momentum in the 1970s, the Islamic approach to opposition gained popularity. As James Bill points out "the Iranian people took refuge in religion and flocked the *mujtahids* for social and political shelter. When these centers themselves became the targets of regime attack, the *ulema* decided to fight back to the end".¹¹³ Each step the Shah took to contain the influence of the *Shiite* establishment, albeit, further ensured the Islamic character of the revolutionary trend.

The anti-Shah sentiment and the demand for dramatic change, enabled Khomeini to use Islam as ideology as an effective tool to oust the Shah. Khomeini's ultimate successful plan was facilitated not only by the trend in the 1970s toward an Islamic expression of the opposition movement but also by the popularization of the eclectic doctrines, which articulated an ideology in the language of *Shiite* symbolism.

No doubt the organised opposition to the Shah was fragmented but it had the organizational and financial potential to challenge the government at proper moment. The liberalisation policy of the Shah provided this opportunity since the liberalization coincided with the economic reversal of the 1976-79 which had created tension between the state and the merchants, shopkeepers, and industrialists. It facilitated the organised opposition to channel the people s deep-seated grievances into collective action.

The opposition took advantages of liberalization and started protest against the Shah. On the eve of 1978, the President of the United States, Jimmy Carter visited Tehran and applauded the Shah for creating an

---

112 Gustav Thaiss, "The Bazaar as a Case Study of Religious and Social Change," in Ehsan yar-Shater, ed., *Iran Faces the Seventies* (New York: Praeger, (1971), P. 193.

113 James A. Bill, "Power and Religion in Revolutionary Iran", *Middle East Journal Winter*, 1982, P. 27.

oasis of stability in a troubled area. Soon after Carter's visit, Tehran's crisis entered into a new phase. The poorly-organised, reformist, non-violent, and decentralized movement that was confined within Tehran gradually transformed into a more coordinated, radical, violent, and centralized movement that extended to the major urban center of the country. It is noteworthy that the *ulema* captured the leadership of the movement, Khomeini in Iraq and Kazim Shariatmadari in Iran. "Shiism became the umbrella under which divergent groups came together and destabilised the government."[114]

Since the last two decades, the revival of *Shiism* as an ideology of protest had been alarming visible. The religious literature circulated in the masses. Religious periodicals gained wider circulation and religious books became ever more popular. In the period 1954-63, religious books had constituted about 10 percent of the total published books, by 1975 their share had risen to 35.5 percent. From 1965 to 1975, "twenty-six exclusively religious publishing houses were established in Tehran alone, and religious books, considered innocuous by state censors, had the highest circulation of any category".[115] In the universities there was visible increase in the number of veiled women and Islamic student associations. The hundreds of student rioted against co-education at Tehran University in 1976 was symbol of the resurgence of Islam.

The peculiar features of Iranian society was a rapid mobilization of the opposition; Iran was a society with a number of significant urban centers in which opponents of the Shah-clerics, *bazaaris*, students, workers, professionals, urban poor, and so on - were highly concentrated. The protest that started in 1977 greatly accelerated in 1978 and came to be massive in size. Some of the agitations were scheduled according to the Islamic practice of commemorating deaths (i.e.; previous protesters killed by agents of the Shah) at specified intervals. Religious and other opponents of the Shah protested together. The unity of hatred for the Shah greatly overwhelmed their differences and diverse factions came closer to fight against the Shah's autocracy. Educational establishments often closed in acts of protests, and some students radicalized through the *Mujahidin*,

---

114 Mohsen M. Milani, *The Making of Iran's Islamic Revolution: From Monarchy to Islamic Republic* (San Francisco and Oxford: Westview Press, 1994), P. 112.

115 Said Amir Arjomand, "Shiite Islam and the Revolution in Iran", *Government and Opposition*, Vol. 6, Summer, 1981, PP. 311-312.

actively participated in demonstrations.

Islam became not only the language of political opposition for the socially and economically deprived groups but on the other hand, the manifestation of this discontent became mythified through the use of *Shii* symbols. When the grievances of rural migrants to urban areas became entangled in sacred religious symbols and myths, these grievances with great intensity could connect to the Iranian political community in a successful way. Such as *Shiism* was not only a tool in addressing the deeper grievances but also essential to instill these grievances with the mythic force which they could motivate others to revolutionary solidarity and action.[116]

In early January 1978 in Tehran's two newspapers, Khomeini was presented as an agent of colonialism and traitor of non-Persian descent. This news complicated the situation. In support of Khomeini, the *ulema* organised a peaceful rally in Qum on January 9. In support of the protest, *bazaaris* closed down their shops. After arriving the police, rally turned into violent and more than a dozen people were killed. Soon after the Qum episode, riots broke out in seven other cities. The *bazaars* in these cities closed in sympathy with the *ulema*, marked the entry of the shopkeepers and merchants into the revolutionary movement and their historic alliance with the *ulema*. This episode manifested that the religion had gained ground for averting the Shah's any move that perceived anti-Islam and anti-people.

---

[116] See Hamid Dabashi, *The Theology of Discountent* (New York: New York Univ. Press, 1993), which deals with ideologies and idelogoue of the Iranian Revolution. Ayatollah Khomeini was the dominant leader of the revolution in so far as he came to incarnate a *Shiism* which incorporated themes of nationalism and social justice within the symbolics confines of a putatively indigenous, traditional discourse. However, other leaders were also extremely important in forming a *Shia* ideology which was a compelling alternative to the political authority of the Shah. The interesting points about these other ideological leaders is that, though quite different and appealing to different sections of Iranian society, came to work basically, within a religious idiom. Even the *Tudeh*, eventually, accepted the leadership of Khomeini. As *Shiism* became the symbol of absolute rejection of both the Shah and the West, a Paris educated, Shariti looked to, Shiism and, more particularly, a radically politicised *Shiism* such as Khomeini's as the troublebearer of an emphatic rejection of the Shah and the West. Each of these various leaders were important in their own right and each had an appeal to certain sections of Iranian society. Shariati to students, and Bazargan to the middle class. These leaders had very different agendas and followings, but they each helped to create ideological climate which looked to *Shiism* as the alternative to the Shah. Eventually, it was Khomeinin who embodied this alternative

The use of *Shii* symbols and rituals manifested in an uprising in Tabriz in February 1978. The *ulema* planned to commemorate the fortieth day of the death of the martyrs of Qum, an Islamic tradition, in the mosques of Tabriz, the home of Shariatmadari. But the government determined to prevent the escalation of riots to Tabriz, ordered the police to block people from entering mosques. The angry mob went on rampage in which the police fired upon the people and killed. The pulpits were used by the *ulema* to attack the Shah. The *ulema* relied on thousands of mosques, *heyat*, Islamic associations, and the *bazaar* to mobilise the masses against the Shah. The massive network of mobilisation proved effective, and became extremely difficult for the authorities to contain it.

The monarchy as an institution and the Pahlavi Dynasty as the Royal house of Iran became completely unacceptable to Khomeini. During his long exile, he had rebuked the regime and the Shah for having failed to defend Islam, for promoting despotism, insulted the clergy and permitted foreigners to exercise control over the country's resources. In his strong opposition to the Shah's imperial traditions, he stated that Islam opposed the system of monarchy.

However, he declared in his proclamation of January 1978, "Mohammad Reza Khan (Shah) is a traitor and rebel whose overthrow is ordained by law."[117] In November 1978, he called for the establishment of an Islamic Republic in Iran and asserted, "our Islamic objective is the toppling of the monarchical regime and the overthrow of the Pahlavi Dynast."[118] In his support, the Iranian people organised demonstrations against the policies of the regime. To put pressure on the government, he adopted various tactics like the vast demonstrations within the context of the general strike, recompensing striking workers, peasants, functionaries, artisans, desertion by members of the armed forces and fraternization with civilians.

As *Muharram* came closer, banks went on strike, on 26 November 1978 general strike was announced. Most *bazaars*, stores and government offices closed down. Such processions were central to the observance of the particularly holy days in this period, and the government's restriction was perceived not only as a political gesture but as a form of religious repression.

---

117 Akhavi, no. 28, p. 167.

118 Ibid., p. 167

Islam An Ideology

As a result, large numbers of Iranians defied the ban, and in Tehran alone almost 100 people killed by martial law authorities. Khomeini called for "rivers of blood" to flow on the 10th *Muharram (Ashura)*, or the 11th of the December 1978, in order to topple the monarchy.[119]

On the first day of *Muharram* all was calm until late in the evening when worshipers were on their way to home from mosques, broke up into groups and rampaged through the streets shouting anti-Shah slogans. The slogans were *Marg-bar Shah* (Kill the Shah), *Allah-o Akbar* (God is Great), and *Khomeini-ra baz arid* (Bring back Khomeini).

"Death to the Shah!" was a central slogan and theme of demonstrations in 1978. The Shah was widely represented with the deaths of prominent opposition figures and his troops killed demonstrators helped to depict the evil nature of the regime, especially the Shah himself. The slogan "Death to the Shah!" first emerged in February 1978, and used throughout the Revolution. Khomeini referred to the protests that included closures of *bazaars* and universities, stated in a speech while he was in Iraq:

> These closings represent a form of active protest against the person of the Shah... The people have identified the true criminal. Bearing to the themes of the demonstrations, a week later he congratulated those who have risen up...with the crises of "Death to the Shah!"[120]

At the first day of *Muharram*, shooting continued throughout the country where a large member of people being killed. The government rescinded its ban on processions for *Tausha* and *Ashura*, the two holiest days in the important month of *Muharram*. The government was compelled to lift ban on processions in the month of *Muharram* because people had defied the imposition of ban for the procession. "At the same time it banned the use of motorcycles and vans, ostensibly to keep traffic down, although automobiles were not banned."[121]

The *Tausha* came finally with major processions throughout the country. In Tehran alone, around two million people marched through

---

119 *The New York Times*, 4 December, 1978, quoted in Akhavi, no. 28, p. 168.

120 Khomeini quoted in Shaul Bakhash, *The Reign of the Ayatollah: Iran and the Islamic Revolution* (New York: Basic Books, 1984), p. 45; Said Amir Arjomand, The Turban for the Crown (New York:Oxofor Univ. Press, 1984), p. 103.

121 Jerrold D. Green, *Revolution in Iran: The Politics of Countermobilisation* (New York: Praeger Publishers, 1982), p. 128.

the streets. On the following day came *Ashura*, when large processions took place. As the previous day, most formal activity was absent. In Tehran procession was less organised and a little bit rowdier. People openly shouted "Death to the Shah!" but there was no apparent tension. Similar demonstrations took place throughout the country.

This formalized national amalgamation of politics and religion set the tone for the revolution. Events of *Tausha* and *Ashura* firmly established Khomeini and his supporters as the leaders of the popular revolution against the Pahlavi Dynasty. As early as 1972, Hamid Algar pointed out that in Iran "protest in religious terms will continue to be voiced and the appeals of men such as Ayatollah Khomeini to be widely heeded".[122] This anticipation of Hamid Algar was proved in 1979 when Khomeini mobilized people in the name of religion and all factions of society came together under the banner of Islam to fight against the Shah. "The Iranian Revolution was both a religious Islamic Revolution and a political revolution cloaked in a religious idiom".[123]

It was commonly accepted that discontent should be voiced in the symbols and language of Islam, and not in terms of other possible universal ideologies because Islam was the uniting force among the different factions of society. One of the most important reasons for the use of religious idioms in the course of Revolution was that the Shah had swept away many secular centers of power, such as political parties. The Shah also tried to outstrip the *ulema*, but could not affect their power, which was seemingly beyond his reach. It is also important that hostility to the Shah was generalized into a hatred for all things– the Shah was identified by virtue of his US ally with a poisonous secular westernisation.

Shii religious symbols were used in the course of Revolution in discrete ways by these different leaders. It provided a space on which the Iranian political community could most easily form the consensus necessary for a united revolutionary front to work against the Shah. These symbols were employed to unite the people of the different factions in opposing the Shah. These symbols were being invested with the cultural myth of a collective consciousness in which those symbols took on a structural power which deeply affected the self-articulation of such a collectivity.

---

122 Algar, n. 89 P. 225.
123 Green, n. 121, p, 130.

Religion became a medium to spread message. Public emotion was aroused and used by Khomeini under the banner of religion. Religion united diverse community that could forge a revolutionary consensus to overthrow a political order. It is in this sense that religious ideology is the key and the corner-stone to the Iranian Revolution, a sense which does not preclude the importance of social economic, and political factors.

Khomeini was victorious in this revolution. Theocracy emerged because Khomeini and his followers successfully built an institutional apparatus and avoided political division over the meaning of Islam and anti-imperialism. "In a revolution, ideology takes over politics, transcends social differences among participants moving them in a communitarian relation and orienting them to act directly against the Shah. It is ideology that distinguishes revolution from routine contentious for power."[124]

The collapse of the political system culminated with the departure of the Shah (16 January 1979), the resignation of the caretaker government of Shahpur Bakhtiyar (11 February 1979) and the referendum in favour of the Islamic Republic was, however, directed by the *ulema*. Their participation, providing centuries of *ulema* quietism and aversion to overthrow regime, was an unprecedented act in Iranian history.

In the aftermath of the Revolution, Islam has been institutionalized with the expression of *Velaya-e Faqih* (guardianship of Jurisconsult). The political culture of Iran has been completely changed after the Revolution. At the social level, un-Islamic norms and mores have been divorced and Islamic culture has been introduced.

The 1979 Iranian Revolution is a unique *Shiite* phenomenon in itself because throughout Revolution Islam was used as ideology. In the long history of Iran, Islam has been used by the *ulema* as an instrument of protectors and defender of the masses against the suppressive and repressive policy of the monarch and foreign encroachment in Iran. As had been seen in the Reuter Concession in 1872 and Tobacco concession in 1892, the *ulema* directly confronted with the state against the granting concessions to the foreigners. But during the Safavids, situation was very different. The Safavid Shahs managed to maintain good relations with the *ulema* in one way or other even through making matrimonial relations

---

[124] Mansoor Moaddel, "Ideology as Episodic Discourse: The Case of the Iranian Revoluition" *American Sociological Review*, vol. 57, 1991, p. 354.

in the families of the *ulema*. The Qajars were failed to do like this and confrontations became an inevitable which raised the question of legitimacy of the monarchy. The constitutional movement was the culmination of the previous developments which brought monarchy's foundation at stake.

The volatile condition of the Qajar was exploited by Reza Shah, buried the Qajar dynasty and became king of Iran. Initially, relations between the *ulema* and Reza Shah were good, but not at later stages. Even his son, Mohammad Shah, sought to maintain good and healthy relations with the *ulema* but could not materialize. In 1951 during the agitation over nationalization of Anglo-Iranian Oil Company, monarchy was in shaky position. The decades of 1960s and 1970s were the decades of the *ulema* because they successfully mobilized the masses against the Shah in the name of Islam and diverse factions of society came under the umbrella of Islam in opposition to the Shah. Finally, under the leadership of Imam Khomeini uprooted the monarchy and Iran entered into a new phase and became a theocratic state.

ISLAMISATION OF POLITICS

The Islamic Revolution (1979) was a unique revolution in the history of Islam which was erupted in the name of religion. The monarchy's demise, and the revolutions rapid metamorphosis into the Islamic Republic reflected the *ulema's* maneuvering capability. Islam became the determining object for the system as a whole. This revolution changed the structural nature and functional scope of the three branches of the government, namely legislature, executive and judiciary. The 1979 Revolution's unique feature has been seen in form of the creation of the post of the *Velayat-e Faqih*[1].

The term *Velayat-e Faqih* is coined by Khomeini. The concept of *Velayat-e Faqih* has been derived from the *Imamate* system, as *Imam* had authority and power to rule over society and only legitimate ruler, in the same way, the *Velayat-e Faqih* has all these powers. This theory is not innovation at theoretical and conceptual level rather than replica of the *Imamate* system where the *Faqih* is all in all in the governance of the country, and only this post is the source of legitimacy for the system as whole in the absence of the *Twelfth Imam*. Only the *Faqih* has right to rule over society and is a legitimate ruler. On this conviction, Khomeini developed the theory of the *Velayat-e Faqih* and became first *Velayat-e Faqih* of the Islamic Republic of Iran.

The structural changes were brought in the three branches of the government in the post-Revolutionary Iran. The President of the Islamic Republic of Iran is the head of the executive, is directly elected by the people, and is next to the Leader (Spiritual Leader). Any problem created within or among these branches, is sorted out by the *Velayat-e Faqih*, who is the leader of the nation. The President cannot appoint his Council of Ministers at his own will, but he has to propose the name of the Council of Ministers before the *Majlis*, and the *Majlis* has right to approve or disapprove proposed names of the Council of Ministers.

---

1 The term *Velayat-e Faqih* is a persian term which means the Guardianships of the Jurisprudent.

There is an independent constitutional body, the Council of Guardians, which evaluates and examines the legislation of the *Majlis* that a bill is passed in the *Majlis* is according to *Sharia* or not. This body's function is not only confined to legislation but also interprets the constitution whenever needed. The permanent nature of this body has reflected its significance in the Iranian political system.

"And you God is One God. There is no God but He."[2] "He is Allah, The One; Allah, the Eternal, Absolute."[3] "All authority belongs to God alone."[4] The whole Islamic political philosophy is rotating around the notion that Allah (God) is sovereign, all in all, and only He is the law-giver. He is the real sovereign and all others are His subjects. He is the law-giver, and absolute legislation authority vests in Him. Even no one in this world, is parallel to Him. The Islamic political theory is based on this notion, and all theoretical and conceptual sketches of the Islamic State are drawn on the basic faith of Islam.

> Islamic government is neither autocratic nor absolute but constitutional. Although it is not constitutional in the current sense of the word i.e., based on the approval of laws in accordance with the opinion of the majority. Islamic government is constitutional in this sense that the rulers are subject to a certain set of conditions in governing and administering the country, conditions that are set forth in the Quran and the Sunna of the Most Noble Messenger. It is the laws and ordinances of Islam comprising this set of conditions that must be observed and practiced. That is why the Islamic government is defined as the rule of divine-law over men.[5]

The Islamic government is nothing but the rule of God, and the divine-law is the source of all laws, and on this God-gifted law, the foundation of the Islamic State is based.

The twenty five hundred years old monarchical system of government demised in February 1979 after a glorious Revolution. Khomeini dismissed monarchy and hereditary forms of government as being unIslamic. The 1979 Revolution is watershed in Iranian history that culminated into

---

2   *Al-Quran*, 2:163

3   Ibid, 112:1-2

4   Ibid, 3:154

5   Ayatollah Rouhollah Khomeini, *Hukumat-e Islami* (Islamic Government) (Tehran, 1971), pp.45-46

the establishment of the Islamic Republic. The 1979 Revolution's rapid metamorphosis into an Islamic Revolution, was a product of the *ulema's* political manoeuvreness and shrewdness. A close alliance between religion and state was made an attempt to legitimise political power by a religious ideology. The ascendancy of clergymen to power, led an ideological Islamisation of Iran. After Revolution, Iran's political culture changed in two ways, first, existing monarchical system and its pervasive effect demised and eroded during Revolution; and second, at the same time, the revolution gave birth to the Islamic government that was envisioned by Iran's religious community for long time.

The unique and the most important feature of post-Revolutionary Iran is the institutionalisation of the post of the *Velayat-e Faqih*. The concept of the *Velayat-e Faqih* legitimizes the *Faqih's* role as the guardian of the people. The three branches of the government, executive, legislative, and judiciary are under the influence of Islam.

Genesis and Development of the *Velayat-e-Faqih*

The *Shii*[6] political theory is based on the doctrine of *Imamate*. The first person who gave "a theological exposition of the doctrine of the *Imamate* is said to have been Ali Ibn Mithan."[7] Ali Ibn Mithan said that on "the Prophet Mohammad's death Ali was *afdal an-nas* (the most excellent of man) who was designated by Mohammad.[8] It is faith of *Shia* that the Prophet Mohammad designated his successor to Ali to lead the community. "Prophet Mohammad was the first person in the history of Islam who undertook the implementation of laws, the establishment of ordinances, and administration of the society, thereby bringing into existence the Islamic State."[9] Thus, the Prophet Mohammad is the founder of the Islamic State in the history of Islam, and who also designated his successor to maintain its continuity.

---

6 The term *Shii* will be used to denote '*Ithna Ashari*' 'Twelver' or *Jafari* branch of *Shiism* unless otherwise noted.

7 W. Montgomery Watt, "The Significance of the Early Stages of Imami Shiism", in N. R. Keddie, ed, *Religion and Politics in Iran: Shiism from Quietism to Revolution* (New Haven and London: Yale Univ. Press, 1983), p.24

8 Ibid, p.24

9 Mohsen AzimiEtemadi, "Political Thought in Islam", *The Message*, Quarterly, vol.5, no.2, Dec. 1995- Feb 1996 (*Rajab-Ramadan* 1416), p.17

Those who were busy in theorizing the concept of *Imamate* doctrine on the basis of the Prophet Mohammad's designating successor that their basic aim and principle seems to have been that "authority must come from above and cannot be conferred by the vote or acclamation of ordinary people."[10] This is the corner-stone of the *Imamate* system that each and every *Imam* is appointed by their predecessors, those have had divine authority to do it. It is crystal-clear that authority can only be conferred by someone who already has authority, so, the method of appointment of an *Imam* must be designated by his predecessor as the Prophet Mohammad had designated Ali. So in *Shia*, *Imam* has prerogative, discretionary and legitimate right to appoint his successor and no one has right to say anything on the issue of designating successor. The people have nothing to say and will have to obey without any question because they are only follower of the line of *Imam*. Here is a question, why the people should obey their *Imam* appointed by his predecessor without questioning? These *Imams* legitimize their succession by connecting themselves with the Prophet Mohammad and they believe that they are the descendant of the Prophet.

It is the *Shia's* belief that the only Prophet's cousin and son-in-law, Ali ibn Abu Taleb, and his direct descendant *Shiite Imams* have had the divine authority and ability and capacity to understand Islamic law and implement it. According to *Shia*, Ali is the first *Imam*, who was designated by the Prophet. The Prophet during his life-time ruled over society, he had absolute authority over society in all matters then he designated his successor to Ali, Ali had also the same authority like the Prophet, to tackle and handle the affairs of society in all matters. Such as *Imam* should have absolute authority like Ali. *Imam* ought to be a divinely inspired and guided man and has right to speak last word on any disputed question of God's law.

When we see the long history of *Shii Imamate* system, we find that except Imam Ali Abu Taleb, "no *Imam* ever held the reins of government, the *Imamate* provide an alternative, heaven-inspired government for *Shia*."[11]

The Eleventh *Imam* of the series, Hasan Al-Askari died in January

---

10 Watt, n.7, p.25

11 Homa Omid, *Islam and the post-Revolutionary State in Iran* (London: Macmillan Press, 1994), p.5

874. One or two year afterward, his son, Abu al Qasim Mohammad, mysteriously disappeared, the date is often used as 878, but the whole matter is very obscured and even the *Imami* sources are not unanimous on this issue. It is a matter of faith among *Shias* that Imam Hasan Al-Askari's son, Mohammad is mysteriously disappeared and who is the Twelfth *Imam* of the *Shia*.

According to *Imami* theory, the disappearance was a voluntary going into occultation or concealment. It also implies that in this state, the Twelfth *Imam* was not subject to mortality but who would return as the Mehdi at an appropriate time. It is the *Shia's* faith that Mohammad went into occultation but he is still mysteriously present as *Imam-al Zaman* (the *Imam* of the day, often described as the *Hidden Imam*) and he is fulfilling and performing the requirement for the permanent presence of the *Imam* and at the appointed time, he will return as the Mehdi to bring salvation to the earth.

It is also common belief among the *Shia* that the Twelfth *Imam* was represented on earth by a *Wakil* (agent), who had been contacting to the *Imam*. In fact, there was a succession of four agents, in which fourth, the last agent died in 940 and the time up to that date is known as the period of the Lesser Occultation (*al-Ghaibah al-Sughra*). After the death of the fourth *Wakil* in 940, there was no *Wakil* (agent) who could contact with the Twelfth *Imam*, this period is called the Greater Occultation (*al-Ghaibah al-Kubra*), and still continues. After the occultation of the Twelfth *Imam*, Imam Abu al-Qasim Mohammad ibn Hasan in the ninth century, the *Shii ulema* gradually acquired the mantle of the Prophet.[12]

According to *Shiite*, theoretically all temporal and spiritual authority is vested in the Twelfth *Imam* who is into occultation, since he is into occultation, the exercise of that authority is not possible. Such as, the *Shia* community is left leaderless, so, leader has authority to govern society such as *Imam* governed society before going into occultation. To exercise these functions, the *ulema* would act collectively as *al-naib 'al Imam* (vice-regent), they have an obligation and duty to exercise all the *Hidden Imam's* powers and functions which include ruling or governing the community. Only they are the rightful successor of the *Imam* to lead the community which has been left leaderless.

---

12 For Detail see Roy Mottahedeh, *The Mantle of the Prophet: Religion and Politics in Iran* (New York: Pantheon Books, 1985)

To lead the leaderless *Shia* community, Ayatollah Khomeini's doctrine of *Velayat-e Faqih* is not an innovation in the *Shia* political theory rather it is a revival of an old dormant doctrine. His notion of the *Velayat-e-Faqih* is based on the *Imamate* doctrine, and even we can say it is a replica of the *Imamate* system.

Khomeini has defined *Velaya* (guardianship) clearly, *Velaya* is either existential (*takwini*) or relative (*itibari*). The erstwhile is a spiritual pre-eminence exclusive to the Prophet and the *Imams*; the latter is the social and political duty of the *Faqih* to "administer and rule the state and to implement the laws of the sacred paths."[13] Only *Faqih* has the right to rule and administer the society because he has the legitimate right in this regard and this legitimate right has been derived from the sacred-law.

The *Quranic* verse clearly manifests the rank and status of Prophet Mohammad. "The Prophet has a greater claim on the believers than they have on themselves".[14] The position, status and rank of the Prophet is higher than any other in this world, and even no one id parallel to him in this world. His spiritual status is higher to the rest of the human being in this world. The *Faqih* follows the sayings and doings of the Prophet and implement the *Sunna* and its *Quarnic* precepts.

The term *Velayat-e Faqih* means "authority" or "governance" of the jurisprudence[15] over the affairs of the Muslim community. According to *Shia* tradition, a *Velayat* (guardianship) has been derived from the universal authority of the Twelve *Imams* "descendants of the *Prophet* through his daughter Fatima and his son-in-law Ali, each designated by his predecessor, all immaculate and infallible, who possess a universal authority... in the

---

13 Two types of *Velayat*, the first *takwini* (existential), and the second, *tashri'i* (Legislative) or *shari* (Canonical), the first is the exclusive to the Prophet and the Imams and the second is the duty of the *Faqih*.

14 *Al-Quran*, 33:6

15 "Jurisprudent(s)" will be used to translate *Faqih* (pl. Fuqaha). To avoid any terminological confusion it is to be noted here in order. Religious leaders in *Shiism* consist of the *alem* (pl. *Ulema*), "Scholar", who is learned in religious science; The *Faqih*, "Jurisprudent", who is expert in *Fiqh* (Islamic jurisprudence); and the *mujtahid* who is authorized (possesses the *ijaza*) to exercise the *ijtehad*. These distinctions should not be confused with the hierarchy of the mujtahid based on erudition and size of following: *hujjatul-Islam wa al- Muslimin, Ayatollah fial-almin*, and *Ayatollah al-Ozma fi al alamin*.

things of religion and of the world."¹⁶ Each and every *Imam* is designated by his predecessor who has divine-authority, so, successor has also the divine authority.

According to *Shii fiqh*, there are four types of functions of the *Faqih* (jurisprudent) who exercises over the community. First, guardianship over persons and properties of those who might victimize and maltreated these embody orphans, foundlings, widows and persons of restricted capacities in any way and any form. Traditionally, the *Velayat* assigns powers to the jurisprudent to overrule, dismiss and replace a incompetent, dishonest and corrupt executor or ruler without any delay. Second, the *Faqih's* function is related to religious matters. The *Faqih* has to exercise guardianship over the properties and activities upon which the religious life of the community depends. For instance, these *Faqih* administers the pious charitable, endowments, mosques, *madarssa* and shrines. It falls under the authority of the *Faqih* to supervise religious educational institutions, to arbitrate and divide disputes within the community and to serve as judges and delivers verdict in properly constituted *sharia* courts. These verdicts and judgments are binding to the community as a whole. Third, jurisprudent may exercise a general guardianship over the weal of the Muslim community, covering the responsivly of serving as a social force, aimed at carrying out and implementing the *Quranic* injunction to "command the good and forbid the reprehensible."¹⁷ This type of *Velayat* (governance) must indulge in such type of activities to compel the authorities to release scarce good and commodities, provide social welfare facilities and perdition against the authorities and administration on behalf of the victim of oppression and injustice.¹⁸ Guardianship of *Faqih* over the first three is unanimous among the *Shia ulema*, but, the fourth, is controversial and has lack of unanimity over this guardianship. The unanimity does not take place on the fourth claim that has been forwarded by some *Shia* scholars, that jurisprudent enjoy a *Velayat*, empowering them to exercise direct political authority to conduct the day-to-day operations of the government, particularly, in

---

16   Al-Babul Hadi Ashrar Hasan ibn Yusuf al-Halili, *A Treaties on the Principle of Shiite Theology*, Trans. by W M Miller (London, 1928), p.62

17   *Al-Quran*, 9:112

18   Nikki R. Keddi, *Religion and Rebellion in Iran: The Tobacco Protest of 1891-1892*, (London, 1966). The author has highlighted *ulema's* activities who opposed injustice and oppression in society.

the times of danger or impeding chaos on behalf of the *Hidden Imam*.[19] There has been no disagreement over the rights of the *Faqih* to indulge and engage in political activities aimed at redressing injustices done by the ruler or protecting and preventing from declining the religious. Nonetheless, the fourth claim that has been put forward by some *Shii* theoreticians extends beyond the actual administration of government and brings political processes under institutional control, powers which belong to the universal authority of the Imams which is coming down form the Prophet and his designates successor, Ali.

Universal authority was vested in Ali with his appointment as caliph. There was no such question during the lifetimes of the remaining the *Imams* except Hussein to whom *Shia* claim universal political authority, only Husein sought political power. He fought a historic battle at Karbala with Yazid to hold and retain his political power. In this historic battle, he lost himself and entire his family members and got martyr in the history of Islam. This battle is historic in itself because in spite of losing his all family members, did not bow and surrender his political authority to Yazid. That is why, the later *Imams* sough political authority to redress injustice and oppression and run society. Al-Murtada's treaties "concerning the tenure of office on behalf of the oppressor and nature of the doctrine about its propriety or impropriety assumes that the *Twelfth Imam* is the only rightful ruler of the Muslim community."[20] The *Twelve Imam* is the only rightful ruler of the Muslim community.

The traditional view legitimized participation in governmental function under very restricted circumstances, in which the traditional jurisprudent could intervene in political matter only to redress injustice and to guard and secure Islamic moral standards. But Khomeini's thesis of *Velayat-e Faqih* differs from the traditional point of view. The *marjaiyat* allows that a believer must follow (*taqlid* to) a qualified legal scholar (*mujtahid*) in matter of religious practices if believer himself is not a *mujtahid*, he could be denied political role. Sheikh Murtada Ansari was a *mujtahid* during his lifetimes, advocated that the political activity of jurisprudent should be limited and they should intervene in

---

19 Imam Khomeini supported the idea of political *velayat* in his book *Hukumat-e Islami* that *Velayat-e Faqih* must use the universal authority in the absence of Twelfth Imam.

20 W. Madelung, "A Treaties of the Sharif al Murtada on the Legality of Working of Government (Mas ala fil-amal ma alsultan)", *Bulletin of the School of Oriental and African Studies 43*, (1980), p.24.

political matters only to secure justice and Islamic morality, except this, should not be intervened by jurisprudent. His view was also supported by Ayatollah Mohammad Hasan Shirazi, who invoked *fatawa* (religious decree) against the British Tobacco Concession in Iran in 1892, his *fatawa* was an intervention to secure justice for the peasants of Iran and prevent the expansion of *kafir*[21] influence in the Muslim community. Ayatollah Mohammad Naini also belonged from same school of thought. He was a *mujtahid* as well as leading theoretician of the constitutionalist Revolution. Naini advocates "it is true that the *ulema's* responsibility as General Agents of the *Imam* in all other offices, i.e. rulership is not unquestionably recognized."[22] However, his concept of the political role of jurisprudent is more than simply intervention for securing justice and protecting Islamic norms and values.

Traditionally, *Velayat-e Faqih* in political matters is limited. The *Shii* authorities had claimed political authority for jurisprudent only in the 18th century. The political *Velayat* of jurisprudence has been taken into account only for occasional intervention into political matters to redress injustice and safeguard religion and Muslim society. But Khomeini's notion of the *Velayat-e Faqih* is distinct form theirs because he blends political and universal authority in one and made the *Velayat-e Faqih* a spiritual and political leader like Church and State as was blended in medieval period. He placed to the *Velayat-e Faqih* in licensing position to rule over society in the absence of *Imam* because society is a leaderless society. Khomeini's theory of the *Velayat-e Faqih* is a synthesis of spiritual and temporal affairs.

Khomeini's Notion of the *Velayat-e-Faqih*

The concept of the *Velayat-e Faqih* of Khomeini is incorporated in the constitution of the Islamic Republic of Iran[23] and has acquired a central place in the Iranian political system. This politico-religious post is the source of legitimisation of all the government acts and the government's day-to-day business. Khomeini's exposition of his theory of *Velayat-e Faqih* clearly states that "the Faqih has authority over the ruler."[24] The

---

21   According to Islamic tenets, those who do not believe in Islam, they are called *Kafir*.
22   Abdul Hadi Hairi, *Shiism and Constitutionalism in Iran: A Study of the Role Played by the Persian Residents of Iraq in Persian Politics* (Leided, 1977), p.193
23   Article 5
24   Khomeini, n. 5, p.52

Faqih is the actual ruler of society and has universal authority. If the ruler follows Islam and its rules and regulations, "he (ruler) must submit to the *Faqih*, asking him regarding the laws and ordinances of Islam in order to implement them."[25] Thus, the true rulers are the *Fuqaha* themselves, and rulership ought officially to be theirs unquestionably.

The *Faqih* must possess excellence in moral and belief, and he must be just and untainted by major sin. God assigns powers to administer the affairs of His creature must not be a sinner. God says in this support "My covenants does not embrace the wrongdoer."[26] His covenant Prophet Mohammad and covenants were free from sins and they were the rulers of the Muslim community, in the same way, the *Fuqaha* are the covenant and have the right and authority to rule over the Muslim community.

It is imperative for the *Fuqaha* (rulers), they must have two qualities: Knowledge of the provisions and ordinances of Islam; and justice excellence in belief and morals. These two qualities of the knowledge of the law and justice are present in the *Fuqaha* of present day. If a individual having these two qualities and establishes a government, "he will have the same authority as the Most Noble messenger in the administration of society, and it will be the duty of the people to obey him."[27]

When we talk about the Prophet Mohammad's status, rank and position, and authority over the Muslim community, we must keep in mind that the Prophet's position, status and his spiritual position is higher than any other, but in the matter of administration, the *Fuqaha* and others have the same authority to rule over society as Prophet Mohammad had. "The prophet has higher claims on the believers than their own selves."[28]

> The virtues of the Most Noble Messenger were greater than those of the rest of mankind, and after him, the commanders of the Faithful were the most virtuous persons in the world. But superiority in respect of spiritual virtues does not confer increase in governmental powers.[29]

---

25 Ibid

26 *Al-Quran*, 2:124

27 Khomeini, n.5, p.55

28 Al-Quran, 33:6

29 Khomeini, n.5, p.55

God has granted upon government in the present age, the same powers and authority that were held by the Prophet Mohammad and the Imams in respect of equipping and mobilising armies, appointing governors and levying taxes and expending them for the weal of the Muslims.[30]

There is no difference in exercising the governmental powers between the Prophet and the *Fuqaha*, here difference lies between them only in the spiritual status where the Prophet has the greater virtues than others.

Khomeini's theory of the *Velayat-e Faqih* is based on the notion of the Occultation of the Twelfth Imam that "the just *Faqih* has the same authority and power that the Prophet and the *Imams* had,"[31] barring that his authority does not extend to other *Faqih* and a "*Faqih* does not have authority over all other *Fuqaha* of his own time, being able to appoint or dismiss them."[32] However, Khomeini himself denies "the status (*manzleh*) of the *Faqih* is identical to that of the *Imams* and the Prophet "[33] and asserts that "the *Velayat* (governance) of the Faqih is a rational and extrinsic matter,"[34] and it is only a type of appointment like the appointment of a guardian over a minor. In this way, there is difference between the Prophet and the Imams on the one hand, and the just *Faqih* on the other, because we do not talk here about the status but rather of function. Here authority means government, the administration of the country and implementation of the sacred laws of the *Sharia*. Khomeini emphasises that the *Faqih* enjoys the extrinsic position that is social and political powers of the *Imam*.

The authority and power that "the Prophet and the *Imam* had in establishing a government, executing laws and administering affairs exist also for the *Faqih*."[35] It is the duty of the *Fuqaha* to set up a government in order to implement the laws and protest its territory collectively or individually. If this task falls upon a single *Faqih*, he must fulfill his duty, otherwise, it is a duty that falls upon all the *Fuqaha* as a whole. "Even if, it is not possible to fulfill the task, the authority vested in the *Fuqaha* is not

---

30   Ibid, p.55
31   Ibid, p.55
32   Ibid, p.57
33   Ibid, p.55
34   Ibid, p.56
35   Ibid, p.57

voided because it has been vested in them by God."³⁶ The *Fuqaha* are the real ruler of the society, and society must be governed by them.

The Prophet and the *Imams* had the governmental authority, its does not mean that they have no spiritual status.

> Government and authority belong to the Imam, its does not mean that the imam has not spiritual status. Indeed the Imam has spiritual status that is unconnected with his function as a ruler. The spiritual status of the imam is the universal divine vice-regency that is now and then stated by the imams. It is vice-regency relating to the whole of the creation, by virtue of which, all the atoms in the universal humble themselves before the holder of authority.³⁷

Imam's status and rank is not like the status and rank of the Prophet but his governmental authority is the same as the prophet had.

"It is the duty of the *Imams* and the just *Fuqaha* to exercise governmental institutions to execute divine law, establish the just Islamic order and serve mankind… The governance of the *Faqih* is nothing but the performance of a duty."³⁸ It means that the involvement of the *Faqih* in the day-to-day administration is nothing, but the performance of a duty that has been assigned by the God. The *Fuqaha* are bound by God to perform their duty whatever has been assigned by God and they can not run away form performing these duties, their duty is to govern society and serve mankind. For running the administration and serving the mankind, the ruler "must know the law and be just,"³⁹ these two qualities are prerequisite for the governance of the *Faqih*. The commander of the Faithful put two necessary qualities for the ruler, and the whole discourse revolves around these two points, 'knowledge' and 'justice'. "He should not be benighted and unaware of the law lest in his ignorance he may mislead the people,"⁴⁰ here emphasis is upon the knowledge, but in the remaining sentence the emphasis is upon justice, in its true sense.

---

36   Ibid, p.57
37   Ibid, p.57
38   Ibid, p.60
39   Ibid, p.60
40   Ibid, pp.62-63

The *Mujtahids* and the *Fuqaha* are the successors of the Prophet, disseminating the divine ordinances and instructing men in the sciences of Islam. The Prophet prayed before God and said "O God! Have mercy on my successors."[41] The *Fuqaha's* principal duty is to implement the divine ordinances upon which Islam is based, so, their first and foremost duty is to implement the divine law. The successors of the Prophet are "the *Fuqaha* of Islam. Dissemination of the ordinances of Islam, as well as the teaching and instruction of the people, is the duty of the *Fuqaha* who are just."[42] The governance of the *Fuqaha* means that all acts of the government will be done in the name of the *Fuqaha*, and the *Fuqaha's* action will legitimize the government's function. The *Fuqaha* are the successor of the Prophet, which means to succeed to all the functions of Prophethood. The *Fuqaha* are the sole guardian and the successor of the Prophet to protect the Muslim community form inflicting injustice and oppression.

It is the saying of the Imam that "those believers, who are the *Fuqaha*, are the fortresses of the Islam,"[43] it actually refers to the *Fuqaha*, the duty of being guardian of the faith and beliefs, ordinances, and institutions of Islam. The *Imam's* statement sheds light on the meaning that the *Fuqaha* are the fortress of Islam is that they have duty and are bound by duty to protect Islam and they must perform their duty whenever is necessary to fulfill that duty. This is one of their indispensable duty, moreover, an absolute duty, not a conditional one.

Islam came into being to bring order in society, leadership[44] and government are for the sake of ordering the affairs of society. It is the duty of the *Faqih* to establish order in society since they are the protector and the fortresses of Islam. The *Fuqaha* are the trustees of the Prophet, so long as they do not indulge themselves in the illicit desires, pleasures and wealth of this world.[45] The just *Fuqaha*, who are the successors of the Prophet and do not have any worldly pleasure and desire.

---

41   Ibid, p.68

42   Ibid, p.68

43   Ibid, p.71

44   The expression translated here as "leadership is *imamate itibari*. The "governance" (*Velayat of the Faqih* is *itibari* (extrinsic) to his person, he exercises it only by virtue of the acquired attribute of just *Faqih*.

45   Khomeini, n.5, p.57

If a *Faqih* has aim to accumulate the worldly wealth and pleasure, he is no longer just and can not be trustee of the Prophet and the executor of the ordinances of Islam. It is only the just *Fuqaha* who can correctly implement the ordinances of Islam and establish just society in which the people will lead their life in accordance with Islamic values and norms.

The expression, "the *Fuqaha* are the trustees of the Prophet" is not that the *Fuqaha* are trustee only in respect of pronouncing juridical opinion but they also take into account and solve the various problems in the light of Islamic precepts which have been arisen in society. The most important function of the Prophet was the establishment of a just social order through implementation of laws and ordinances. This notion is limpidly manifested in the verse, "verily, we have sent our Messengers with clear signs, and sent down with them the Book and the Balance in order that men might live in equity."[46] It is obvious from aforementioned that the main purpose for sending down the Prophet was to ensure men's life in order on the basis of just social relation, and true humanity may be established among men. It may be possible only by establishing just government and implementing divine laws, whether it was accomplished by the Prophet himself, as was the case with the Most Noble Messenger or by the followers who came after him.

God appointed the Most Noble Messenger the head of the Muslim community and instructed them to obey him, "obey God and obey the Messenger and the holders of authority from among you."[47] Obey the Messenger means, obey the religious matters that had been revealed by the Prophet. Here obedience to God is the conformity to the ordinances of religion, all activities are conducted in the conformity to divine ordinances, whether they are rituals or not, are a form of obedience to God. Obeying the Most Noble Messenger is in certain sense, to obey God, we obey the Prophet because God has commanded us to do so. Those who have authority in accordance with religion, God has commanded us to obey them because they are the preserver and protector of the Muslim community.

Just as the Prophet was entrusted to implement divine laws and establish institutions of Islam and God set him up over the Muslims as their leader and ruler, making obedience to him obligatory, so, too, "the

---

46   *Al-Quran*, 57:25

47   *Al-Quran*, 4:59

just *Fuqaha* are leader and ruler and they must implement divine laws and establish the institutions of Islam."[48]

"The Islamic government is a government of law...the *Fuqaha* must administer its function. The *Fuqaha* supervise all executive and administrative affairs of the country along with all planning."[49] When a government of law is established, all will live without fear, and no ruler will have the right to take any step which is contrary to the provisions and laws of the immaculate.

Imam Reza said, "an honest and trustworthy *Imam* is *sine qua non* for the community in order to preserve it from degrading, and he also reasserted that the *Fuqaha* are the trustees of the Prophet."[50] Thus, the *Fuqaha* must be the leader of the people in order to prevent Islam from declining. It is the duty of the *Fuqaha* to prevent Islam from its declining.

It is fact that the *Fuqaha* do not have the status and rank of Prophethood but must be the legatees or successors of the Prophet, the legatees of the Prophet is *sine qua non* of them, otherwise, who will govern society, if they will not rule over society. the expression "legatee of a Prophet" is generally assumed to refer to his immediate successors. The concept legatee of a Prophet includes the *Fuqua*. According to this concept, the immediate legatee of the Prophet was, of course, the commander of the faithful, who was followed by the other *Imams*, and the affairs of the Muslims were entrusted to them, but no one should think that the function of government is a form of privilege for the Imams. But it is a grave responsibility. Governmental functions are entrusted to them because only they are the best to serve a just government and implement social justice among the people. "Spiritual status and position qualify a man for the assumption of government and social accountability".[51]

Imam Jafar Sadiq[52] stated "avoid from judging, because judging is reserved for an *Imam* who has knowledge of the law and legal procedure and who behaves just to all Muslims; it is reserved for only a Prophet or

---

48 Khomeini, n.5, p.80

49 Ibid, p.80

50 Ibid, p.82

51 Ibid, p.86

52 Imam Jafar Sadiq : sixth of the Twelve Imams. He is referred because played an important role in developing the religious science.

the legatee of a Prophet."⁵³ Thus, the *Fuqaha* are the legatees of the Prophet and all tasks entrusted to the Imams are also incumbent upon the *Fuqua* and that task had been performed by the Prophet, they also had been performed by the commander of the faithful.

A person who desires to sit as a judge, first, he must be an *Imam*. *Imam* means "leader", "guide". Those who want to sit as a judge; they must possess three qualifications being a leader, being knowledgeable, and just. The tradition confirms it that these three qualifications can be found only in a Prophet or the trustee of the Prophet.

Only the just *Faqih* has right to sit as a judge, not any *Faqih*. The term *Faqih* refers to one who is learned not only in the laws and judicial procedure of Islam, but also in the doctrines, institutions and ethics of the faith. Thus, the *Faqih* is a religious expert. "The *Faqih* is just."⁵⁴ His third qualification is that, he should be an *Imam* in the sense of leader. The just *Faqih* occupies the position of leadership and guidance in capacity as judge in accordance with the appointment by the *Imam*. These three specific qualifications are not found in anyone except a Prophet or the legatee of a Prophet.

> Since the *Fuqaha* are not the Prophet they must be the legatees or the successors of the prophet ... the *Faqih* is the legatee of the Most Noble messenger, over and above, during the Occultation of the imam, he is the leader of the Muslims and the chief of the community. Only he may act as judge and no one else has any right to occupy the position of judgeship.⁵⁵

The doctrine of 'proof of God' means that "like the Prophet was the proof and authoritative guide of all the people, in the same way God had appointed him to guide people in all matters, so, the *Fuqaha* are also accountable for all affairs and are the authoritative guides of the people."⁵⁶ The *Fuqaha* are the legatees of the Prophet, in the same way they are also the 'proof of God'. The person who is a 'proof of God' to "whom God has assigned to conduct affairs: all his deeds, actions and sayings constitute of

---

53   Khomeini, n.5, p.86
54   Ibid, p.87
55   Ibid, p.88
56   Ibid, p.90

proof for the Muslims."⁵⁷ Without being the *Faqih*, a person cannot claim for the universal authority, is rest only with the *Fuqaha*. The *Fuqaha* of Islam are proofs to the people. "Just as the Most Noble Messenger was the proof of God; the conduct of all affairs of society being entrusted to him... so, the *Fuqaha* are also the proof of the *Imam* to the People."⁵⁸

"O you who believe, obey God and obey the Messenger and the holders of authority among you."⁵⁹ The verse, "O you who believe" has been addressed to the entire Muslim. God commands them to obey Him by adhering His divine-ordinances and to obey His the Most Noble Messenger as well as the holders of authority by following to their teaching and the governmental decrees. The decrees of the *Fuqaha* must be followed by the people, it is the command of God. There is difference between the obedience to the God and the obedience to the Prophet. All ordinances of divine law, whether they concern to the worship or not, are the commands of God and their implementation is the obedience to God. The Prophet did not issue any command regarding prayer, he impelled men to pray, it was the way for confirming and implementing the God's laws. When we pray we also obey God. Obeying the Messenger is different from obeying God. The command of the Prophet are those that he himself issued in the course of exercising governmental function; for instance, he commanded the Muslims to follow the army of Uthman.⁶⁰

The Commander of the Faithful exercised powers, appointed governors and judges whom all Muslims were bound to obey. In the same way, Imam Sadiq also held an absolute authority and empowered to rule over all the *ulema* and the *Fuqaha*. He named the *Fuqaha* as "rulers", so, that no one might presume that their function was restricted only to judicial affairs and divorces form the other concerns of government.

"*Imam* assigned to exercise the functions of the both government and judgeship to the *Fuqaha*. It is the duty of the Muslims to obey this

---

57 Ibid, p.90

58 Ibid, p.92

59 Al-Quran, 4:59

60 Uthman: Uthman ibn Zaid, was a third caliph, and a beloved companion of Prophet Mohammad who was placed in-charge of a military expedition when he was only eighteen. He died in 59/679.

decree of the *Imam*."⁶¹ Obeying the *Imam*, is the duty of the *Fuqaha* since they have been appointed by him.

"The judicial and governmental functions granted by the *Imams* to the *Fuqaha* of Islam are held perpetually."⁶² The political authority is held by the *Fuqaha*, is permanent in nature since they have universal authority to run society. "*Imam* has appointed the *ulema* of Islam to the positions of ruler and judge, and these positions belong to them sempiternal."⁶³

It is coming down form the tradition that those who are learned, they must rule over society. The learned man must take the reins of government to rule over society. As a matter of fact, the scholars are the heirs of the Prophet; the Prophet endowed not a single *dinar* or *dirham*: instead they endowed knowledge and whoever acquires it, has acquired a generous portion of their legacy. Here "the Scholars", means the *ulema*. Those ordinances have been left by the Prophet are a form of legacy, and those who take these ordinances are his heirs. His heirs inherited "only of his ordinances and traditions, for the tradition states that the Prophet bequeathed knowledge."⁶⁴ In fact, the prophet left things that could be bequeathed, "was his exercise of rule over the community, which was handed down by him to the Commander of the Faithful and then to each and every successive Imam."⁶⁵

Ahmad Kasravi, a noted historian denounced the *Shiism* and clerical pretensions to authority. In the defence of secularism against the superstitions of clergy, published *Shiagari* (*The Shia Tendency*) where he questioned the very core of *Shia* belief. His view on the leadership is very much different from Khomeini. He argued against an absolute wisdom and innocence of *Imams* which entitled them to rule, judge and interpret the laws of Islam. He did not assign the leadership of Muslim community to the clergy. Kasravi dismissed the very foundations of *Shia* beliefs as well as its practices and concepts of honour and innocence:

---

61   Khomeini, n.5, p.105
62   Ibid, p.109
63   Ibid, pp.109-110
64   Ibid, p.117
65   Ibid, p.119

With all its turns and shades, *Shiagari* has concluded that authority and government of our time in the hand of the absent *Imam*. *Mullayan* follow this and say: we are the representatives of the Imam and we should be the rulers today… but even though they think that they should govern.⁶⁶

Ali Shariati was also against the institutionalization of the role of the *ulema*. He endorsed Kasravi's skepticism and questioned the very legitimacy of the *ulema's* claim to represent the *Imam* and act as the protectors of the oppressed and needy. He made distinction between the clergy before and after the Safavid period. When the Safavid adopted *Shiism* as the official religions of Iran the clergy became institutionalized. But once *Shiism* became institutionalised, the religious establishment became part of the ruling elite and endangered the religious despotism.

> From the moment that *Shiism* succeeded in gaining formal recognition, from that moment it was vanquished… form the moment that the power that ha been ranged against it began to accommodate it, they observed it, it ceased to be a dynamic movement, it became a powerful ruling institution.⁶⁷

That is why Shariati was against the institutionalisation of religion.

Bazargan did not justify the government of the jurisconsult *(Velayat-e Faqih)*. Khomeini's edict of January 1988, proclaimed absolutist government of the jurisconsult. The total monopolisation of power in the hands of the governing jurisconsult is an unprecedented religious innovation that is neither rooted in the *Quran* and the *Sunna*, nor reflects democratic *Quranic* principle that "affairs of the people should be conducted on the basis of mutual consultation."⁶⁸ Freedom Movement of Iran (FMI),Bazargan's political organization pointed out that the absolute power of the jurisconsult subjects religion to political imperatives, but the distinguish feature of an Islamic State is that religion would be in command and politics would be a dependent function of it. Therefore, it has been argued that Khomeini's edict is contrary to the *Quran* and the *Sunna*, since it equates the powers of the governing jurisconsult with that of God.⁶⁹

---

66   Ahmad Kasravi, *Shiagari* (Noor Publication, n.d.), p.99

67   Ali Shariati, *Tashiiyeh Alvi va Tashiiyeh Safavi* (Tehran: Husseinie Irshad Publication, n.d), p.47

68   *Al-Quran*, 42:38

69   Nehzate Azadi-e Iran, *Tafsil vo Tahlil-e Velayat-e Motlaq-e Faqih* (Tehran: Nehzat-e

The Blueprint for Islamic Government

Shiism permits political leadership to the *ma'soum*[70] (immaculate), those descendants of Prophet Mohammad who are protected from sin. It is noteworthy, only the descendants of the Prophet are free from the sin. The powers were exercised by the Prophet and *Imams*, "are also the prerogative of the *Fuqaha*."[71] The core idea of the political analysis of the *Velayat-e Faqih* is the notion of a benevolent ruler, who have universal authority. Motahhari, like his teacher Khomeini, had idea that only the clergy has had the cultural background to become the natural leader of any Islamic government. Only the clergy has the essential quality and ability to lead the Islamic government.[72] Khomeini himself stated in his book *Hukumateh-e Islami* that "the scholars are the heirs of the prophet." Here scholars mean the *ulema* of the Muslim community. They are the heirs of the tradition of the prophet, they did not bequeath a single *dinar* or *dirham*, they bequeathed his sayings and tradition. It means, they inherited only the knowledge. It is reason, they are called the heirs of the Prophet. So, *Shii* political theory endorses it as along as the Twelfth Imam is in occultation, "it is our duty to obey the *Velayat-e Faqih*."[73]

It is to be noted that Khomeini himself endorsed that notion of collegiate government by a group of clergy, who repeatedly referred to the *Fuqaha* (religious jurisconsultants) who are just and would fight in God's way to implement the laws of Islam and its social system, as a natural emerged leaders of the Islamic government:

> as long as they do not concern themselves with illicit desires and wealth of this world... If a *Faqih* has as his aim the accumulation of worldly wealth, he is no longer just and can not be the trustee of the prophet and executor of the ordinances of Islam... Only the just *Fuqaha* who may correctly implement the ordinances of Islam and firmly establish its institutions, executing the panel provisions of Islamic law.[74]

Azadi-e Iran, 1988), pp.97-118

70 Khomeini in his book *Hukumat-e Islami* has elaborately explained the notion *masoum*.

71 Khomeini, n.5, p.149

72 Murtada Mutahhari, *Barresiyeh Ejmali-e Manabi-e Eqtesad-e Islami* (Tehran: Enteshrat-e Hikmat, 1982), p.83

73 *Kayhan*, 23 February, 1988

74 Khomeini, n.5, p.149

In a nutshell, the implementation of all government laws devolve upon the *Fuqaha*. Who are just. Khomeini states furthermore that no *Faqih* has "an absolute authority over all other *Fuqaha* of their own time, being able to appoint or dismiss them. There is no hierarchy among the *Fuqaha*, and no one *Faqih* is higher than another or endowing one with more authority than another."[75]

The rise of single *Faqih* is to be the natural outcome of the model of government that Khomeini projects. He always argues about the *Velayat-e Faqih* which refers to *Fuqaha* than *Faqih*. At the time of his heyday, he brought the theory, the *Velayat-e Faqih* into practice. He advocated only a singular male *Faqih*, would be the ruler of society.

> When a *mujtahid*, religious leader, who is just and learned, struggles for establishing an Islamic government and succeeds, he will have the authority and rights in the affairs of society that were enjoyed by the prophet. It is the duty of the people to listen and obey this *Faqih*. He will hold the supreme power in the government and management and control of social and political lives of the people in the same way as the prophet and Ali had.[76]

Just like Motahhari, Khomeini too, has a notion of guardianship of minors, paternalistic rule by a theocrat, is a threshold of his notion of the Islamic government. In fact, "there is no difference between the guardianship of a minor and the guardianship of a nation."[77] Just as a minor is looked after by his guardian in each and every matter, in the same way the guardian of a nation looks after his people in all matters. The guardian of a nation is accountable in the same way as the guardian of a minor if minor commits any mistake. So, there is no difference between the guardian of a nation and the guardian of a minor. The method which Khomeini has employed in analyzing the Islamic government, indeed it is a hallmark of the Islamic government as outlined by him. In Khomeini's view, there are no elections and no legislation because all laws are made by God, man cannot alter the laws of God, it is only the *Faqih* who rules, and everyone must obey willingly. The blueprint for Islamic government envisages that there is no need of an extensive bureaucracy and judiciary to administer

---

75 Ibid, p.57

76 Ibid, p.55

77 Ibid, p.56

the country.

The theory of the *Velayat-e Faqih* had been projected by Imam Khomeini on the religo-politico basis, which postulates a future government would be led by a high-minded and high-spirited clergy who will have to submit himself to the Will of God that is the Supreme Will and only Will prescribes the Islamic dictum for the people to follow them. As had been assumed by Khomeini that the people are deeply-devout, simple-minded, will accept the rule of religious men and follow their instruction. Religious taxes meet all the expenditure of the state whatever is incurred by the state in maintaining its social and political fabrics, and the religious courts will deliver the verdict without procrastination. There is no need for elections and representative government, in the sense of Western representative governments because the laws are God-gifted. These laws are prescribed by Islam and the representative body only delineates the laws on the Islamic lines. They will abandon the malpractice in the name of religion. All people will adhere the decrees of the *Velayat-e Faqih* and follow the path which will be led by the *Faqih* and protect form degrading the moral standard of Islam and the public face of Islam, and prevail peace and tranquility in society.

Bazargan denounced all forms of autocracy. Bazargan envisaged a clear separation between faith and its rituals and government and the state. His movement intended to return the country to its constitutionalised base and to implement the constitution which guaranteed the freedom of all individuals and the welfare of the people. He did not envisage at any place an absolute rule by the *Faqih*. A number of religious leaders, including Ayatollah Mahmud Taleqani (who passed away suddenly in September 1979) and Kazim Shariatmadari supported Bazaran's views that the state and the religious classes should be clearly separated and the integrity of the boundaries between religion and government should be maintained,[78] a view not shared by Khomeini's disciples in the Revolutionary Council.

Taleqani was against the religions despotism. He saw there is no conflict between a representative secular government and the demands of Islam. He stated about the autocratic theocracy:

---

78 Mehdi Bazargan, "Marz Mianeh Madhab va Omoureh Ejtemayi", in *Madhab dar Ouropa (Religion in Europe)*, (Tehran, 1965), pp.145-46

> The most dangerous of all forms of oppression are laws and restrictions forcibly imposed on people in the name of religion... This is the most dangerous of all impositions because that which is not from God is thrust upon the people to enslave and suppress them and present them from evolving, depressing them of the right to protest, criticise and be free.[79]

He did not endorse the concept of the *Velayat-e Faqih*, government by religious leader. On this issue, he was supported by other amongst the clergy, who did not share his left wing tendencies, but had a high regard for a constitutional democratic form of government. The best known among this group is Ayatollah Kazim Shariatmadari.

Shariatmadari was a liberal clergy. He was the *marjay-e taqlid* of the Azarbaijanis, the powerful minority group of the north-western provinces. Shariatmadari was first and foremost a scholar, politically he demanded a return to the 1906-9 constitution. He though it is not necessary for the *ulema* to govern the country at any time and they should supervise the temporal powers. According to Shariatmadari, politically, the *ulema* were the provider of protection for people against injustices by the government; their role was an oppositional one. During the Revolution 1979, he began demanding reforms and return to parliamentary democracy.

After the Revolution 1979, Shariatmadari called for a pluralist political system where all groups should participate and elect officials, and not the clergy, wielded power. He was against the institutionalisation of the role of the clergy. He thought that the *Faqih* should be consulted in cases of major crisis and the clergy intervene only if the government contravened religious laws. His notion of government is a non-clerical notion of government.[80]

Function of the Government

In the post-Revolution Iran, structure, nature, and function of the government changed. The post of the *Velayat-e Faqih* became the source of legitimacy for government functioning. The three branches of the government – executive, legislature, and judiciary – came under Islam's influence. The *Velayat-e Faqih* has vast power under the constitution, and all governmental functions perform with his consent. The President is the next to the Leader in the system and performs his duties under guidance of the *Velayat-e Faqih*.

---

79 Suroosh Irfani, *Revolutionary Islam in Iran* (London: Zed Book, 1983), p. ii
80 Omid, n.11, p.55

Position and Status of the *Velayat-e Faqih*

The post of *Velayat-e Faqih* is a hub of all activities in the post-Revolutionary Iran, and the whole system is rotating around it just like the earth is rotating around the sun. It is a center of the magnate form where the entire system is controlled. The post-Revolutionary Iran has institutionalized this pious post by incorporating in its constitution, and the state apparatus derive their legitimacy from the institutionalized post. The constitution states status, position, powers, functions and the duties of the *Velayat-e Faqih* in a very lucid way. Theoretically and practically, the *Velayat-e Faqih's* position remains the locus of power in the Iranian political system around which the other offices of the states are spinning. The very basis of the legitimacy of the Islamic Republic is to be found in the doctrine of the *Velayat-e Faqih*.

The *Velayat-e Faqih* has got a central position in system of power in Republic form where powers are devolved and get its legitimacy. Khomeini once told Council which seemed to have forgotten its duties and responsibilities for obeying the *Velayat-e Faqih*, "*Velayat-e Faqih* has legitimate right to rule over society is a basic faith in Islam."[81] The *Velayat-e Faqih's* ruling over society is *sine qua non* since he has legitimate authority due to occultation of the twelfth Imam, that is why, the rule of the *Faqih* "is not a privilege but a grave responsibility."[82] His is accountable for each and every matter in society if society is facing problem either religious or political, he has the right t to issue *fatawa* to settle down crises. Mohsen Armin stated,

> The *Valiye-Faqih* legitimises the Islamic government who leads it: It is the *Valiye-Faqih*, who is accountable for each and everything and rules over everyone, and is in-charge of the nation... Islamic society is governed in accordance with the views of the *Valiye-Faqih*. He is beyond required to take into account any one else's opinions.[83]

The *Faqih* has supernatural entity, and he is above the state because all requirements of the state is determined by it and the state will have to obey.

---

81   *Kayhan*, 11January, 198
82   Khomeini, n.5, p.79
83   *Kayhan*, 17 January, 1988

ISLAMISATION OF POLITICS

> In Islam the *Faqih* has right to issue Fatwa, Islamic decrees, and to legislate and impel polices. These rights are granted to hem by virtue of his Islamic Knowledge. It is his erudition and superior learning which legitimises his rule... by virtue of his erudition and astuteness, God has entitled only the *Faqih* to rule over the Muslim community.[84]

The *Faqih h*as the same power in the governing of society as the *Prophet* and the *Imams* had.

The *Velayat-e Faqih's* presence is entrenched in the political system of Iran. The *Faqih* has pivotal position in the system. It is nucleus from where powers are devolved. The three branches of government in exercising their powers and functions derive legitimization form this post. The position of the *Velayat-e Faqih* is such that all acts of government are legitimised from here, it is a source of legitimization. The constitutions has granted the *Faqih* overwhelming powers. He is the actual ruler of the country, his word is final in the matter of law and administration, and all will have to obey his directives. He has the supernatural identity in the political system and no one is above him.

After the Revolution 1979, a new constitution was framed along Islamic line to fulfill the aspirations of the Revolutionaries, but it was revised in 1989 due to some constitutional shortcomings and domestic compulsion. The revision of the constitution was started in April 1989 when Khomeini was alive and completed in July while Khomeini had died on 3 June, 1989. By 11 July, 1989, the final amendments to the constitution had been made and it was put to referendum on 28 July, while the presidential election was held. The revision of the constitution required because there was weakness in the 1979 constitution which vaguely left undefined powers and responsibilities among the various centers of power in the republic which was overlapping one another. The undefined powers led to power struggle in 1980-81 between President Bani Sadre and Prime Minister Rajaii and his Islamic Republican Party. There was continuous fighting between the theocrats and Bani Sadre for controlling the state power. In the struggle, the Islamic Republican Party (IRP) played major role.

In the post-Revolutionary Iran, the *ulema* played crucial role and controlled the state where all policies were made by them. Both centers of power were competing each other to control the state apparatus. IRP and

---

84   *Kayhan,* 23 January, 1988

Bani Sadre had opposite idea about the nature and function of the state. The theocratic state closed down all oppositional newspapers whereas Bani Sadre was against it. Bani Sadre in his daily paper made apprehension for the danger of theocracy. By using reminiscent of Ali Shariati, he indicated the threat posed by `religious fascism', "sacking to reestablish political despotism under the guise of religion."[85] This fierce struggle for power proved costly for Bani Sadre. The struggle for power eventually culminated into the dismissal of Bani Sadre form the presidential post (through exercising a vote of no-confidence motion against the president by exercising its constitutional right by *Majlis*), which underlined the vagueness of the constitution. At the same time, the leader was limpidly aware of the destabilizing consequences of such uncertainties on the entire system, especially in the absence of Khomeini and the interceder and the ultimate arbitrator. The 1989 revised constitution, institutionalized the doctrine of *Velayat-e Faqih* and the authority of the *Faqih*.

Khomeini got support not only from the cleric side, but from the non-cleric side also. A number of Muslim intellectual, who supported Khomeini though they did not have cleric back ground like Hasan Bani Sadre, Sadeq Qutbzadeh and Ibrahim Yazdi. Unlike Khomeini, this group sought to set up a form of democratic socialism in Iran. Like Shariati, Bani Sadre had firm belief in Islam with a conviction that Islamic rule would be representative, democratic and welfare oriented – which he already expressed widely in his writing on Islamic politics and economics.[86]

Powers and Functions of the *Velayat-e Faqih*

The *Faqih* is the supreme Commander of the armed forces and has the right to declare war.[87] It is the most important function of the *Faqih*. He is all in all of the armed forces, and issues ordinance regarding forces and has also power to declare war and peace on any country. He is the sole authority to declare war and peace and has also sole authority concerning mobilization of general troops. The movement of troops within or outside the country depends upon the instructions of the *Faqih*. The *Faqih* can send the troops outside the country to defend or offend other country.

---

85 *Enqelab-e Islam*, 14 May, 1980

86 See for instance, Bani Sadre's *Bayanieyeh Jamjourieh Islami* (*Manifesto of the Islamic Republic*) published in Paris in 1971

87 Article 110

His power is not only restricted to the armed forces but also play an important role in determining the general policies of the Islamic Republic of Iran (in consultation with the Expediency Council). It has been already mentioned earlier that all centers of power rotate around it since it is a nucleus of power. The entire government policies are determined by the *Faqih*. He supervises the general implementation of agreed policies. The *Faqih's* decision is final in all the matters and will be accepted by all unquestionably.

Not the President but the *Faqih*, who issues order for referenda. There is provision in the constitution that the major changes in the constitution can be brought through referenda. In referendum, the people cast their votes either in favour of or against the changed provisions of the constitution. If they cast in the favour that is approved by the people, and if they vote against it, then disapproved.

Whenever differences brew among the three branched of the government, the *Faqih* settles down it amicable and also regulates relation among these three branches of the government. These three branches of the government come under direct control of the supreme leader, who is the leader of the *umma*.[88] The entire responsibility of the government of the country fall upon the shoulder of the *Faqih*.

The *Faqih* has also the appointing and dismissing powers. The *Faqih* appoints six clergymen in the Council of Guardians. This council examines whether the laws made by the Assembly has conformity with the *Sharia* or not. Being the Supreme Commander of the armed forces, the *Faqih* appoints and dismissed Chief of Staff of the Armed Forces, Commander-in-Chief of the IRGC, and the Commander-in-Chief of the military and security forces. These appointing and dismissing powers are very important for the *Velayat-e Faqih*. The Supreme Leader controls directly over the entire armed forces through appointing and dismissing these armed forces. Not a single appointment can be made without his consent.

The *Faqih* appoints Director of Radio and Television networks. It is one of the most important and sensitive post because it is an instrument of the propaganda. Both print media and electronic media plays an important role in making opinion regarding government policies. The mass-media feeds the information to the people at every level and plays an important

---

88 *Umma* : The entire Islamic community without territorial or ethnic distinction.

role in the formation of the public opinion in this modern world, the minds can be controlled by the media,, the coercive force cannot be always used to control the minds of the people. So, the control of the mass media by the *Faqih* is very important.

The *Faqih* signs the decree naming the President after election. The President is directly elected by the people and after electing the president, the *Faqih* certifies his name. These powers of *Faqih* are most important in carrying out the day-to-day administration of the country. These powers are necessary for discharging the duty because he is only the right-full ruler of the Muslim community.

Succession

In Khomeini, so much power and authority were vested. Therefore, the question of succession became central importance to the politicians. The constitution required the Council of Guardians to set up an Assembly of Experts (*Majlis-e Khebregan*), with eighty-three members elected to choose a successor for Khomeini.[89] It is provision that there should a natural leader emerge, and be accepted and endorsed by the Council of Guardians and the people, and then he could take on the mantle of the Prophet. If it is not possible, then the constitution return to the traditional solution usually adopted by the religious institution, namely that of having a "collegial leadership."[90] The Assemble of Experts is to select three to five suitable Jurisconsults to take over the leadership.

When Ayatollah Montazeri, the heir-apparent of Khomeini resigned in March 1989, then the crisis of succession precipitated, and the Republic lost its stability due to uncertainty of succession. His departure precipitated a constitutional crisis because there was no suitable candidate to fill the post of the *Faqih*. Khomeini's thesis prescribed that it could only be a male theocrat; who had excellent knowledge and be a religious leader who would not only have to take responsibility of office but also lead to the nation both by his own exemplary virtue and by his extensive and superior learning and erudition. The constitutional solution had been collegial.[91] If a single *Faqih*, who is accepted and recognized by the majority of the people, had

---

89 Article 108
90 Article 107
91 Article 107

failed to emerge naturally, then a council of three or five religious leaders would take charge of the leadership.

The revised constitution 1989 removed the collegial option for leadership,[92] and the idea of *Velayat-e-Faqih* radically revised. Khomeini insisted that the leader would have an immense religious knowledge and vision and be a '"oath" politician was replaced by the need to select a person who had the "correct political vision". It is clear from the amended constitution that the individual who shall have stronger insight in matters involving jurisprudence and politics shall have preference.[93]

The revised constitution has given political precedence over religion and the political vision and farsightedness is more important than religious erudition. The new leader no longer had to be a fearless sources of enlightenment (*marja* or exemplary) in terms of justice and probity; instead he had to be prudent and have good political judgment and sufficient religious knowledge.[94]

The amended constitution has made specific provision in order to ensure stability in the event of death, resignation ore removal of the *Faqih*. Until such time as the new leader will be introduced, a council comprising the President, the Head of the Judiciary, and one of the jurists of the Guardians Council appointed by the congregation for determining the Expediencies shall provisionally assume all duties of the leader.[95]

The single *Faqih* doctrine is incorporated in the revised constitution in order to maximise stability at the highest level in the post-Khomeini era. The collegial leadership option regarded as an attractive formula in situation where a clear *Faqih* figure may have not emerged, was obstacle to the survival of the post-Khomeini period. So, collective leadership formula was left because in collective leadership, the judgment might lead to indecision.

The leader's demotion to ranks and position of mere mortal posed a serious problem of legitimacy for a state which is carried on the basis of absolute obedience to the sacred laws of God. Who (the *Velayat-e Faqih*) is

---

92   Article 91
93   Article 109
94   Article 109
95   Article 111

the shadow of God on earth. The *Faqih* is the highest source of emulation, the *Faqih* is not one and the same as the *Vali*, then who has absolute authority and the right to rule in the name of God. But the theses has been put forward in favour of a fallible and removable religious leaders who will rule over country. Khomeini has stated in his book that the powers of the *Velayat-e Faqih* are in no way inferior to those exercised by the Messenger of God and his son-in-law, Ali; his power and authority for governing society is exactly the same as they had. It has been assumed the infallibility of the leader that has made obedience to his ruling a religious duty, without it how would people be expected to be obedient? The infallibility of the leader is the prerequisite for the obedience of the people which has made obedience a religious duty. The *Majlis* representative Seyed Hosein Hoseini stated,

> Our country has been saved by leader from numerous dangers. He has acted in this way because of the absolute obedience of the people to his ruling. His commandments and decrees have been above and beyond the law and the constitution. Neither council nor government can claim to such sanctity infallibility.[96]

The revised constitution had made the leader a mere human being, fallible without superior religious learning and without absolute probity, to rule over the country. In spite of this, the people are expected to obey the ruler.

> It cannot be separated the leadership from *marjayiat*, being the source of Islamic knowledge and emulation. The leader is *marjaeh taqled* or not, we must be ruled by him. He is a religious leader, *mujtahid*, and he is just we must obey his decrees....... On matters of politics and the state it is the leader who rulers absolutely. We must obey him as a matter of religious duty and we have no right t to question his judgment, even if we are the most learned scholars of Islam and higher ranking *ulema*. Just as now the Imam's decrees are binding, so in the future it is absolutely essential that we obey the decisions of our future leaders.[97]

The *marjayiyat* cannot be separated form the leader because the theory of the absolute obedience of people will be surrounded in controversy and how the people could obey a mere fallible man? The *marjayiyat* legitimises

---

96   *Kayhan*, 20 April, 1989
97   *Kayhan*, 20 April, 1989

his absolute authority to be obeyed by the people. It is the *mujtahid* who will issue decrees whatsoever problem has been come to surface and settle down it through using decree, and the people obey it willingly. To obey commandments and the decrees of the leader, is the religious duty of the people.

Executive (President)

The office of the President is one of the most important constitutional post next to the *Velayat-e Faqih*. The President holds the highest official authority of the country who is directly elected by the people through universal adult franchise. This post is politically viable and lucrative because it is next to the leader. "Next to the leader, the President of the Republic is the highest official authority of the country who is responsible for the enforcement of the constitution and presides over the executive power with the exception of those matters which directly relate to the leader."[98] The president is the next to the leader (spiritual leader) means that he is constitutionally head of the state but under the control and surveillance of the *Velayat-e Faqih*, and the *Faqih* has universal authority in running the state. The *Faqih* signs the name, and issues the decree of the elected candidate for the post of the President.

The constitution 1979 created both the post of the Prime Minister and the President but it did not clearly define and allocate their powers and functions separately. There was no clear-cut demarcation of their authority in exercising their powers and was overlapping each other. The constitution's revision was completed in July 1989. The revised constitution abolished the post of Prime Minister and made a powerful President by assigning all executive powers to the President. The President exercises these powers. The Prime Ministerial powers were merged with the Presidential powers. The overlapping powers ceased to operate after abolition of the Prime Ministerial post. The president is in-charge of both the Cabinet and all branches of the government.[99]

The elected president selects his Cabinet Ministers to run the Government. The President nominates his Cabinet Ministers. But nominations require voting in the *Majlis* for their approval. When *Majlis* passes it by majority vote then they become Ministers, and if they fail to

---

98 Article 113
99 Article 57, 60, 64, 69, 70, 87, 88, 89, 124, 126, 127, 130, 131

secure the majority vote in *Majlis* then they cannot become the Ministers. Therefore, *Majlis's* ratification is essential to be a Minister. The president also controls all branches of the government. Ministers are hired and fired by the president subject to *Majlis's* ratification.[100] The President is responsible for all omission ad commission of the cabinet. He has the power to remove an individual Minister from his Ministry. At the same time, it has been explicitly stated in the constitution, the President can not hold any Ministerial Portfolio.[101] The constitution does not permit to hold any Ministry to the President in any circumstance. Thus, it avoids concentration of power in one had, and to be an omnipotent ruler of the country.

The President can not take the decision contrary to the Islamic tenets, rules and regulation. His decision will be in conformity with the Islamic rules and regulation. So, an aspirant for the post of the president, will apply for his candidature, and his candidature will be clear out by the Council of Guardians. Without clearance for the Council of Guardians, a candidate cannot contest the election for the post of the President.

Legislative

Legislation is one of the most important function of every government because changes in time and circumstances require a new law to fulfill the needs of society. The legislature is one of the three branches of the government, whenever any shortfall is perceived in the existing laws, the legislature makes laws for overcoming these shortfalls. But the story of legislation in Iran is different. According to constitution, Iran is governed under Islamic tenets, and Islam does not admit anyone sovereign except God, and does not recognize anyone law-giver other then Him. So, here in Islam, legislation belongs only to God. The individual has no any role in legislation. "Human legislation, according to Islam, is and should be subject to the supremacy of Divine law and within the limits prescribed by it."[102] Legislation in Islam is permitted only within prescribed *Sharia*, there is no scope for legislation beyond *Sharia*, man can not make laws because all laws are mad by God. The *Sunnis* believe that there are four sources of

---

100 Article 133, 135, 136

101 Article 141

102 Sayyid Abdul Ala Maududi, The Islamic Law and Constitution (Lahore: Ripon Printing Press, 1960), p.77

law: the *Quran*, the *Sunna, Ijma* (consensus), and *Ijtihad (qiyas)*; the *Shias* also have retained the same number and order concerning the sources of jurisprudence the *Quran*, the *Sunna, Ijma*, and *Aql* (reason) substituting reason for *qiyas*. These four sources of law are used in legislation. Whenever laws are made to solve a problem, only these four sources have to be used in making the laws. There is no scope for legislation in Islam outside these four sources. "Islamic law is to form the foundation of all legislation."[103]

In Iran, there is three competing legislative agencies which perform their respective role in making the laws. These three competing agencies are the *Majlis Shorayeh Islami* (the Islamic Consultative Assembly), Council of Guardian, and the Council for the Determination of Expediency. The originating place of the bill is the Islamic Consultative Assembly. First, it is passed in the assembly, then it moves to the Council of Guardians for its approval, and if it is not passed by the Council of Guardians due to not conformity of the bill to the Islamic precepts, then it moves to the Council for the Determination of Expediency to examine the bill. If the bill requires an urgent need to pass it for national interest, then it is passed by the Council for the Determination of Expediency.

Majlis Shorayeh Islami (Islamic consultative Assembly)

The new Iranian National Assembly was created after 1979 Revolution. At the outset, the name of the House of Representative, was *Majlis Shorayeh Melli* (the National Consultative Assemble) but its name changed after Khomeini's instruction and became *Majlis Shorayeh Islamic* (Islamic consultative Assembly). The total strength of the Assembly is two hundred ninety and its representatives are directly elected by the people for the term of four years. The main function of the *Majlis* is to fulfill its duty to the electorate. It falls duty upon the people that they submit before the will of *Majlis*. Khomeini stated, "we must submit to the will of the *Majlis* and that would be submitting to the will of Islam and the Muslim.... Obeying the *Majlis* and its laws is part and parcel of our religious rituals and duties and is like paying homage to God."[104] At the same time, he said, the *Majlis* is sovereign only so long as it follows the Islamic tenets.

Here is a question which the constitution has failed to solve the basic contradiction that is inherent in the concept of an Islamic government.

---

103 Article 4

104 *Kayhan,* 28 May, 1981

The concept of an Islamic government has differed form the concept of other forms of governments. According to Islamic tenets, all laws are made by God, they can not be changed and they are eternal and only God is law-giver and no one has anything to say regarding the laws of Islam. If God is the sole source of all laws and no one has to say anything concerning the laws; and if the laws of God must be obeyed unquestionably, then how can an Islamic government accommodate any notion of democracy at least in the matter of elected legislature? The legislature makes laws for institutions and delineates administrative paths for running the state.[105] The Islamic government does not require an elected legislature to make laws but this elected body is needed to delineate the administrative paths for the implementation of the Islamic laws. The constitution has designated the *Majlis* to be an elected representative body whose representatives would delineate the path for the implementation of the Islamic laws which have been given by God to cope up with problems. This legislative assembly is the single assembly for making laws which needs to be checked that does not deviate from its assigned path. To make ensure that this single legislative Assemble does not stray form its path, its decisions have been to scrutinized and ratified by the council of Guardians and the *Faqih*. An elected representative body is created in Iran only for the implementation of the Islamic laws and not to make or alter it.

Ayatollah Motahhari, a *Shia* political theoretician had also argued explicitly that the laws of Islam were eternal, so, there is no question of altering them according to the needs of the time and circumstances. The Islamic laws can not be changed in any circumstances. It is common acceptance among the *Shias* that the true Islam had been ephemeral, so it could not delineate all paths of the Islamic rules, and is needed to accommodate with day-to-day problems. To solve these day-to-day problems, the concept of *Ijtihad* has been used. "*Ijtihad* means the capacity to give expert opinion in matters of religion."[106] Whenever any problem comes to surface, then a *mujtahid* issues decrees in this regard and becomes a law.

Legislation is an important function of the government, the laws are made by the elected representatives of the people or by the people

---

105 To get detail see Khomeini's *Kashful Asrar*; S A A Maududi, *Political Theory of Islam*

106 Murtada Mutahhari, "Ijtehad in the Imamiyyeh Tradition", *Al-Tawhid*, A Quarterly Journal of Islamic Thought and Culture, vol.4, no.1, *Muharram-Rabial-Awwal* 1407 (September-November 1986), p.26

themselves through public vote (referendum), must necessarily be based on Islamic tenets. Only that law has legitimacy and enjoys legality which may not be repugnant to the Islamic criteria. Hence, there cannot be formulated any law which is contrary to the Islamic precepts and such law cannot be enforced and acted upon. In Iranian system, the legislature has no right to draft a law which is contrary and repugnant to the Islamic injunction and the Divine decrees. The constitution of Iran has been limpidly expressed that the Islamic Consultative Assemble has no right to formulate laws repugnant to Islam and all laws must be based on Islamic injunctions.

The constitution stipulates "all civil, penal, financial, economic, administrative, cultural, military, political and other laws and regulations regarding natural resources should be based upon Islamic precepts..."[107] At the same time, the constitution also specifies the role of the Islamic consultative Assembly: "the Islamic Consultative Assembly can not pass laws in contravention of the principles and precepts of the constitution or the official religion of the country."[108]

Shorayeh Negahaban (Council of Guardians)

The Revolution 1979 gave birth to the new constitution in Iran, this new constitution created a new constitutional body, namely the Council of Guardians to "guard Islamic laws."[109] Without its ratification, the *Majlis* can not legislate on any matter. So, this body is the *sine qua non* for legislation, and not only for legislation but the existence of the legislature also depends upon this body. The constitution stipulates: "until the Council of Guardians is not formed the proceedings of the Assembly has no legal validity as such, and can approve only election of its own members besides electing six jurists belonging to the Council of Guardian."[110] This Article stresses the importance of the Council of Guardians, until and unless the Council of Guardians is formed, the proceedings of the Islamic Consultative Assembly is legally invalid.

The constitution has made the Council of Guardians an independent

---

107 Article 4

108 Article 72

109 Article 91

110 Article 93

body and does not form part of any of the three branches of the government, namely: the judiciary, the executive, and the legislature. However, on the one hand, its members are directly nominated by the leader, who is supreme and officially accepted by the absolute majority of the people. Under the provisions of the constitution, it is he, under whose supervision all the three branches of the governments. On the other hand, this body is also related to the legislature and the judiciary (which elects the members of the Council of Guardians). The constitution states,

> The Council of Guardians shall be composed of 12 members out of whom six are to be qualified and just jurisprudents well-acquainted with the need of time and issues of the day. These individuals are to be appointed by the Leader or the Leadership Council. The other six shall be jurists qualified in various branches of law and must be Muslims and committed to religion. The Supreme Judicial Council shall introduce some qualified Jurists (generally twice the number required) and introduce them to the Islamic consultative Assembly. Later, the Assembly shall take vote on them and those securing the majority votes shall be elected as members of the council of Guardians.[111]

The members of the council of Guardians are appointed for fix tenure.

> The members of the Council of Guardians are elected for a six-year term but in the first round after three years, half of the members each group (Jurisprudents and Jurists) are to be replaced by new members by drawing lots. This has been duly carried out in the first term of the council of Guardians.[112]

The constitution does not say any thing for the re-election of the members of the councils of Guardians at the end of the six-year term. However, the constitution is silent over this matter. The silence on the part of the constitution has been construed as non-prohibition of re-election and some of the members at the end of the six-year tenure have been re-appointed and re-elected for the next six-year tenure.

After passing all the laws by the Islamic Consultative Assemble, it must be sent to the Council of Guardians to overhaul it, and after close scrutiny unless ratified by the council of Guardians, it is not constitutionally passed.

---

111 Article 91

112 Article 92

The laws have been passed by the Assembly upon which the Council of Guardians has right to determine their compatibility and incompatibility with the provisions of the constitution, and it is not confined only for particular laws and proposals. Prior to assent of the President, all the laws without any exception and without request of any individual or official, must be sent to the Council of Guardians after being passed by the Islamic Consultative Assembly.

> All legislations passed by the Assembly must be sent to the council of Guardians for examination. The council of Guardians, in a maximum period of 10 days, must ensure that the contents of the legislation do not urn contrary to Islamic precepts and the Principles of the constitution. If there is any contravention, it should return the legislation to the Assembly for re-examination and if not referred back, the legislation shall be enforceable.[113]

After passing the bill by the Assembly, it is instantly sent to the Council of Guardians. The Council of Guardians will have to peruse the law form two aspect; first, the law has been passed by the assembly is not contrary to the provisions of the constitution; and second, it is not abhorrent to the Islamic precepts. Both jurisprudents and jurists members of the Council of Guardians are competent to examine a bill in order to ensure its conformity to the constitution. The majority of the members of the Council of Guardians will decide the consistency or inconsistency of a bill which is passed by the assembly, and the constitutional validity will be ensured. The Council of Guardians has authority to pursue the law in terms of conformity to Islamic injunction and it falls under sole jurisdiction of the *Fuqaha* (the jurisprudent members) of the Council of Guardians, and they reach on decision by majority vote, then it has to be accepted for its enforceability.

> The division as to whether legislation passed by the Assembly complies with Islamic precepts rests with the *Fuqaha* of the Council of Guardians. As regards the question whether it complies with the constitution or not, is to be determined by the majority of the council of Guardians.[114]

When a bill is approved by the assembly, the bill is sent to the Council of Guardians for its approval. The Council of Guardians has only two

---

113 Article 94

114 Article 96

options, either endorses it or rejects it. If the bill is passed by it then does not matter, but if it does not pass, then further creates problems. The Council of Guardians passes the proposed bill of the Assembly after scrutinising that it is either contrary to the Islamic precepts or not, if they finds the proposed bill is not contrary to Islamic tenets then its decision is conveyed to the Assembly, and the bill is sent by the Assembly to the President for his assents. The President issues notification to the Government for its enforcement. But majority of the members of the Council of Guardians find that the proposed bill by the Assembly is either contrary to the constitution or Islamic injunction, then it is sent back to the Assembly. The Assembly is obliged to amend in accordance with the exceptions taken by the Council of Guardians to the proposed bill, and return it to the Council. Eventually, the Council of Guardians declares that the proposed bill is not contrary to the constitution and the Islamic tenets, then the bill becomes a law after getting signature of the President.

But there is prescribed time-limit under which the Council of Guardians has to examine and approve or reject the bill which is proposed by the Assembly. According to article 94 of the constitution, the Council of Guardians has 10 days time from the date of it receipt to overhaul a legislation and express its opinion on it. It is further said in the Article, if the Council fails to express its opinion within prescribed time-limit then the Assembly bill automatically shall be passed and it shall be sent to the President for his assent. There is also provision in the constitution for the extension of time-limit. "If the Council of Guardians feels that 10 days are inadequate for the examination of the legislation, it can ask the Assembly to extend the period or a further 10 days, giving its reason for such a request."[115]

> In case when an emergency bill is on the Assembly agenda, members of the Council of Guardians are obliged to attend the Assembly session and express their views right there in this regard. In such cases, in view of the presence of the members of the Council in the Assembly, the ratification does not require to be referred to the council.[116]

It is also provision in the constitution. "If possible the Council of Guardians must express its opinion without any delay, and if not, then

---

115 Article 95
116 Article 97

within a maximum period of 24 hours following the Assembly's opinion."[117]

There is a clear procedure for the voting system in the Council of Guardians. The quorum of the Council of Guardians is complete with the presence of its nine members. But in emergency cases, it holds its session with the participation of seven members only. Nevertheless, the decisions have been taken by the absolute majority of votes. The decisions will be taken by majority votes at least seven out of 12 members in the cases of constitution and four out of six members in the matter of determining the compatibility of a law with Islamic precepts and injunctions.

The Council of Guardians is so important that the interpretation of the constitution "lies within the jurisdiction of the council of Guardians, and the courts have not been authorized to interpret the constitution."[118] Moreover, the need for approval of the qualification of the presidential candidates by the Council of Guardians;[119] necessity for holding the oath-taking ceremony of the president inside the Islamic Consultative assembly in the presence of members of the Council of Guardians;[120] and the Council of Guardians' assigning task for supervising the presidential election and the Islamic consultative Assembly elections, and its task of holding referendum,[121] are in themselves the guarantor of the permanent presence of the council of Guardians and as a non-suspension body.

Majmaeh Tashkhiseh Maslehateh Nezam (the Council for Identifying the National Interests of the Government)

There was clash between the Council of Guardians and the Islamic Consultative Assembly over the legislation matter. The Council of Guardians is an independent body which has authority to declare any

---

117 Article 86

118 Article 98

119 Article 110 (4) "... The competence of the candidates for presidency of the Republic regarding the qualifications set forth in the constitution should be confirmed by the Council of Guardians before elections and in the first presidential term, by the Leadership"

120 Article 121: "The President shall take the following oath and fix his signature to it in a special session of the National (Islamic) Cnsultative Assembly attended by the Chief Justice of the Supreme Court and the members of the Council of Guardians…"

121 Article 99: "the Council of Guardians has the responsibility for the elections of the president of the Republic, the elections for the National (Islamic) Consultative Assembly, general elections and referendum."

law invalid which is contrary to the constitution and that does not have conformity to the Islamic precepts. It has been already stated earlier, the assembly sends the bill to the Council of Guardians after passing to get its approval, without ratification of a bill by the Council of Guardians, can not become a law. Not the judiciary, but only the Council of Guardians has overwhelming power in the matter of legislation. This overwhelming power of the Council of Guardians bring collision with the Assembly. To avoid these clashes, the constitution has created a body, namely, *Majmaeh Tashkhiseh Maslehateh Nezam* for smooth legislation. To sort out this problem, constitution has created the 13-member Expediency Council, and recognized the body,

> formed for the purposes of determining the proper acts and things deemed expedient in cases where ratification of the *Majlis* shall be rejected by the Guardians' Council on grounds of inconsistency with the principle of Holy Sharia or the Constitution. The congregation shall be formed upon the instructions of the leader.[122]

To avoid day-to-day clashes between the Council of Guardians and the Assembly needed an institution. The day-to-day clashed between two constitutional bodies might be aggravated crises for the system. With creating this body, the brewing problems of the system is positively thwarted.

The Council's membership is to be determined by the leader, who will appoint its members either permanently or temporary, and the leader will ask advice from these members. "This council's role is to arbitrate between the laws of Islam, as expressed by the council of Guardians, and the political expediency as expressed by the *Majlis*."[123] The Council's role is to compromise between the Guardians' Council and the Assembly when they are in deadlock on any issue. This council takes into account the political compulsion of the country in the formulation of the laws, and this political compulsion and expediency play the greater role in deciding the matters, and it mediates between both these actors by taking into account the argument of both parties.

---

122 Anoushirvan Ehteshami, After Khomeini: The Iranian Second Republic (London: Routledge, 1995), p.41

123 Article 112

Judiciary

Judiciary is one of the important organ of the government in the political system of Iran. The main function is to dispense the justice to all people without any distinction and discrimination. In politico-ideological state, the ideology has its influence over each and every institution of the country, and the judiciary is not spared without its sway. The whole judicial system has come under Islamisation. The structural alteration in judiciary along Islamic lines was needed to fulfill the purpose of the Revolution. The courts had been remodeled in such way that they could oversee the implementation of the *Sharia* laws. In august 1982, the government declared null and void "all pre-Revolutionary laws that were considered un-Islamic, including the Family laws."[124] The new Islamic system of *qisas* (retribution) has been introduced in 1983 and made emphasis on speedy justice. The Western codes and conducts of the judiciary had been changed.

The previous regimes adopted the western procedures in the functioning of the judiciary, had been changed by the Islamic regime. The Revolutionary regime introduced Islamic procedures, codes, and conducts in functioning the judicial system and dispensing justice to all people. The style of functions of the new restructured judicial system is not as the pre-revolutionary regimes had. The new regime has introduced Islamic system of retribution both in form and substance, is closely resembled to the Saudi Arabian model. It has introduced dismembering and amputation of fingers or a hand of theft, flogging for fornication and violation of the code of dress for women and stoning for adultery. "The execution aspect of the judicial practices have also been stepped up especially in regarding to Islamic codes and conduct."[125]

The constitutional amendment 1989 did not only affect the other organs of the government but affected also the judicial system of the country. The amended constitution 1989 abolished "the five-member Judicial High Council as the highest judicial authority in the republic and replaced it with a single appointment (made by the *Faqih*) to be known as the Head of the Judiciary (Chief Justice)."[126] Constitutionally,

---

124 Meherdad Haghayeghi, "Politics and Ideology in the Islamic Republic of Iran", *Middle Eastern Studies*, vol.29, no.1, January 1993, p.39

125 *Kayhan*, 21 November, 1989

126 Article 157

the Chief Justice is appointed for a five years term and he is accountable for all judicial administrative and executive matters. For each and every matter of justice, the Minister of Justice is responsible to the Chief Justice despite he is appointed by the President. Minister of Justice is to be chosen by the President form "among those proposed to the president by the Head of the Judiciary."[127] It is provision in the constitution that "it is the religious leader and not the Minster who is empowered to appoint the judges"[128], including the "Head of the supreme Court and the National Public Prosecutor, both of the whom has to be religious leaders."[129] The religious leader constitutionally has firm control over the judicial system of the country because he makes an important appointment in the judicial system. "The Head of the Judiciary is empowered to change or remove a judge after consultation with the Head of the Supreme Court."[130] The Head of the Judiciary is appointed by the *Faqi*h and the Head of the Judiciary has authority to change or remove a judge with the consultation of the head of the Supreme Court, it means that the judicial system has been moved towards the centralization. It is the process of Islamisation, which has moved towards centralization of the judicial system:

> The powers of the government in the Islamic republic are vested in the legislature, the executive and the judiciary, functioning under the supervision of the *Velayat al-amr* and the Leadership of the *Ummah*, in accordance with... Articles of the present constitution. These three powers are independent of each other, and the liaison between all three of them is provided by the President.[131]

The unprecedented Revolution in the name of Islam in the history of Iran, and demise of the old system, was an unique. In the post-revolutionary Iran, the post of the *Velayat-e Faqih* has been created and institutionalized. The *Velayat-e Faqih's* un-parallel stature and position and overwhelming power in the Iranian political system has been derived from the *Imamate* system. It implies that the *Velayat-e Faqih* is the legitimate ruler over the country since Twelfth Imam is into occultation. In the absence of the Twelfth Imam, no one but only the *Velayat-a Faqih* is a true leader and

---

127 Article 60

128 Article 160

129 Article 162

130 Article 164

131 Article 57

legitimate ruler. On this theoretical concept, Khomeini developed his theory of the *Velayat-e Faqih* and became first *Velayat-e Faqih* of Iran.

Legislature, executive and judiciary have come under Islamic garb and under the control of the *Velayat-e Faqih*. An independent constitutional body, the Council of Guardians has been created in the process of Islamisation of the political system to see whether the legislation is according to *Sharia* or not. The Council of Guardians functions under the guidance of the *Velayat-e Faqih* who is the supreme authority in the land. Although the President is directly elected by the people but he has no so vast authority as the *Velayat-e Faqih* has. The whole system is rotating around this post because it is only legitimate source of power from where the entire system driving its legitimacy. Islam's penetration in the political system of Iran is deep, vast, and indelible. At the theoretical and conceptual level, Islam has apparently restructured the whole system.

ECONOMY IN THE POST-REVOLUTION IRAN

The Revolutionary regime had sought to reshape economic policies. One of the basic thrust of the Islamic Revolution was to end the economic dependency on the US and West, and to be self-reliant economically. The Islamic regime debated the role of the state in the economy and the limits of private property rights.[1] In the process of formulation of economy policy, the Iranian leaders and theoreticians had to resolve the issue of private property rights.

The resolution of the *Ashura* march (11 December 1978) served as a reflection of the economic orientation of the revolutionary movement. The resolution demanded, "honourable economic independence, rejuvenation of agriculture and independent development of industries to the limits of self-sufficiency and liberation from dependence from foreign domination, and an end to exploitation and colonialisation of, and dependence on, imperialism of East and West."[2] The Islamic Revolution's slogan "Islam and independence" was also reflected in its formulation of its economic policies in the post-Revolution Iran.

The dominant tendency in the Islamic Republic, however, followed a populist-statist orientation. It emphasized the role of *mostazafin* (the oppressed) and perceived the Islamic Republic as an interventionist state that would impose extensive limitations on private property rights. The mixed-economy was adopted by the revolutionary regime. According to Article 44, the economy consists of state, co-operative, and private sectors, in that order. Such as the constitution of Islamic Republic reflects the Iranian Revolution as a movements aimed at the triumph of the oppressed and deprived over the oppressor.

---

[1] Sohrab Behdad, "Property Rights in Contemporary Islamic Economic Thought: A Critical Perspective," *Review of Social Economy*, 47/2, 1989, pp.185-211

[2] This resolution was reprinted in Akbar Khalili, *Gam be Gam be Enqelab* (Tehran: Soroush, 1981), pp.114-16

The Revolution, decline in oil revenue, Iran-Iraq War, economic mismanagement, population growth, and political instability had led to major structural crisis in the Iranian economy. The crisis affected Iran's economic growth, per capita income, trade, and virtually every other aspect of its economy. The war with Iraq and the glut in the international oil market, from 1985 to 1989, and since 1993, aggravated the economic crisis. The Revolution and the Iran-Iraq War had negative impact on Iran's economic growth. The economy of this period can be called war-managed economy. After Iran-Iraq War, Iran faced many problems at domestic level: infrastructure problem, erratic real economic growth, a steady rising population, and declining per capita income.

Iran's external trade was severely affected as a result of the Revolution. The drop in the oil revenues and decline in the total exports affected the economy as a whole because oil was the main source of revenue. Iran's near total dependence on oil and gas related exports for foreign income, its growing dependence on exports, its growing trade deficit and problems with its current account showed its sever economic crisis.

To cope up with these problems, Iran moved to adopt from unplanned economy to planned economy. First economic plan was initiated in 1989/90. Rafsanjani and his supporters sought to implement their strategy of reconstruction. It was consisted of several integrated elements: economic reconstruction and development, economic reform of highly distorted economy, and an economic opening to the outside world. Economic reform implied a clear-cut rejection of the political economy of the radicals. It adopted reforms as advocated by the International Monetary Fund (IMF) and the World Bank. They advocated privatization of inefficient of state enterprises, removal of price controls, the elimination of the system of subsidies and unification of the anarchic system of multiple exchange rates. They wished to strike root and branch at the factors which had caused massive distortion in the economy and contributed to the decline in the standard of living of all socio-economic strata. But the second-five years plan was more balanced than the first plan.

Economic Policy and Developments Till 1989

The Iranian Revolution 1979 brought changes at both micro-and macro-economic levels. The Revolution was interpreted as a populist movement intended at income and wealth distribution and at restructuring and remodeling in a rentier economy. After Revolution, the government adopted populist step in the formulation of the economic policies. The new economic policy remained a war-managed economy that continued till the beginning of the First-Five year plan.

The constitution says, "the Iranian Revolution... has been a movement aimed at triumph of all oppressed and deprived persons over the oppressor."[3] The constitution also declares, "economic independence from foreign domination and elimination of poverty and deprivation"[4] to be among the basic goals of the Islamic Republic of Iran. It is evident, the constitution's basic aim was to create an equality in society through minimizing gap between the rich and poor and side by side its also aim was to be an independent from foreign domination.

Islamic flavour in economy entered in the arena of social and political thought in the last-phase of the Revolution. However, its actual development took place only during the early phases of the Islamic Revolution. Islamic influence in economics was natural and spontaneous because the state itself had been coming into Islamic garb. Just after the Revolution, provisional Revolutionary government was formed and established the Office of Revolutionary Project (ORP). This Office of Revolutionary Project, defined the Islamic Revolution of Iran's goals, "the establishment of a social, political and economic system based on the teaching of Islam and toward a classless society of Divine Unity (*Jame-ye bi tabaqe-ye Tawhidi*)."[5] According to teaching of Islam, society should be a just society in which everybody will have to fulfill his/her basic needs.

The populist and redistributive nature of the revolution had been ushered in the policies and programmes of the Islamic Republic of Iran. Islamic revolutionaries sought to surpass the capitalist and socialist models of development and create a new Islamic economic system in which no one be deprived and oppressed in any way and to establish a just society. By the end of the 1980s, the Islamic Republic managed to create a mixed-economic system in which the Public sector played a dominant role. The Islamic constitution clearly expresses that "the economic system... is to be

---

3   *Constitution of the Islamic Republic of Iran*, p.19

4   Ibid, p.43

5   *Office of Revolutionary Project*, "Summary of the Preliminary Report on Determination of the Economic Social Policies in the Islamic Republic of Iran", *Murdad* (1358) (August 1979), p.5

based on orderly and correct planning."⁶ However, the economy remained unplanned and its policies were largely ad hoc till the beginning of the First-Five-Year Plan 1989-90.

While economy was in restructuring process, two prominent schools of thought were operating at that time to give the economic direction. First, the *Hojatieh*, had clear policy concerning economy. This school openly advocated the right to private property and free market economy and opposed radical socio-economic legislation, high taxation and statist policies and advocated more cautious and traditional Islamic approach. This school argued that high taxation and efficient collection of taxes by the government might undermine the authority of the religious establishment and reduce the flow of annual revenues to the mosque.

Second, the *Maktabi* (also known as the Followers of the *Imam's* Line) advocated centralized economic planning, higher taxation, material support for the poor, the confiscation of land without compensation and its redistribution to the poor. By and large, the *Maktabi* line had been followed in the process of the restructuring of the economy. *Hojatieh's* power in the government considerably declined in the mid-1980s. Despite the official demise of the *Hojatieh* society, many in the regime continued to press the case for a strengthening of the private sector. Even Ayatollah Khomeini himself stated more than once in favour of the *Bazaar* and the private sector, "we promise that as long as there is Islam there will be free enterprises also."⁷

However, the economic policies were formulated in the light of the *Maktabi* line since populist orientation was inherited in this school. The new regime was bound to adopt the populist schemes because it was aspiration of the people and was the cause of the outbreak of the Revolution. The populist schemes required the government's greater role in the economy, that is why after the Revolution, the state played a dominant role in the economic sphere.

The revolutionary upheaval was mainly a popular, urban, multi-class and traditionalist movement which legitimized itself through invoking an egalitarian and puritan interpretation of Islam. The primary aims and

---

6   *Constitution of the Islamic Republic of Iran*, trans. H Algar (Berkeley, Calif: Mizan Press, 1980)

7   *The Sunday Times*, 10 January, 1983

purposes of the revolutionaries were, (a) the redistribution of income and wealth towards the lower income echelons of society: (b) the self-reliant economy and political and economic independence from the West; (c) favourable policies towards the agricultural sector.[8]

The economic redistributive nature of the Revolution manifested in the form of the expropriation and reallocation of property, formulating the agricultural policies, reorientation of the government expenditures toward the lower-income and rural sectors, increasing minimum wages, and the rise of new para-satatal institutions for the subsidisation of the living standard of the lower income segments of society. These para-satatal institutions are the Foundation for the Oppressed (which took over the assets of the *Pahlavi* Family), the Reconstruction Crusade (for the construction), the Housing Foundation (for rural and low-income housing), the Martyr Foundation (for the help of those families of the military and the para-military personnel who killed in the war with Iraq), and the foundation for the affairs of the Refugees of the Imposed-war.[9] These para-satatal organizations were run and financed through return from confiscated property along with public subsidies in the form of both fiscal aid and assistance and foreign exchange allocation.

Nationalization:

The economy was about to collapse as a result of the Revolution, Iran-Iraq War, and sharp decline in exports. The revolutionary regime tried to address the challenges by initiating economic reforms. Imam Khomeini intervened and asked the government to take appropriate measures. The government started confiscation and nationalisation policies and issued directives in this regard. The government nationalised those properties which were owned by the Royal Family and its close associates. The nationalization of those properties whose owners had left the country. The nationalization of any firm which owed more than half its assets to the banks.

In February 1979, the government confiscated the movable and immovable properties of the *Pahlavi* Family and its close associates. The

---

[8]   These points are stated in the *Constitution of the Islamic Republic of Iran*. See for detail Algar (1980).

[9]   The rise of the para-satatal organizations in Iran is parallel that of Nicaragua under the Sandanistas. For a detail of Nicaraguan experience, see Ocampo (1991)

Foundation for the Disinterested was set up to administer these properties. The immovable properties of the Royal Family included two hundred large factories, farms, bank, hotels and trading companies.

The government took over industries because the industry's owners, managers, and technicians left the country, and the industry itself was under heavy debts and depended on government funds. This law was also applied for those who had closed or unable to run, and had asked the government for help. The law also obliged the government to determine the ownership of those industries within the "framework of Islamic law."

In July 1979, the Revolutionary Council approved the law for the Protection and Expansion of Iranian Industry which nationalized the three categories of the private industry. Strategic industries were nationalised such as metals, chemicals, shipbuilding, aircraft manufacturing; industries belonged to 53 individuals and families who were closely associated with the *Pahlavi* Family; and industries whose liabilities exceeded their net assets and those which were indebt to the government. The owners of industries of the first category could receive compensation according to their net assets. The industries of the last two categories were nationalised without compensation. The government entered for participation in those enterprises whose assets were greater than their liabilities in proportion to the value of the debt to the banking system.

The Revolutionary Council on 7 June, 1979, "nationalised twenty-seven privately owned banks, of which thirteen were joint-ventures with foreign share holdings and on 25 June, fifteen privately owned insurance companies were nationalised."[10] Justification for the nationalization of banks was the heavy domestic and foreign trade debts of some of the banks, especially, the development banks, the feasibility of bankruptcy of others and capital flight.

On the eve of summer 1979, 36 government and newly nationalised banks were reorganized and integrated into ten banks; the Central Bank; three commercialized banks in the fields of industry and mined, housing and construction and agriculture; and six commercial banks.

---

10 Farhad Nomani and Ali Rahnema, *Islamic Economic System* (London: Zed Book, 1994), p.162

Public Distribution System

The severe financial crunch in the mid-1980s due to fall in the oil revenues, economic embargo and imposed-war, led the budget deficits and hightened inflationary pressures on the economy. To avert the impact of inflation on the standard of living, and to alleviate the severe shortage of major commodities, the government introduced a complex system of rationing for a large number of commodities. At the outset, government started rationing on petrol and fuel. Rationing was soon extended to essential commodities such as sugar, meat, vegetable oil and cloth. The Foundation of Economic Mobilisation was set up to administer rationing, and local mosques distributed ration cards. This policy improved the distribution of essential goods.

Food price policy of the government during the war consisted of a combination of measures, such as subsidisation, direct control of prices and two- tier pricing based on coupon allocation for certain products. The price of wheat was regulated through direct-price subsidies and provisions of public supply through wheat imports and purchase form domestic suppliers to support the low relative prices. According to government budget, "the cost of wheat subsidies increased form 37 billion *rials* in 1982 and peaked at about 68 billion rails in 1986, then declined to 39 billion *rials* in 1989."[11] In the government's food subsidization policy, the price of flour, provided to the bakeries, was kept constant throughout the 1980s.[12] In fact, relative to the overall consumer price index, the price of flour declined by more than 90 percent between 1980 and 1993.[13] A number of other consumer goods were also came under government subsidies and controls in this period. In the post-Revolution, the price of energy did not increase even war was on.

---

11   Mosoud Karshenas and M. Hashim Pesaran, "Economic Reform Under the Reconstruction of the Iranian Economy", *The Middle East Journal*, volo.49, no.1, Winter 1995, p.102

12   It is noteworthy that the cost of flour sold to the bakeries was fixed by the government during this period, the price of bread in the final product market was not fixed. The increase in labour and other costs would have implied a rising trend in bread prices despite the fixed flour prices. Flour is a major input in bread production, fixed flour prices would have implied substantial subsidies on bread consumption.

13   Taking into account this 90 percent decline, it is to be noted that the price of bread was already subsidised in 1978.

Alternative schemes to Direct price subsidies

The government introduced three types of scheme to avoid adverse impact on the poor and other vulnerable groups in society: (a) Universal Direct price subsidies, (b) Targeted Direct price subsidies, (c) and Income supplement for the poor.

(a) **Universal Direct price subsidies:-** Under this scheme, the effect of the unified exchange rate on the domestic price of certain essential and strategic goods was alleviated by maintaining the final consumption prices of these goods at, or close to, their pre-reform levels. The government wanted to maintain *status quo* with regard to the prices of certain essential and politically sensitive commodities. This was a costly programme which covered both the rich and the poor.

(b) **Targeted Direct price subsidies:-** This scheme provided subsidies to the targeted groups through a two or multi-tier pricing system. Through thee scheme, different targeted groups were provided with different degree of subsidies at different levels through bread or other coupons, while the final price for consumer, in general, remained the unregulated 'free' market price. This scheme had many advantages. From the point of view of efficiency, the market price distortions were removed to a large extent. The scheme was more equitable than the first since subsidies were targeted at the poor and other vulnerable groups in society. Its main problem was implementation because the identification of targeted groups and the administration of the system were difficult.

(c) **Income supplement to the poor:** - This third scheme was similar to the second scheme barring that, instead of received bread coupons, the targeted groups received the implicit premium in their bread coupons in the form of food stamps of certain value, that can be spent in shop. The advantages of this scheme was that, it was administratively less cumbersome and less costly to implement. In addition, it gave a degree of overall more flexibility the consumers and the government. It did not require to create a separate markets in different types of coupons like bread, meat, sugar, etc. and it provided the consumer more flexibility in solving his/her expenditure allocation problems.

Land and Agricultural policy

In 1979, the Revolutionary Council nationalised almost all dead or underdeveloped land in urban areas. The implementation of land policy in rural area was slow and more conservative. The Revolutionary Council approved a land distribution bill in March 1980 during Bani Sadre presidency which permitted the division of the large assets without indemnification. But it was protested a prominent clergy, Qumi of Mashhad, who condemned the expropriation of private property an un-Islamic. So, Ayatollah Khomeini asked Ayatollah Montazeri, Beheshti, and Meshkini to see whether or not the bill was in accordance with Islamic law. They reviewed the bill and did not find any thing un-Islamic. The bill ordered the distribution of land to the landless and poor peasants, high school and college graduates, civil servants and other who desired to cultivate the land. Landlords were to be indemnified net of their debts to the government and any outstanding religious dues. When the land distribution at village level was stated, it was vehemently opposed by landlords and they succeeded in obtaining fatawa (religious decree) against the distribution of land. Government was under heavy pressure on the issue of land distribution, and finally, Khomeini ordered the suspension of land distribution in November 1980.

The new government's major agricultural policy was to promote self-sufficiency in basic staples through a whole range of incentive policies. These included subsidisation at the production (output and input prices) and consume levels. The fixed prices were set on basic staples such as meat, sugar, beets, cotton and oil seed. The prices of these commodities were based on production cost, inflation and input prices. Moreover, there were other incentives, for instance, farmer may used a percentage of the money which they received from the government for their wheat to purchase consumer goods or tractor at official rates far below market prices. The government also bought part of the farm's surplus staple produce and milk, thus, limiting the role of the private sector in marketing, especially in the wheat market.

The government also subsidized on agricultural inputs, e.g. fertilizers and pesticide. At consumer level, basic staples (except rice) wererre subsidized, and their prices were controlled. There was two-tier pricing policy with the use of ration coupons where wheat was heavily subsidised. There was dual market for meat: the controlled prices of meat, and the free market. Milk was bought by the government at a high prices, and consumer bought it either at a lover price with ration coupons, or at a free market price.

Iran and the OPEC (Organization of the Petroleum Exporting Countries)

The Islamic Republic played a significant role as a OPEC member in the world energy market. In the matter of oil, Iran's policy tilted towards the so-called 'hawks' - Libya and Algeria – who tried to keep the price as high as possible because high price of oil would benefit Iran. Thus, Iran left its earlier middle path policy. Iran's OPEC policy had a political motive as well. The Iran-Iraq War divided OPEC members into two groups. Some OPEC members sided with Iraqis, whereas Libya was with Iran. Any decision in the OPEC during this period further created problem for Iran, and Iraq was better treated.

The tension within OPEC eventually led price collapse in 1986 due to excess supply of oil in the world market that reduced Saudi production from 10 mbd in 1980 to 2.5 mbd in 1985. Saudi Arabia first threatened to cut prices and was ignored, but it switched to the infamous netback pricing policy that ensured Saudi oil was the cheapest in the world.[14] The political division within OPEC created inability to control members' output at this juncture, OPEC needed to adjust the price downward without backbiting.

Iran's oil production policy was also affected by a view of OPEC as a price-setting agency where the world price was decided in bargaining over price rather than output, in this situation Iran's decision to adopt a production ceiling of 4 mbd made sense. Prices were so high and foreign

---

14   Iran blamed for the price collapse entirely on Saudi Arabia, declared act as a 'treason' and 'declaration of war' (MEES, 10 October, 1988). For price collapse, see Jacques Cremer and Djavad Salehi Isfahani, eds., *Models of the Oil Market, Fundamentals of Pure and Applied Economics* (Switzerland: Harwood Academic, 1991).

exchange so abundant that not a single country was thinking of expanding production, much less doing so while cheating or acting against the interest of fellow OPEC members.[15]

After the price collapse of August 1986 and the end of the war in august 1988, Iran decided to abandon its production ceiling and to expand capacity. Iran made statements in 1991 for a production capacity of 5 mbd and started to lobby for a higher quota. To gain OPEC's blessing to increase production, Iran decided to improve its relations with Saudi Arabia, which was in a position to help Iran in gaining its OPEC share.[16] Iran got Saudi support for a higher Quota.

In the early 1990s, Iran's policy had been changed and adopted middle path and wanted to get its natural place in OPEC as one of the two most important producers in the organization and as the mediator between the hawks and doves. However, external oil policy of Iran was more precisely adopted by its rivalry with Saudi Arabia for leadership of OPEC. The Gulf War 1991 made Iraq out of picture, so Iran moved in to fill the vacuum. But in purely commercial term, Iran was in no position to mount a serious challenge to Saudi Arabia by capturing its market share, it applied considerable pressure on other fronts. Iran used Saudi weakness by portraying the kingdom's oil policies in general, and its decisions in OPEC in particular, as motivated by its subservience to the consuming nations' interests, particularly that of the United States. Iran depicted Saudi Arabia alternatively as friend and foe. President Rafsanjani initiated a call to King Fahd of Saudi Arabia to break deadlock in OPEC's September 1993 negotiations, which resulted in a compromise and ended the stalemate in favour of a boost in Iran's quota form 3.4 to 3.6 mbd. But within six month, the moderate language toward Saudi Arabia turned into a war of words. At the time of the next OPEC meeting of March 1994 in which Iran advocated a drop of 1.4 mbd in the OPEC ceiling (from 24.52 mbd), most of which

---

15 This is the argument behind the backward bending supply curve for oil which argues that OPEC was not a cartel before 1982, and thereafter only an unsuccessful one. See Jacques Cremer and Djavad Salehi Isfahani, "The Rise and Fall of Oil Prices: A Comparative Review", *Annale d'Economie at the Statistique* 15/16 (July-December 1989), pp. 427-54.

16 Iran's share in OPEC output infact declined from around 20 percent in 1970s to 10 percent in 1980s. In 1994 its share rose to 15 percent.

would presumably have come form Saudi Arabia. In this meeting Saudi prevailed and OPEC froze its ceiling for another nine months.

Iran accused Saudi Arabia of maintaining a high output of 8 mbd against its own interests and solely for the purpose of pleasing the Unites States. Although, oil issue dominates in the relations between Iran and Saudi Arabia, the two countries interact at several other levels, competing for leadership in the Persian Gulf and in the Islamic world.

Monetary policy

The Central Bank of the Islamic Republic of Iran is formally responsible for the monetary policy. The Central Bank forbids the use of interest, the monetary policy can not be in the way of fixed interest rates. Various measures are taken to determine the level of liquidity. The Central Bank intervenes and supervises the banking system's operation in various ways. It is the Central Bank which fixes minimum or maximum rates of profit for banks in their joint venture and *muzaraba*[17] contract; minimum anticipated rates of return for various investment and partnership projects; and minimum and maximum profit margins for installment and hire-purchase transaction. The Central Bank determines maximum and minimum rates of Commission for banking services and fees charged on investment accounts; it determines the types, account, and minimum and maximum bonuses paid to depositors.

In the 1980s, the Iranian economy was in deep trouble due to erratic oil revenues and other economic performances. The ups and downs of oil revenues not only effected the level of consumption of government revenues, expenditure and deficit, but budgetary deficit also determined the monetary base of the economy. Increasing dependency on Central Bank credits to finance these deficits had obstructed the implementation

---

[17] The term *muzaraba* means profit-sharing in trade. This term is derived from the word *'zarb'* means walking or traveling, which applied to the function of the agent or the merchant-labour who works for the commercial capitalist, who owns capital. The agent and the commercial capitalist may each comprise more than one person. The condition for the establishment of a profit sharing-enterprise in trade or *muzabara* resembles to that in *muzara*. *Muzara* is considered an Islamic type of share-crop, where one party provides land and the other provides labour. In this contract profit-sharing can be based on a predetermined fixed quantity of output or sum of money. They take their shares according to an agreed proportion of total output.

of monetary policies for specific macro or micro-economic objectives. In spite of decline of real GDP in 1984-89, the growth of private sector liquidity had always been higher than that intended by the government. Despite the government's official policy of curbing the growth of commercial credit in favour of industrial and agricultural credit, it was the commercial credit that had the highest growth rate during that period. Moreover, the dependence on imports of intermediate and capita goods, poor management, and the overall lack of co-ordination within the industrial sector gave rise to structural problems. Budgetary deficit, which increased demand for goods and services that pushed up prices and led to high inflation. In 1980s, this problem arose by the fall in output which contributed to unprecedented stagflation. However, inflation was lower than many underdeveloped economies, primarily because increase in liquidity was held back through price control by the private sector. "The high level of liquidity indicates that there was a high inflationary potential during the recovery and the reconstruction period."[18]

Monetary base was expanded rapidly which was used to finance public sector-borrowing that led to transfer of resources form the private to the public sector mainly for consumption purposes. The Central Bank took measures and enhanced reserve requirements and set credit ceilings to provide extra sources for government deficit financing. The banking system was also used to divert resources to the public sector. The increased private liquidity was transferred to the public sector since the swelling in credit was bound to the expansion of private liquidity. This was the main cause of the expansion of monetary base through public sector borrowing. Thus, the Central Bank was in position to control in swelling the private liquidity through monetary expansion base. The expansion of the monetary base and inflation led to depreciation of the *rial* in the free market, that made the free market exchange rate an important outlet for private savings. The inabilities to control the money supply and give stability to the currency were major factors in economic policy changing of the Rafsanjani government.

---

18 Ali Rahnema and Farhad Nomani, eds., *The Secular Miracle: Religion, Politics and Economic Policy in Iran* (London: Zed Book, 1990), pp.286-87

Foreign Exchange policy

Changes in foreign exchange policy was felt to break the economic stagnation that persisted since the revolution. The decline of oil revenues as foreign exchange as a result of military import and capital flight, led to a severe balance of payment crisis. The government responded by imposing capital controls and bringing a system of multiple exchange rate. At the same time, the foreign exchange constraint was further deteriorated as a result of the freezing of Iran's foreign assets in the west/US and the repayment of her outstanding foreign debt according to the 1980 Algiers's Agreement, that led to the reduction of Iran's foreign exchange from eleven billion dollars to about four billion dollars.[19]

The government adopted a very complex system of multiple exchange rates which comprised at a time ten different rates. Bilateral real exchange rate (BRER) and multi-lateral real exchange rate (MRER) was adopted by the government to stop further deterioration of the country's economic condition. The official exchange rate was set artificially at low level. The balance of payment crisis and macro-economic disequilibrium contributed to a remarkable long period of real exchange rate misalignment. The real exchange rate indices illustrated the accumulation of relative price distortions in Iran.

A policy of dual exchange rates could be viewed as a justifiable short-term response to the temporary balance of payments problems.[20] This dual exchange rate was only for short-term in order to maintain balance of payments under control. This policy was taken in order to maintain low prices for essential goods and reducing capital flight. The foreign exchange policies contributed to massive distortions of the price system, high budge deficit and distortion of the non-oil current account and other macro-economic distortions.[21]

---

19 For detail of the Algiers Agreement, see report of the *US Congress Committee on Banking, Finance and Urban Affairs (1981)*

20 See Agenor (1990), Dornbusch (1986 A and B), for detail of the use of multiple exchange rates as a tool for temporary balance of payment adjustment.

21 Behdad (1988) and Pesaran (1992) discuss the consequences of an over valued exchange rate for the Iranian economy.

Fiscal policy

The government adopted a restrictive fiscal stance. The ratio of government expenditure to GDP declined form 42.6 percent in 1977/78 to 16.0 percent in 1988/89. This ration of decline in government expenditure was not entirely of deliberate policy rather it can be interpreted as a result of the decline in oil revenues. The overall fiscal position of the government is illustrated in table1.

Table 1. shows regarding expenditure that expenditure was shifting away form capital to current expenditure. The ratio of capital expenditure in GDP declined in 1977/78 from 15.6 percent to 3.1 percent in 1988/89. As an outcome of this decline, maintenance and improvements in the infrastructure of the country had been put off at a heavy and long-term expenses. The shrinkage in development expenditure had several explanations. The Iran-Iraq War and the decline in oil revenues was the main factor in the reduction of the allocation of sizeable funds for development projects.

The US economic sanctions against Iran at international level created many economic difficulties for Iran to interact with other countries in having trade relation. The ascendancy of clergy to power deteriorated relations with the European countries which were its main partners in the pre-revolution period after the US. Second, the situation where political instability and uncertainty was high and there was intensified redistributive measures, long-term projects sacrificed and pushed back, and the government concentrated on the short-term projects. Since 1978-79, the current expenditure constantly increased except 1986/87, in 1986/87 the economy was in grim condition and foreign exchange reserve came down at the lowest ebb as never touched ever before.

In regard to revenues, the decline in oil revenues pushed pressure on non-oil revenues that increased the proportional share of taxes in total revenues. Despite increase the proportional share of taxes in total revenue, tax revenues, remarkably shrinked since the revolution. Taxes as a percentage of GDP declined from 8.4 percent in 1978/79 to 3.7 percent in 1988/89. The decline in real tax had several reasons. Fluctuations in tax revenues were largely determined by economic institutions and macro-economic policies of the government. Particularly, in Iranian case, the decline in tax revenues had been partly because of expansion in the size of parallel economy and service sectors. The expanded economy and service sectors were more difficult to monitor and tax than other sector of the economy. Government's incapacity to finance its budget deficit form the banking system and the cost of raising income taxes in a political instablity was one of the most important reason behind the shrinkage in tax revenues. The drastic reduction in imports, the tariffs on which comprised a major chunk of the government's tax revenues.

The para-statal organisations had also a significant fiscal impact. They had been not only the recipients of both budgetary assistance and subsidies through the receipt of foreign exchange at the official rate but also they had been largely exempted form taxation.

Despite restrictive expenditure stance, the government was under heavy deficit that sharply increased form 458 billion *rials* in 1977/78 to 2125.6 billion *rials* in 1988/89. Table 1 also demonstrates the rise of the budget deficit in relation to the GDP. This budget deficit was largely covered by borrowing from the banking system due to certain limitations were imposed on foreign borrowing by political conditions in Iran. Except short-term credit, government was not in a position to borrow abroad long-term credit. Consequently, Iran' long-term foreign debt decreased form 2875.9 million dollars in 1980/81 to 255.6 million dollars in 1989/90.[22]

---

22 Iran's long-term foreign debts decreased sharply after the revolution and the government was able to obtain some short-term credit. In the end of 1990-91, Iran's foreign obligation was at about 4.7 billion US dollars.

Table 1. The government budget (in billions of current rials).

	1977/78	1978/79	1979/80	1980/81	1981/82	1982/83	1983/84	1984/85	1985/86	1986/87	1987/88	1988/89
Rerevnes	2034.2	1598.9	1699.6	1325.9	1770.1	2501.9	2773.7	2714.8	2666.2	1707.3	2171.3	2085.0
Oil & gas	1497.8	1013.2	1219.7	888.8	1056.4	1689.5	1779.4	1373.2	1188.7	416.8	766.2	667.9
Taxes	443.6	465.9	368.3	340.4	554.1	613.9	796.5	898.7	1033.7	1024.6	1030.0	986.2
Services & Sale of Goods	20.0	15.5	21.9	29.2	37.0	72.0	81.1	312.3	220.4	146.1	243.6	321.5
Others	72.8	104.3	89.7	67.5	122.6	126.5	116.7	130.5	223.4	119.8	131.5	109.4
Expenditures	2492.2	2207.8	227.9	2298.4	2707.1	3167.4	3672.3	3353.6	333.2	3156.8	3640.4	4210.6
Current	1565.4	1550.7	1594.8	1730.3	2032.4	2252.4	2523.7	2475.6	2548.1	2410.3	2911.2	3394.2
Fixed Capital formations	926.8	657.1	633.1	568.1	674.7	914.8	1148.6	878.0	765.1	746.5	729.2	816.4
Deficit / GDP (%)	7.8	11.0	8.3	14.7	11.2	6.0	6.4	4.2	3.9	8.0	6.9	8.1

These exclude special revenues and expenditures.

These include the sale of foreign exchange.

Source: The Central Bank of the Islamic Republic of Iran.

The Islamic Banking System and the Financial Institutions

In 1979, banks and insurance companies and the "Law of Usury-Free Banking was approved by Parliament in August 1983."[23] Under this law, "banks perform the function of a profit-sharing institution."[24] The bank introduced two types of deposits: *qard al-hasanah* (interest-free) deposits (both current and savings); and term-investment deposits. *Qarz al-hasanah* current account is similar to earlier current accounts and *qarz al-hasanah* savings account are interest free savings account. These both types of accounts are operating in Iran. Moreover, banks can bewitch deposits through non-fixed bounces in cash; absolving depositors from payment of commissions and fees; or giving priority to depositors in the utilisation of banking facilities.

There are two types of term-investment deposits: short-term (3 months) with a minimum amount of 2000 *rials*, and long-term (1 year) with a minimum amount of 50000 *rials*. Banks have right to utilize their resources in investment projects, sharing the profit (or loss) in proportion with the depositors' funds, in that case a commission is charged by the banks. Theoretically, the profits earned as an outcome of the bank's investment are divided among depositors, after deduction of the bank's fees. The return is calculated in proportion to the total value of investment deposits, excluding the required reserves. Moreover, bank must announce their profit rate every six months, when the share of profit of the depositors is due to be paid. If deposits are withdrawn before maturity or reduced below the required minimum, no profit will be earned. The term investment funds can be used by banks according to Islamic criteria like *muzaraba*, *musharaka*[25], direct investment, hire-purchase forward transactions, credit sale in industrial, agricultural and the service sectors. Consumers can receive *qarz al-hasanah* loans and enter into credit sale contracts for consumption purposes.

Hire-purchase is a leasing contract and forward transaction is the cash purchase of products in advance at a fixed price. Credit sale is sale

---

23 Nomani, n. 10, p.178

24 Ibid, p.178

25 The *mushraka* contract is the Islamic form of a partnership in which two or more people invest their capital in a single enterprise and the profit is divided between/among them at the end term of contract. Joint stock companies or corporations have been considered as legitimate Islamic entities.

by investment where in the bank may acquire a commodity and sell it to applicants in installments.

In March 1985, according to the balance sheet of the banking system at the end of the first year of operation of the new system, 39.2 percent of private sector deposits had been transformed into *qarz al-hasanah* and term-investment deposits; the rest were in the form of saving and time deposits. *Qarz al-hasanah* deposits are considered simply as demand deposits and can be withdrawn at will.

The Central Bank determines the rate of profit on term-investment accounts on the basis of the overall profits of the banking system. In 1985-87, the "official rates of profit" (or interest rates) for short-term and long-term investment accounts were 6 percent and 8.5 percent respectively. In real terms, these rates were negative after adjusting inflation. Banks are allowed to change a commission on loans given to borrower; the lowest rate being on housing loans. "Some banks have been ordered by the Central Bank to finance government projects."[26]

The specialized banks were not allowed to receive private sector deposits, so, they depend on the Central Bank and the government deposits. It led to a paucity of funds for the specialized banks. The commercial banks lend their excess liquidity tone another on a fixed rate of return.

As far as interest-free banking is concerned, there is a device that facilitates evasion of Islamic practices, discounting. The purchase of debt or discounting is legitimate in *Shii* banking law in Iran.

At present, the largest and economically powerful private enterprise in Iran is the Islamic Economic Organisation (IEO). The IEO originally came into existence after the Revolution to work as an interest-free loan fund, accepting deposits and granting loans. Initially, it was called Islamic Bank. When all banks were nationalised after the Revolution, it was spared from nationalisation due to personal intervention of Khomeini. But soon changed its name to IEO. This IEO is not under control of the Central Bank, it is a "non-profit" oriented enterprises. It has expanded its activity to cover trade, construction, and imports and exports in order to increase its capital. It competes with the nationalised banking system and does not always co-ordinate its policy with the government's monetary policy.

---

26 Rahnema, n.18, pp.281-82

The Performance of Economy Before the Beginning of the First-Five-Year Plan

The profound institutional changes and the economic shocks had adverse impacts on both aggregate supply and demand as Table1 shows. The decline in oil revenues consequently led to sharp reduction in real aggregate expenditures. On the other hand, shortage of foreign exchange for import of intermediate goods for industries, and increase in real wages, among other factors, created severe supply-side problems.

Table 2 demonstrates the changes in various components of aggregate demand. After the Revolution, the private investment dramatically declined, and by and large remained stagnant despite some recovery in the period from 1983 to 1985. In the aftermath of the Revolution, the government was determined to contain expenditures as Table 2 shows. The expenditure's trend is in declining. Gross national income is not upward mood but very much erratic, and more or less stagnant. The shortage of foreign exchange, and the heavy dependence of Iranian industries of imported intermediate goods, lowered the rate of capacity utilisation in the manufacturing sector to about 30 percent. It is noteworthy that in 1979/80, nearly 57 percent of the value of output in the manufacturing sector, was consisted of imported inputs. This heavy dependency of Iranian industries on imported intermediate and primary goods was due to basically in the continuation of import-substitution policies prior to the Revolution. The diminution in the availability of credit to the Private sector, and the dawn of Islamic banking system, contributed to the decline in private sector accumulation.

The sectoral changes came in response to the decline in oil revenues and the macro-economic policies of the government. There was a significant decline in the manufacturing sector owing to decline in foreign exchange receipts, and the erosion of property rights. On the other hand, expansion of government intervention in the economy like price control, massive distortions in prices and incentive system, and adoption of multiple exchange rate system, led to the expansion of the service sector and parallel economy.

Table 2. Gross National Expenditure in billions of rials, 1974/75 prices

	1977/78	1978/79	1979/80	1980/81	1981/82	1982/83	1983/84	1984/85	1985/86	1986/87	1987/88	1988/89
Consumption	2638.3	2542.3	2162.6	2039.5	2368.0	2317.7	2548.8	2626.2	2721.4	2410.8	2317.9	2260.9
Private	1839.1	1745.0	1525.9	1458.0	1761.3	1715.7	1951.5	2026.7	2127.6	1936.4	1868.2	1797.0
Public	799.2	797.3	636.7	581.5	606.7	602.0	597.3	563.5	593.8	477.4	449.7	463.9
Gross domestic Fixed capital formation	1074.7	928.3	575.8	562.4	572.8	587.2	809.4	814.3	707.3	843.7	444.8	427.0
Private	412.2	280.7	258.2	268.4	271.1	202.0	417.4	444.5	397.8	297.3	255.3	238.4
Public	662.5	647.7	317.6	294.0	301.7	367.2	392.0	369.8	309.5	246.4	189.5	188.6
Changes in Inventories	-122.0	-308.7	53.6	308.6	437.9	-105.2	211.0	-74.0	43.5	357.7	366.7	286.7
Net exports	94.7	67.0	182.6	-342.9	-447.1	-100.7	-380.8	-385.0	-258.5	-127.6	-80.4	129.9
Statistical discrepancies	357.6	130.8	94.6	-74.4	-243.9	375.8	203.0	522.7	437.4	159.3	257.7	257.7

	1977/78	1978/79	1979/80	1980/81	1981/82	1982/83	1983/84	1984/85	1985/86	1986/87	1987/88	1988/89
Gross domestic expenditure	4043.3	3359.7	3069.2	2491.2	2687.7	3047.58	3391.4	3504.2	3651.1	3343.9	3306.7	3362.2
Net factor income from abroad	-37.7	-71.9	58.6	32.7	51.6	31.1	47.7	38.3	19.2	19.3	6.4	7.8
Gross national expenditure	4005.6	3287.8	3127.58	2523.9	2739.3	3105.9	3439.1	3542.5	3670.3	3363.2	3313.1	3370.0
Terms of trade adjustment	107.7	-0.7	255.1	256.7	269.5	335.2	386.3	366.3	247.4	-85.3	-5.1	10.1
Gross national income	4113.3	3287.1	3382.9	2780.6	3008.8	3441.1	3825.4	3908.8	3917.7	3277.69	3318.2	3380.0

Source: The Central Bank of Islamic Republic of Iran.

Table 3 demonstrates the sectoral composition of GDP. The most important development, which this table shows the decline in the share of petroleum sector. But it should not be interpreted as indication a declining dependency of the Iranian economy on oil. However, oil has had the most important source of foreign exchange for the government. Industrial sector was very much in trouble after the Revolution due to not clear-cut policy of the government. In the post-Revolution, the industrial sector as has been illustrated in the Table 3, either stagnant or recession due to intermediate goods' shortage on which the Iranian industries were dependent, and these goods were not imported owing to shortage of foreign exchange. It was the reason that the Iranian industry did not perform well. Table 3 demonstrates the expansion in the share of agricultural output. Real agricultural output increased at an average annual rate of 5.2 percent between 1979/80 and 1988/89. The continuous growth in agricultural output is largely due to the least disturbance by revolutionary upheaval and the Iran-Iraq War. In addition, particularly agricultural sector has been the recipient of the special attention and subsidization by the government and the government's determination to decrease reliance in importing food.

Since the Revolution, the most important development has been the hypertrophy of the services and the informal sectors. Particularly, this trend has been noticed in the area of trade activities. The main cause of the expansion of the service sector is rooted in the decline in the manufacturing sector and in large-scale economic production units, both of which has forced a large portion of the labour force into the service sector. The sizeable parallel market premium and the rents involved in trade activity also provided strong incentives for the rapid expansion of the trade activities. This phenomenal rise in trade activity occurred when the country was significantly less open to international market.

Table 3: The Sectoral composition of GDP (in billions of rials, 19974/75 prices, percentage shares in parenthesis.

	Agriculture	Oil	Industry	Services	GDP
1975/76	320.0 (10.3)	1264.5 (40.1)	532.5 (16.9	1029.1 (32.7)	3150.1
1976/77	341.7 (9.7)	1384.6 (39.2)	630.4 (17.9)	1173.2 (33.21)	3529.9
1977/78	340.9 (8.7)	1363.4 (34.8)	645.6 (16.5)	1753.8 (44.7)	3992.3
1978/79	352.6 (10.8)	929.8 (285)	553.9 (17.0)	1620.4 (49.6)	3266.9
1979/80	356.3 (11.6)	767.6 (25.0)	511.9 (16.7)	1560.7 (50.8)	3070.5
1980/81	360.3 (14.8)	230.6 (9.5)	520.6 (21.4)	1319.0 (54.3)	2430.5
1981/82	400.0 (15.1)	251.1 (9.5)	598.8 (22.6)	1397.6 (52.8)	2647.5
1982/83	438.7 (13.8)	557.3 (17.5)	521.4 (18.3)	1471.0 (48.7)	3018.4
1983/84	453.9 (13.8)	547.6 (17.5)	630.0 (19.2)	1625.0 (49.5)	3283.5
1984/85	486.9 (14.4)	454.3 (13.8)	684.5 (19.1)	1773.8 (52.5)	3374.5
1985/86	526.0 (15.0)	470.3 (13.4)	673.5 (19.1)	1847.3 (52.5)	3517.1
1986/87	548.5 (17.0)	401.5 (12.4)	632.0 (19.6)	1648.8 (51.0)	3230.8
1987/89	562.9 (17.6)	457.1 (14.3)	599.3 (18.7)	1584.0 (49.4)	3203.3
1988/89	584.9 (17.9)	486.8 (14.9)	592.7 (18.1)	1608.6 (49.1)	3273.0

Source: The Central Bank of the Islamic Republic of Iran

Table 4: Selected Economic Indicators

	Money supply Growth (M2)	CPI Inflation	Foreign Reserves Growth	Real GDP Growth
1975/76	44.1	12.8	1.8	2.6
1976/77	39.1	10.9	30.5	12.1
1977/78	14.7	27.6	23.2	11.1
1978/79	41.1	11.7	1.8	-16.7
1979/80	37.7	10.5	37.4	-6.0
1980/81	20.8	26.0	-41.8	-20.8
1981/82	16.6	22.4	44.6	8.9
1982/83	22.7	19.2	-12.0	14.0
1983/84	17.2	17.7	-13.5	8.8
1984/85	5.9	10.5	-16.9	2.2
1985/86	12.3	4.1	17.0	4.2
1986/87	18.3	20.8	0.1	-8.1
1987/88	19.1	27.8	-4.8	-0.1
1988/89	22.3	28.9	-4.7	2.2

Source: The Central Bank of the Islamic Republic of Iran

The real economic activity was virtually stagnant during 1978/79 and 1988/89; real GDP, measured in constant 1974/75 prices, increased only slightly from 3226.9 billions of *rials* in 1978/79 to 3273.0 billion rails in 1988/89. However, table 3 illustrates fluctuations in the GDP, in 1980/81, it was at the lowest point. In the post-Revolution period, the highest growth of the GDP is 3517.1 billion *rials* in 1985/86. Table 4 indicates the real GDP growth rate is by and large stagnant, and economic condition is not positive, and there is high fluctuation in GDP growth. The foreign reserves growth is negative, the decline in foreign exchange is due to the decline in oil revenues, because oil is the main source of foreign exchange. In this period inflation is very high except 1985/86, there is always inflation in double digit. This high inflation severely affected the poor, lower-middle class and the salaried-people. Money supply growth is always in double digit except 1984/85 during the period which has brought inflation.

External trade

Table 5 demonstrates that the overall balance was continuously deteriorating. The country was under balance of payments crises. The main cause in the deterioration of the balance of payments was the decline in both oil revenues and non-oil exports and simultaneous trade sanctions imposed by US on Iran. The oil sector was in erratic position and non-oil sectors was also in downswing. The prime factor in deterioration of the non-oil current account was the sizeable misalignment of the exchange rate. Table 5 show some improvement in non-oil export since 1986/87 was on account of the introduction of preferential exchange rates for exports and the reduction in the current requirement on these exports. As Table 5 illustrates, non-oil exports increase from 284 million dollars in 1982/83 to 1160 in 1987/88.

Import was also on declining trend. Current account was negative, it means, the county was under severe financial crunch. The country's overall balance was incessantly deteriorating.

Iranian Economy Under Plan

Iran-Iraq War had shattered the Iranian economy. War-ravaged economy sought to reconstruct it in a plan way. The problem was not only the availability of financial resources but also the structural and economic mismanagement that had been neglected for many years. After the end of war, government's main agenda was to reconstruct the war-ravaged areas, and a general improvement of the quality of life of the people. So, Iran had to concentrate on medium term development programmes to balance and fulfill the short-term needs of the people against the nation's long-term interests. It was against this background that planners developed First-Five year plan, covering 1989/90 to 1993/94 for economic, social and cultural development.[27]

The first-Five-Year Plan 1989/90-1993/94 started for an organized economic development. Practically, plan's implementation came into delay until early in 1990 due to political and economic debates in the parliament. The thrust of the plan was to increase investment in economy, particularly increase investment in private sector, increase in employment by creating

---

27 The Iranian solar calendar year, which starts on 21 March has been converted to the Gregoian calendar by adding 621 to the solar year.

Table 5. Balance of payments (in millions of US dollars)

	1976/77	1977/78	1978/79	1979/80	1980/81	1981/82	1982/83	1983/84	1984/85	1985/86	1986/87	1987/88	1988/89
Trade Balance	10859	7358	5872	15650	1450	-1307	7900	3480	2358	2169	-3414	-89	101
Export (f.o.b.)	24719	24076	17675	24171	12338	11831	20452	21507	17087	14175	7171	11916	10709
Oil and gas	24179				11639	11491	20168	21150	16726	13710	6255	10755	
Non-Oil	540				645	340	284	357	361	465	916	1160	
Imports (f.o.b)	-13860	-16718	-11803	-8521	-1088	-13138	-12552	-18027	-14729	-12006	-10585	-12005	-10608
Current Account	7660	2816	104	11968	-2438	-3446	5733	358	-414	-476	-5155	-2090	-1869
Capital Account	-4957				-8238	1441	-1847	-2474	-2818	544	3127	2097	
SDR Allocations	75	85	125	220	307	339	331	324	314	361	410	486	156
Net Erros and Omissions	-290	-360	-654	-876	829	1635	1001	867	-904	487	814	155	539
Overall balance	2413	2090	-715	3069	-9847	-370	4887	-1249	-4136	555	-1214	-224	-1010

Source: International Financial Statistics, IMF

new jobs in various sectors, increase in per-capita income and to reduce its budget deficit from 51 percent to 1.5 percent by the end of the plan. The five-year-plan explicitly asserted that, "the change in price policy for goods and service is in such a way gradually equilibrium prices are achieved for economic resources and in this process, prices are determined...based on... demand and supply."[28] According to macroeconomics point of view, this policy seeks to reduce the government budget deficit and a gradual unification of different foreign exchange rates.

The First-Five-Year plan 1989/90-1993/94 started in Iran for a balanced economic development. The aims of the plan had been the following:

1. Eliminating fiscal disequilibrium and reducing inflation;

2. Cope with economic stagnation and increasing output and employment;

3. Curtailing the size of the government, and boosting a greater role for the private sector through denationalization of state owned enterprises;

4. Reducing sectoral imbalances, particularly the growth of the service sector;

5. Unification and liberalisation of the exchange rate system.

Over and above, the government adopted various measures towards reduction of fiscal subsidies, price-liberalisation and trade reform. The liberalization-stabilisation policy was a recognition of the inability of the government to exercise a high degree of centralized control over the economy. The reduction of the state's role in the economic affairs was affected through the transfer of of some of the service to the private sector, and by the complete or partial privatization of some state-owned enterprises. The government also made incentives for foreign investors, particularly those who were seeking the return of expatriates Iranian skilled labourers and entrepreneurs. Therefore, in many ways, the five-year-plan made an attempt to reverse many of the institutional developments and the post-Revolution period's initial policies.

---

28   *Kayhan,* weekly, *30 Aban,* 1369 (1990)

Despite the main goal of accelerating economic growth, the first plan also pursued other objectives, such as expanding and upgrading defence capabilities; reconstructing war-ravaged areas, diversifying the economy; expanding infrastructure; developing the industrial, mining, petroleum, natural gas, electricity and telecommunication sectors, supporting higher education and research, improving medical care; pursuing an equitable distribution of resources; reforming administrative structure; and reorganizing distribution of the population and economic activity nation-wide.

However, the First Plan had some shortcomings, it was reviewed in 1992 and its some policies were reversed. The First Plan's mid-term appraisal in 1992, its success was seen the country's on going Structural Adjustment Programme (SAP), the so-called Rafsanjani perestroika.[29] The SAP included an orderly exchange-rate unification, increased fiscal and monetary disciplines, trade and business deregulation, privatization of money-losing enterprises, restructuring state bureaucracy, attraction of the foreign private investments and the establishment of budgetary control over the semi-independent para-satatal.

On the whole, "the government has been reducing subsides; dismantling price controls; rationings and administrative distribution of essential goods; freeing private participation in imports; encouraging private and foreign investment; setting up free industrial trade zones; reforming multiple currency practices; increasing indirect taxes and selling government enterprises."[30]

Privatisation

The economy was virtually stagnant, the public sector failed to stop this stagnation. The government had little option but to turn to the private sector and the nationalised banks for assistance of national economy recovery. The first concerted effort toward economic liberalization and deregulation was to be found in the government's lifting restrictions on the importation of many essential and luxury items by the private sector. It was to be followed by a comprehensive privatisation policy announced in April 1989 that based on the transfer of ownership of all "non-essential

---

29 Jahangir Amuzegar, "Iran's Economy and the US Sanctions", *The Middle East Journal*, vol.51, no.2, Spring 1979, p.189

30 Nomani, n.10, p.185

and non-strategic" profit and loss-making companies o the private sector.

One of the main components of the liberalization strategy, was the revival of the Tehran stock exchange. Its purpose was to raise investment capital as well as to boost private participation in the reconstruction of the county's economy. The Economic Council directed public organisations to offer more shares on the exchange in the units affiliated to them. Under the Economics and Finance Ministry directive in 1988, any company which had more than a hundred shares was allowed to get registration on the stock exchange.

The denationalization speed accelerated in 1991 and 1992. The plan sought to encourage private investment in the productive-sectors and public participation in decision making process regarding educational and cultural policies. The private sector had to tackle economic hardships, thus alleviate some of the government's burden, the co-operative sector was to grow. It was announced in May 1991 that, "the National Iranian Industry Organisation (NIIO) would sell 100 billion *rials*' worth of shares in state-owned companies to the private sector."[31] In August 1991, was further announced that, "120 billion *rials*' worth of shares in firms and factories controlled by the NIIO would be put on sale through the stock exchange by the end of March 1992."[32] "By the end of March 1991, 77 factories had been sold to the private sector from which the government had earned some 37 billion *rials*."[33]

The government privatized all mines except those regarded as holding "strategic reserves". The Supreme Council of Mines, extended the duration on mine extraction from 6 to 15 years to encourage the greater participation on the private sector in mining. Iran's National Steel Company announced to provide financial assistance to the private sector in regard to the exploitation of mines. So, the state was giving subsidy for the re-entry of the private sector into large-scale mining and mining related-operations. "Within the first 17 months of this policy, over 150 mines extracting coal and various minerals were transferred to the private sector."[34] All coal, industrial dolomite and chalk mines were privatized.

---

31 *BBC's Summary of World Broadcasts (SBW)*, ME/W0180, 21 May, 1991

32 *BBC's Summary of World Broadcasts (SWB)*, ME/W0193, 20 August 1991

33 *BBC's Summary of World Broadcasts (SWB)*, ME/W0195, 3 September, 1991

34 *BBC's Summary of World Broadcasts (SWB)*, ME/W0161, 8 January, 1991

By July 1992, as many as 1400 national mines had been transferred to the private sector.

Even heavy industries had not spared from the privatization. Many heavy industries had been privatized that heavy industries were nationalised in 1979. During the first Plan, a number of large industrial projects initiated by the public sector, were also handed over to the private sector upon completion, in addition to 9 petrochemical projects. Furthermore, not only the state sector was sold to the private sector but they also allowed to invest their capital in new construction and industrial plant of the state. Such as the First Plan created mixed-economy.

The Construction *Jehad Ministry* transferred some of its assets to the private sector, like milk and the production industries, haymaking livestock breeding, farms and pasture land, forestry resources and fisheries. Privatisation of public undertakings companies and assets began while Hashemi Rafsanjani was president from 1989 to 1997. He introduced privatization to improve economy but could not materialize due to economic sanctions.

Mohammad Khatami (1997-2005) continued privatization policy of the previous administration and privatized several public undertakings companies and entities. His policy of privatization led economic growth simultaneously fuelled inflation. The rising inflation caused economic hardship to people. Privatisation also caused replacement and displacement of workers from public undertakings companies and entities and brought pressure over employment. Unemployment increased during the Khatami period and people faced economic difficulties.

Mahmoud Ahmedinejad (2005-2013) reversed previous economic policies and discouraged economic privatization that fuelled price rise and unemployment. Ahmedinejad discouraged economic privatization policy and increased state regulation over economic affairs. He awarded several economic contracts to the Islamic Revolutionary Guard Corps (IRGC), a state entity institution. He increased participation of the IRGC in Iran's economic management. He strengthened public undertakings companies and entities to develop Iranian economy. Thus, Ahmedinejad discouraged private sectors in participation of Iranian economic management.

Economic growth and investment

Economic growth was the main objective of the first plan. Rapid population growth rate and unsatisfactory economic performance, resulted sharp declines in per-capita income, consequently fall in living standards for the average Iranian household. The plan sought to exploit the petroleum sector and other under utilized resources to alleviate and minimize structural deficiencies, and to introduce rational management to accomplish its main purposes. The plan wanted to increase the ratio of total investment to gross domestic product which sharply declined in the pre-plan period. It also wanted to control domestic consumption in order to increase savings and investment.

The economic growth was favourable in the plan period than the pre-plan period. On 1974 prices, gross domestic product was 3922 billions *rials* in 1977, where as in 1988 it had fallen to 3142 billions *rials*. The main reason for the decline in GDP, was the high population growth rate in this period, and consequently per-capita in real terms fell by almost 50 percent. After implementation of the first plan, this trend was reversed.

Table 6 demonstrates that GDP rose by an average rate of 7.2 percent per annum in constant prices that slightly below the target rate of 8.1 percent per annum. Population growth rates declined in this period, and consequently per-capita production increased, but this increase did not lead to a rise in living standards and simultaneously sharply increased in the cost of living. Table 6 shows that whatever the projection of the plan was, that did not materialise and the target had been achieved less than the planned target.

One of the important indicator to assess the plan, is the ratio of investments to GDP. The plan projected an average annual growth rate of 19.7 percent investment to GDP, but its actual rate in the first four years of the plan was 10.6 percent, that only 54 percent of the expected rate. Thus, only a small portion of the GDP was invested in the economy. The figure of net investment was even less significant because the population growth rate was 2.2 percent per year. On the other hand, 27.4 percent of the GDP was invested in 1977, while in developed countries is 30 percent investment to GDP. The adverse effect of this trend was corroborated by the fast increase in consumption. The First plan failed to contain consumption in both the

Table 6 : GDP and its sectoral distribution during the First Plan 1989/94: Planned and actual (billion rials, 1988 prices)*

	1989/90**		1990/91		1991/92		1992/93		1993/94		1989/94	
	Planned	Actual	Planned	Actual	Planned	Actual	Planned	Actual	Planned	Actual	Planned	Actual
Agriculture	5430	5404	5678	5842	6026	6139	6454	6594	7001	6957	6.1	5.9
Oil	2500	2218	2741	2659	2834	2954	3156	3016	3250	3125	9.5	8.7
Industry & Mining	1864	1765	2149	1991	2462	2358	2866	2397	3262	2419	15.0	8.3
Industry	1623	1527	1835	1698	2090	2031	2415	2043	2750	2043	14.2	7.6
Mining	241	238	314	293	372	327	451	354	512	376	19.5	12.4
Water, Electricity & Gas	490	512	526	611	587	706	618	766	714	840	9.1	12.7

	1989/90**		1990/91		1991/92		1992/93		1993/94		1989/94
Construction	1593	1214	1844	1249	2073	1449	2282	1563	2429	1591	14.5	5.2
Services	12758	12395	13664	13598	14651	14944	15681	16139	16794	17350	6.7	7.4
GDP***	24635	23508	26602	25950	28633	28550	31057	30475	33450	32282	8.1	7.2

Notes: Whenever there is a difference in reported data, the latest data is used. It should be noted that there are differences among data reported by the Central Bank, Plan and budget organisation. ** The Iranian year begins 21st March. *** Does not include the net factor earning.

Source: First Economic, Social and Cultural Development Plan of the islamic Republic of Iran (1989/94), Plan and Budge organisation, Tehran, 1990; Central Bank, "Economic Report(s), Pland and Budget Organisation, Tehran, 1990, 1991 and 1992.

private and the public sectors.[35]

Sectoral changes

Table 7 shows the oil sector grew at 8.7 percent annually less than the projected rate. The oil sector grew rapidly in 1990/91 and 1991/92 due to the Gulf War 1990-91. But after the Gulf War, oil sector dropped sharply. Despite of decline in the sector oil, oil revenues remained the main source of the economic development. The First-Five-Year Plan put emphasis on the industry and mining sectors but it failed to achieve its target that had the highest growth rate in the plan.

Table 7 demonstrates the agricultural sector grew positively in this period, but its growth was not evenly distributed among its sub-sectors. During this period, agriculture's growth rate was 5.9 approximately 90 percent of its projected target of 6.1 percent. The agriculture sector consumed employees about 22.5 percent of the country's labour force, produced about 22 percent of its GDP, and accounted for 32 percent of non-oil exports on yearly basis.

The industrial sub-sector grew an average rate of 7.6 percent yearly that achieved only 53 percent of its projected growth rate. As Table 7 illustrates that industrial growth rate fluctuated greatly. Its record shows that not only it suffered from inter-sectoral shortcomings but a clear-cut strategy for national industrial policy was also lacking. The sub-sector's performance was adversely affected by policies such as unbridled and sudden economic liberalisation, floating exchange rates, and unplanned facilitation of imports in the mid-plan period. Small-sized and medium-sized industries were severely effected, which prior had enjoyed considerable growth under protectionist government policy.

---

35 See Mohammad Hussein Adeli, former Director of the Central Bank of Iran, "Guzaresh –e- Seey-o Chaharomin Ejlas-e Salaneh Bank-e Markaziyeh Jamhouri-ye Eslami-ye Iran" (The Report of the 34 th Annual Meeting of the Central Bank of the Islamic Republic of Iran), *Kayhan International Daily*, Tehran, 23 *Mordad*, 1373 (14 August, 1994), p.2

Table 7: GDP and its sectoral distribution during the First Plan 1989/94: Planned and actual (billion rials, 1988 prices)*

	1989/90		1990/91		1991/92		1992/93		1993/94		1989/94	
	Planned	Actual	Planned	Actual	Planned	Actual	Planned	Actual	Planned	Actual	Planned	Actual
Agriculture	4.2	3.7	4.6	8.1	6.1	5.1	7.1	7.4	8.5	5.5	6.1	5.9
Oil	21.4	7.7	9.6	19.9	3.4	11.1	11.3	2.1	3.0	3.6	9.5	8.7
Industry & Mining	14.8	8.2	15.3	15.6	14.6	17.7	16.4	3.3	13.8	0.8	15.0	8.36
Industry	14.8	8.0	13.0	11.2	13.9	19.6	15.6	0.6	13.9	0.0	14.2	7.6
Mining	15.0	13.6	30.3	23.1	18.5	11.5	21.2	8.4	13.5	6.0	19.5	12.4
Water, Electricity & Gas	6.4	11.0	7.2	19.4	11.7	15.5	5.3	8.5	15.4	9.7	9.1	12.7
Construction	29.0	-1.7	15.7	2.9	12.4	16.0	10.1	7.9	6.5	1.8	14.5	5.2
Services	5.1	2.1	7.2	9.7	7.4	9.9	7.1	8.0	7.1	7.5	6.7	7.4
GDP***	7.9	3.0	9.2	11.8	6.8	10.4	8.5	6.1	8.4	5.0	8.1	7.2

Notes and Sources : as Table 6

The average growth rate in the mining sub-sector never exceeded 12.4 percent per annum, although it was projected to reach 19.5 percent per annum and be a major contributor to the industrial development of the nation and to the diversification of its exports base. But its main problem was proper planning.

Water, electricity, and gas sectors grew fast, only in the last year of the plan did not achieve its target. Its annual average growth rate was 12.7 percent, although it was projected 9.1 percent per annum.

Construction failed to achieve even half of its projected growth rate of 14.5 percent annually. Construction has the highest inter-sectoral linkage within the economy, and its stagnation reflects a poor overall economic performance. Moreover, this sector provides the largest number of jobs for the poorest classes, especially rural migrants, so, its weakness also indicates high rates of unemployment, both seasonal and non-seasonal.

The service sector outgrew its projected rates, except 1989. It grew at an average rate of 7.4 percent annually for the plan period, exceeding the projected rate of 6.8 percent. Financial, monetary, and transportation sub-sectors grew the fastest. But the sector declined in plan's final year.

Monetary Reform

In the pre-plan period, there was multi-exchange rates system. Iran's multiple exchange-rate policy was an instrument of the Islamic Republic's industrial and social policy. Basically, it served two aims. First, it run an industrial structure highly dependent on imports; and second, to minimize erosion of the standard of living of the Iranian population in a stagnating (and even declining) economy with a high-exchange price provided Iranian industries with low-cost imported inputs. The government had introduced multi-exchange rates system for improving the country's international competitiveness through the formulation of a three-tier exchange rates. The three-tier exchange rates system was as such ("official" rate: 70 *rials* =$; "competitive" rate: 600 *rials* =$1; "floating" rate: 1600 *rials* =$1). The government's main agenda from mid-1992 was for a single (market-derived) exchange rate system and finally government introduced "a single floating exchange rate system on 21 March 1993 by devaluing *rial* by 95.6 percent."[36] A single floating exchange rate was introduced. The national

---

36 *Middle East Economic Digest*, 23 April, 1993

currency became fully convertible on 13 April, 1993.

By the end of the 1993, "the *rial* was again devalued by more than 8 percent."[37] As a result of shortage of capital, a number of development projects were also suspended. The deepening currency crisis had severe impact on the rest of the economy and fueled inflation.

The largest proportion of Iranian imports are industrial inputs and there are few domestic substitute for these imports, Iran's demand for imports has a relatively low elasticity. Therefore, only a massive devaluation of *rial* will result in a significant decrease in imports. On the other hand, a devaluation would have only a small effect on exports earnings because the exports of crude oil is not affected by exchange-rate changes.[38]

Owing to devaluation in the currency, a sharp decline in import was seen that adversely effected the country's production units and consumers in general. With devaluation, factories started facing acute shortages of cash and raw materials that were needed for production. The factories began to shut down that led to workers being laid off and had caused severe hardship among the low-income strata of society.

The government's unification policy of three different exchange rates in March 1993, led to a massive devaluation of the *rial* from the highly unrealistic official rate. This led to a steep increase in the price of goods which adversely affected the whole population, irrespective of their income level. Price increases generated a strong opposition. The government faced opposition in the *Majlis* for raising the price of goods and services it provided such as water, electricity, telephone, mail, airline and train tickets, and most importantly petroleum products. A number of deputies introduced a bill in April 1994 which required that any future price increase for goods and cervices be approved by the *Majlis*.[39] As a result, the government was forced to give up on its exchange rate rationalization strategy. Thus, an exchange control was restored, a cap on price movements was also restored. Moreover, many subsidies were to continue in the next

---

37 *Middle East Economic Digest*, 3 December, 1993

38 This is because oil prices are determined in US dollars in the international market, and the volume of Iran's export of oil depends on international market considerations (determined by the OPEC quota, or on its own, not by the *rial* cost of production of oil.

39 *Kayhan*, 9 March, 27 April, and 3 May 1994.

five-year plan.[40]

Fiscal Policy

In the plan period, the government adopted fiscal policy for a better economic development. Government's first objective in this direction was to contain budget deficit. The government took various measures to control the budget deficit. The government entrusted the banking system with allocating funds to public enterprises. Some of the funds were given as loans to the enterprises that was not mentioned in the budget. The net indebt of public enterprises to the Central Bank, for instance, as estimated in 1991/92 to 1056 billions *rials*, it reached to 3657 billions *rials* in 1993/94. In order to reduce budget deficit, the government engaged in foreign exchange dealings on the black (free) market. "Selling dollars on the black market proved profitable; the profits (difference between official and free market rates) of selling foreign currencies in the black market accounted for 41 percent of government revenues in 1992."[41]

Despite government's various measures to contain the budget deficit, government was in budget deficit as Table 8 indicates. One of the features of the budget deficit was the fluctuation in the budget deficit, thus budget deficit was not constantly on increasing trend but this trend was itself downward.

Table 8: The Government Budget (in billions of rials)

	1989/90	1990/91	1991/92	1992/93	1993/94	1994/95
Revenues	3830	6617	8364	12299	22020	32126
Expenditures	4924	7288	9553	13269	22567	32295
Lending minus repayments	-5	-6	-39	-6	-104	-1
Deficit (-) or surplus	-1089	-665	-1129	-964	-443	-168

Source: International Financial Statistics, IMF.

---

40 *Reuter*, "Iran's Parliament Orders Curb on Subsidy Cuts", 8 August, 1994

41 Mohammed Mehdi Rezaii, "Tahavulat-e Arz az Didgah-e Eqtisadi" (Change in Foreign Exchange from a Macro-Economic Perspective), Rouznameh-e Ettela'at Vizeh-e Khariz az Keshvra, 6 Mordad, 1373 (1994).

To balance government expenditures with revenues, structural changes in the budget was perceived in the plan, especially through raising the share of taxation. The plan projected to rise 44.8 percent of total government revenues through taxes. But in fact, from 1989/90 to 1993/94, taxes accounted for 37.3 percent, 30.1 percent, 39.5 percent and 38.1 percent of total government revenues, respectively.

Table 9 illustrates the continuous increase in the tax except 1993/94, the increasing portion of the tax in government revenues contributed in minimizing the budget deficit.

Table 9: The Government Revenues from Taxation (in Billions of rials)

	Tax Revenue
1989-90	1859
1990-91	2655
1991-92	4093
1992-93	6013
1993-94	5515
1994-95	10528

Source: Government Finance Statistics, IMF.

To cope with the budget deficit, the Islamic Republic sought the help of external financial institutions to make foreign borrowing politically more palatable, entail extensive direct participation of foreign capital in the Iranian economy. But external financing, whether borrowing or investments, was, however, deeply objectionable to those in the populist-statist faction who had not been influenced by the pragmatists in the Islamic Republic. They saw it as step towards the reconstruction of "the dependent economy of Iran under the Shah". They believed that "our borders must not be opened to dependent capitalism."[42] This was the slogan of the revolution, as Hashemi Rafsajani mentioned in his Friday prayer sermon on 12 January 1990. He stated that as long as foreign investment or borrowing was used in productive projects they would not

---

42   The title of an article in *Kayhan*, 30 August, 1988

be detrimental to the economy.[43] The Islamic Republic's warm reception of the World Bank-International Monetary Fund (IMF) mission in June 1990 was a symbolic significant step towards normalisation of international financial relations with Iran. Since the Revolution 1979, it was the first World Bank-IMF mission to Iran, and was followed by subsequent visits by these two international financial institutions.

This step had two significant immediate implications. First, it had reflected the failure of the populist-statist faction. Second, it not only made necessary on the part of the Islamic Republic to be more co-operative but it also required a clear demonstration of progress towards free market conditions in the domestic economy. The 1990 World Bank-IMF mission reported, the Islamic Republic officials "expressed their determination to move forward with broadly based macroeconomics adjustment, encompassing a strengthened role for the private sector and a step-by-step opening up of the economy."[44] The move was to return nationalised enterprises to the private sector, the reduction in consumer subsidies, and the liberalization of foreign-exchange controls in 1990-91 were clear signs of Iran's determination toward the "macroeconomics adjustment" of the World Bank-IMF type.[45] The World Bank's loan of $ 250 million in March 1991 was the first clear indication that the Islamic Republic was taking step towards "macroeconomics adjustment".[46] By May 1994, the World Bank had approved $ 850 million for various projects in Iran.[47]

Export-Import Policy

In order to make Iran's economy internationally competitive, the government eased restrictions on imports, thereby developing domestic competition and providing the raw materials and intermediate goods necessary for expansion of Iranian manufacturing and industrial productive capabilities. The private sector's involvement in importation of essential

---

43 *Kayhan Havai*, 17 January, 1990

44 IMF, "Islamic Republic of Iran undergoes profound institutional, structural changes", *IMF Survey*, 30 July, 1990, p.228

45 For a critical analysis of the World Bank-IMF type of macroeconomic adjustment see Peter Korner, Gero Maass, Thomas Siebold and Rainer Tetzlaff, eds., *The IMF and the Debt Crisis* (London: Zed Book, 1987).

46 Middle East Economic Digest (MEED), 29 March, 1991, p.12

47 Under pressure from the US, the executive board of the World Bank rejected $ 400 million new loans to Iran. See *MEED*, 20 May, 1994

and consumer goods was also a good means of addressing economic problems. When control on imports were lifted, the domestic market was flooded with foreign cars, household supplies and the imported consumer goods.

The plan adopted import substitution and non-oil exports promotion both to diversify the economy and to reduce its dependency on foreign exchange earning. Import-substitution policy was adopted to reduce the demand for imported consumer goods, thus, curtailing demand for foreign exchange and reducing the county's dependence on volatile foreign exchange revenues.

The government took various steps for the promotion of non-oil export. Primarily, the plan emphasized import-substitution with export promotion. In fact, the First Plan sought to contain the demand for foreign exchange. It was the strategy for the protection of domestic markets and government provisions for foreign exchange for industries, to enhance production of consumer goods and heave machinery. In the plan, government sought for export promotion over import-substitution and the industries were sought to be self-sufficient in their demand for foreign exchange mainly through exports.

For export promotion, they encouraged competitiveness and quality improvements in domestic production and increased foreign exchange earnings, all of which contributed to economic diversification. But export promotion was not an alternative to import substitution. Available data shows that foreign exchange earned form export goods was generally less than that used in their production, and whatever small positive balance remained, was not return to the domestic production process.[48]

Exports were also offered a variety of direct and indirect incentives. The establishment of a new export promotion bank in 1991 was an another feature of the export derive. Variety of concessions were given to the private sectors in the areas of exports. They were encouraged to participate in joint ventures with foreign firms engaged in projects under the Five-Year Plan.

---

48 See Said Lailaz, "Saderat-e Ghair-e Nafti dar Nigahi Digar", (Non-oli Exports in a Different Perspective), *Ettela'at Siasi va Eqtesadi*, nos. 53-54, *Bahman and Esfand* 1370 (1991), p.80-82.

Table 10: Balance of Payments 1989/96: (in millions of US$)

	1989/90	1990/91	1991/92	1992/93	1993/94	1994/95	1995/96
Trade Balance	-367	975	-6529	-3406	-1207	6817	5697
Exports (f.o.b)	13081	19305	18661	19868	18080	19434	18375
Imports (f.o.b.)	-13448	-18330	-25190	-23274	-19287	-12617	-12678
Current Account	-191	327	-9448	-6504	-4215	4956	3478
Capital and Financial Account	2491	-652	7355	6340	4444	-3545	
SDR	400	442	309	10	144	143	134
Net Errors and Omissions	-770	-947	1322	1637	-1119	-3703	163
Overall Balance	2300	-325	-2093	-164	229	907	2867

Source: International Financial Statistics, IMF.

Despite Article 81 of the constitution, prohibiting the establishment of companies and institutions by foreign investors in Iran, the government was determined to bring Iran's foreign investment law and attitude towards foreign capital in line with other medium sized industrialising economics. Restrictions for foreign investment in key sectors like petrochemical, power generation and distribution, were lifted, and the country's investment law was reformulated to allow up to 49 percent equity holding by the foreign partner (which was allowed under *Pahlavi* regime 35 percent).

The opening Iran's industry and economy was another boost through the establishment of two free trade zones in the Persian Gulf and a number of others in the north, west and south-east of the country.

Although, government's export policy was not successful. Non-oil exports performed well in these years and more than double their share of total exports, though they never achieved targeted goals. From 1989/90 to 1993/94, non-oil exports rose from $1.1 billion to $1.3 billion, $2.5 billion, $2.9 billion and $3.7 billion. During the plan, total $ 11.7 billion was, however, below the $ 17.8 billion projected by the plan.

Table 10 demonstrates the balance of payments from 1989/90 to 1995/96. During this period, export fluctuated, in 1994/95 was at the highest point. On the other side, fluctuations in imports had also been seen, which was the lowest in 1994/95 to 12617 millions of dollars. Trade balance in 1994/95 was 6817 millions of dollars, which was the highest trade balance in this period. Trade balance was not favourable. The lowest trade balance was in 1989/90. Data shows, the overall balance is very much fluctuated, it depicts the negative trend. After 1993/94, overall balance has improved. Current account is very much negative that has left impact on the overall balance as a whole.

Inflation, Unemployment and Poverty

In 1988/89, inflation was 28.5 percent. The First plan intended to reduce it to 8.9 percent by 1993/94. To contain inflation within limit, reducing the country's liquidity expansion was paramount among them, so, certain monetary, financial and commercial guidelines were main measures. In 1988, the liquidity's growth rate was 23.8 percent per year that was very dangerous, so, the plan had to reduce this fast growth to a modest 3.5 percent per annum by 1993 mainly by slashing budget deficit and containing liquidity.

During the plan period, economy's liquidity rose at an annual rate of 25 percent. It was projected to reach 23000 billions *rials*, but it actually rose double to 47000 billions *rials*. In fact, inflationary trend of recent years can be interpreted by comparing the 25 percent average annual rate of increase in liquidity with the 7.2 percent average annual rate of increase in GDP. This clearly explains why the inflation rate which supposed to be contained at 8.9 percent in 1993, reached 30.7 percent in 1992. The actual rate of inflation in 1993 was approximately 20 percent, but instabilities and uncertainties in monetary policies and foreign exchange, resulted in an inflation rate of about 60 percent for 1994.[49]

In the plan period, liquidity grew because of increase in private indebtedness. In 1993, 7237.9 billions *rials* were added to the economy's liquidity of which 5292.5 billions *rials* (73.1 percent) was a net increase in private debt over one year.

The reduction of subsidies and floating exchange rates, were instrumental a driving inflationary pressure in the plan's final years. In pre-plan period, the budget deficit, indebtedness to the country's banking system was the chief reason for the high rates of liquidity.

In the matter of employment, the plan was success in decreasing unemployment form 15.9 percent in 1988 to 11.4 percent in 1992. It is noteworthy that the employment figures include official as well as unofficial jobs full-time and part-time jobs and real as well as under-employment. Mostly jobs were created in the public sector, the private sector showed little growth.

The plan sought to change in the nation's employment structure. Planners wanted to reduce employment in the service form 47.2 percent

---

49 Various sources give different figures for inflation. For instance, in June 1994 issue (p.3), *Iran Business Monitor* (quoting an official of the Central Bank), put average annual inflation rate for the First Plan (1989/90-1993-94) at 40 percent to 60 percent; and the *Economist Intelligence Unit*, 1994-95, reports the average annual inflation rate for 1993-94 at 30 percent to 70 percent, depending on specific economic sectors.

in 1988 to 45.5 in 1993. But happened contrary, employment in service sector rose to 50.4 percent in 1993. In the same period, employment in the agricultural sector fell to 22.2 percent in 1993 from 28.4 percent in 1988. The employment ratio in industry and mining sector increased slightly from 24.4 percent to 27.4 percent. The majority of the jobs were created in the service sector.

The Second Plan did not start immediately after the completion of the First Plan 1989/90 – 1993/94. The government took a year in analyzing the First- Plan's success and failure, so, the Second-Plan started in 1995. The Second plan, therefore, covered the Five-Year period 1995 to 1999.[50]

The primary aim of the Second-Five-year plan was to secure sustainable economic growth, emphasis on social justice, reducing demand for foreign exchange, and expanding educational and employment opportunities. The second plan gave top priority to economic growth, and puts emphasis on stable and sustainable growth. The Second plan envisaged a moderate growth rate in order to maintain stability in economic growth. In the Second plan, the average annual GDP growth rate projected 5.8 percent, that was lower than the First Plan. In the First Plan, it was projected 8.1 percent but actually achieved 7.2 percent.

In the First Plan, petroleum earning were 90 percent and non-oil exports earning were only 65 percent of their projected rates. In the second plan, projection for oil revenues was comparatively lower than the First plan, and the foreign exchange demand was to be contained. The oil sector was projected to generate $73 billion for the entire Second plan period, and the non-oil sector had to raise $ 27 billion.

---

50 See the bill of *the Second Economic, Social and Cultural Development Plan of the Islamic Republic of Iran,* Tehran: Plan and Budget Organisation, 1372 (993).

Table 11: GDP growth rate and its sectoral distribution during the First Plan and the Second Plan (average annual percentage rate).

	Second Plan* (1995-99)**	First Plan 1989/90 – 1993/94	
	Planned	Planned	Actual
Agriculture	4.3	6.1	5.9
Oil	3.3	9.5	8.7
Industry and Mining	6.2	15.0	8.9
Water, Electricity & Gas	8.0	9.1	12.7
Construction	6.3	14.5	5.2
Services	5.0	6.7	7.4
GDP	5.8	8.1	7.2

Notes: *Proposed Plan Bill by the government. Although the Plan Bill has 1994-98 as the plan period, in reality, the Plan will cover the 1995-99 period. ** Iranian year begins 21st March.

Sources: As tables 6 & 7

The Second Plan's another primary goal was to expand educational and employment opportunities. The primary and secondary levels educations were to be expanded, as were higher education, professional training, and physical educational programmes. A central aim of the Second plan was to create a competitive labour force, in line with international trends of giving high priority to human resource.

The Second plan adopted cautious measures because its projected plan, was less than the First plan's actual achievement. There were three cautious measures of the second plan inward looking, more balance than earlier plan, and more conservative and pragmatic.

The revolutionary regime reformulated economic policy in the aftermath of the Revolution. The new regime took various measures to improve the appalling conditions of the masses when the country was facing severe financial crunch due to decline in the oil revenues, Iran-

Iraq War, and the US economic sanction against Iran. The Iran-Iraq War and the glut in the international oil market from 1985 to 1989 created further problems for the Iranian economic, and the economy virtually moved to stagnation. The messy condition of the economy plunged Iran into deep financial trouble and continuous budget deficit created further many other problems which directly affected the price hike and standard of living which the government sought to contain. In this crisis-ridden situation, confiscation, nationalization, and the interventionist policy of the government was required which the government adopted.

After the end of war with Iraq and Khomeini's death, the policy-makers sough to adopt the planned economy, and the First-Five-year plan began in 1989/90. The First-Five-year plan reversed many earlier decisions which were taken during the war period. In the aftermath of war, the main issue before the government was to recover economy speedily which severely affected as a result of war. The government adopted various measures for economic reconstruction and development, and economic reforms for highly distorted economy, and adopted reforms as advocated by the World Bank and IMF. In the process of liberalisation of economy, the government privatized many public enterprises which were taken under the state control after the revolution.

The server financial crunch due to decline in the oil revenues led to budget deficit, forced the government to take the help of the external financial agencies in minimizing the budget deficit. In the way of minimizing the budget deficit, the government sought the elimination of the system of subsidies, removal of price control and unification of multiple exchange rates. The Second-Five-year plan adopted the pragmatic approach to provide stability in economic development.

The Revolution 1979 did not transform only polity, but also economy. Iranian economy was transformed in ideological line, and restructured in Islamic line. The post-revolution economic policy put emphasis on welfare of the common people. *Mustazefin* (deprived) got their share in Iranian economy in the post-revolution period. Islam played major role in deciding economic policy of the post-revolution since it was the uniting force during the revolution. Economic sanctions and Iran-Iraq War caused economic problems but Ayatollah Khomeini managed Iranian economy. Ayatollah Khamenei has been managing Iran's economy in the absence of Ayatollah Khomeini. Iran continues to consider Islamic line in formulations of economic policies despite other economic fundamental issues.

ISLAMISATION OF SOCIETY

Ayatollah Khomeini intended to build a thoroughly Islamic state. The western influences were eroded. The western culture permeated at every level of Iranian society before the Islamic Revolution that virtually disappeared from public view, and society underwent a complete transformation in the post-Revolution 1979. The Revolution 1979 had a distinct cultural overtone. The Islamic Revolution paved the way for extensive transformation in Iran, one of which was the transformation of social culture. The educational system was the main target of the revolutionary regime and new curricula was introduced along Islamic line to inject Islamic tenets in the new generation. The implantation of secular ethos in the education during the Shah was a deliberate policy to lessen the Islamic influence in society. The revolutionary regime brought under its control not only the educational system but the mass media also. In the post-Revolution Iran, the Personal Law has changed, consequently has affected the laws of marriage and divorce, and public veiling has been mandatory to women and their appearance and activities have been restricted.

Before the Revolution, the Iranian society sought its historical identity in imperial history. In the modernisation process, they adopted western norms, values, codes and conducts, and culture. The projection of the imperial history and culture did not suite to new Iranian generation. The designers of Iranian social and historical identity of pre-Revolution days, diverted from their original path and created an artificial culture and identity that was inconsisted and against the Iranians' spirit and culture. "Culture includes a collection of intellectual, non-material artistic, historical, literacy, religious and emotional expressions (in the form of signs, symbols, tradition, customs, relics, mores) of a nation which have accumulated in the course of its history and acquired unique form."[1]

---

1   Ali Shariat, *Civilization and Modernization* (Iranian Student Islamic Association North India), P.7.

It signifies desires, temperaments, life-patterns, social characteristics, social relations, and economic structure of a country. Culture manifests total life-patterns of a society that has been adopted in the course of history. Islam as an effective and all-embracing religion, subdued all aspects of Iranian culture since the very beginning, and created a new cultural fabric under the title of Iranian-Islamic culture. The influence of Islam on Iran's social spectrum is so profound that it has left an Islamic impact even on the most Iranian traditions and has imparted Islamic complexion there to.

The process of modernization, industrialization and westernisation was initiated by the earlier regimes, had deep impact on society as a whole. The cultural changes occurred as a result of industrialisation and modernisation. The western values and life styles were deliberately introduced that brought in conflict with traditional values. Such attempts were perceived by some intellectuals and religious leaders as politically motivated to weaken the traditional culture, and make in road for total domination by a Western-backed elite. "The Islamic Revolution emerged as a coalition of religious and nationalist forces to protest against such perceived deliberated attempts to change the culture (what the religious leaders called ("corruption of soul and society"), rather than as a reaction to modernization, development, or industrialization." [2] Industrialisation, modernization, and development were not primary issues during the Revolution, the real issue before the people was the cultural decadence. It was perceived that the west has perverted the Iranian culture in the name of industrialization, modernization, and development by introducing motley western norms, values, and social codes and conducts which is un-Islamic.

The Revolution 1979 in Iran, has changed the attitudes, beliefs and behaviours of the Iranian people. The change in attitude, belief and behaviour of the Iranian people is clearly visible on social spectrum. Ayatollah Khomeini, the Supreme Leader of the Revolution, emphasised the need to transform the culture of post-Revolutionary Iran. According to Ayatollah Khomeini, cultural task derived from two connected goals. "The first was the destruction of the alien and dependent (mostly Western) value forced on the Iranian people."[3] Entwined in the annihilation of the dependent

---

2   Abbas Tashakkori and Vaida Thompson, "social Change and Changes in Intentions of Iranian Youth Regarding Education, Marriage, and Careers", *International Journal of Psychology,* Vol. No.2, 1991, P.213

3   Ruhollah Khomeini, *Payam-i-Inqilab: Majmu yi Payam-ha va Bayanat-I Hazrat-I Imam Khomeinin* (The Message of the Revolution: the Collection of Imam Khomeini's

value system, would be the creation of an authentic cultural milieu that would recapture the dignity of Iran as a Muslim country. The cultural milieu could be realised only with the ascendance of Islamic Republic in Iran. The revolutionary regime established various organisations and institutions. The Supreme Council of the Cultural Revolutions established in 1980, was in charge of providing general direction and setting cultural policy to be implemented by the Ministry of Cultural and Islamic guidance (MCIG) and its four affiliated institutions: The Islamic Republic News Agency (IRNA); the Organisation for Piligrimage; Religious Endowments, and Charity Affairs; The Institutions of Cultural Documents of the Islamic Revolution; and the Organisation of Press and the Publication of the Ministry of Culture and Islamic Guidance. Outside the MCIG, a few other organization were also involved in the process.

There were many factions had to decide the cultural issue. Although, every faction declared its commitment to Islamic cultural ideals, but there was lack of unanimity on these ideals. Despite various factions on the Iranian political spectrum, by and large Iranian policy was dominated by two factions. One of the factions, is *Jama-yi Ruhaniyat-I Mubariz* (the Society of Militant Clergy 'SMC') considered "moderate" or "conservative". The second is *Majma-i Ruhaniyun-i Mubariz* (The Association of Militant Ulema 'AMU'), labeled "militant" or "radical".

The impression of bifactional polity was strengthened by dominance of representatives of one or the other of these two groups in both Third, and the Fourth elections of parliament. In spite of their differences, many individuals, groups and factions combined and gave voice to two general positions, one conservative and the other liberal.[4] The conservative position was based on a puritanical interpretation of Islamic tenets that made an attempt to limit artistic expression to themes, conserving religion and war.[5] It

---

and Speech (Tehran, 1979), P. 326.

4   Here the positions labeled conservative and liberal one defined in the test in relation to the specific context of cultural debates and attitudes within Iran. Despite difference between cultural attitudes in Iran, on the one hand, and those in Western societies on the other, there are certain things in common that make the use of the two labels meaningful.

5   See, for instance, Ahmad Jannati's views, expressed mostly during Friday Prayers, concerning artistic and cultural development in various issues of the *Iran Times,* such as 12 April 191; 5, 7 June 1991; 5, and 6 Sep. 1991.

allowed heavy-handed censorship of artistic expression[6] and advocated the dominant role for both official coercive forces and vigilantism in enforcing and implementing cultural and personal mores.[7] Its support base was very much wide. Its supporting groups and institutions were the majority of the religious instructors at the most influential centre religious teaching, the Qum centre for Religious Studies; influential members of the *Bazaar*; some ministries such as the Ministry of Information and the Ministry of Culture and Islamic Guidance; members of the influential Guardianship Council; some upper echelon bureaucrats; and some prominent members of the judiciary.

There are two significant factors in explaining the cultural position of the conservatives, one ideological, and the other material. Many conservatives who identify themselves with the *Rast-i-Sunnati* (traditional right) are from the older generation of established clergy and come from conservative theological backgrounds.[8] They follows to *fiqh-Sunnati* (traditional Jurisprudence) based on a static interpretation of Islam and a fearful of cultural change.[9] Followers of the *Rast- Sunnati* are associated with the *Chap-i Sunnati* (traditional left), which adds a leftist flavour to cultural conservatism. The *Chap-i Sunnati* manifests authoritarian position toward issues of culture and lifestyles.

Apart from ideological conviction, many cultural conservatives are concerned about the survival of the Islamic Republic and their position in it. Cultural conservatives are broadly divided into two groups, on the

---

6   See, Abulqasim Khazali's statement, a member of Council of Guardians, in regard to censorship of video products and his criticism of the government in its failure to control them, in *Iran Times*, 18 September, 1992.

7   See Parliamentary speeches published in *"Mashruh-I Muzakirat-I Majlis-I Islamic"* (Comprehensive Proceedings of the Islamic Consultative Assembly) (MMMSI). See agenda speeches delivered by Nafisah Fayazbakhsh, MMMSI, session no. 18, 11 July 1991, and Hishmat Musavi, no. 16, 8 July 1991. In both, the speakers urged stricter and more wide and comprehensive enforcement of restrictions of lifestyle and cultural expression and took care in enforcing the laws.

8   On the social support base of different factions within the elite, see Ahmad Ashraf, "Charisma, Theocracy, and Men of Power in Post-revolutionary Iran", in Myron Cveiner and Ali Banuazizi, eds., *The Political of Social Transformation in Afghanistan, Iran, and Pakistan* (Syracuse, 1994), pp. 101-151.

9   Murtada Nabavi argued for the need to fight against "Western Art" and for an at that is in accordance with "peity, truth and God" For it, see, the editorial by Murtada Nabavi, the chief editor of *Risalat*, 25 September 1991, PP. 1 & 6.

left and the right of different strata of society. For the *Rast-i Sunnati*, its base of support upon which its survival depends, consists of members of *Bazaar*, particularly small shop owners and the members of guild and their apprentices. For the *Chap-i Sunnati*, the base of support consists of the *Basijis*, the martyrs families, and generally many disaffected, less-educated young whose hope for social mobility depends on their religious dedication and involvement in the war effort.

The second, liberal advocates a less restrictive code of censorship and a more tolerant attitude towards art and culture. It also puts emphasis on education and the use of logic and discourse in deciding art and culture rather than repression to establish a good intellectual atmosphere.[10] Those who have come under Western influence fold, argue that technical advances like, world wide satellite telecommunications have made a policy of repression ineffectual.

Those follow liberal position, come mostly from the younger generation of upward mobile, better-educated individuals. Many are devout Muslims, they have attitude that Islam is a tolerant and searching. The liberals advocate *fight-I Puya* (dynamic Jurisprudence), argue that the survival of the Islamic Republic depends on its flexibility and adaptability.

The disagreement between the conservatives and the liberals over the cultural issue still continue. The key cultural positions were in the hands of the liberals since 1980 till early 1990 . The conservatives criticised the Ministry of Culture and Islamic Guidance and Guidance, accusing the agency and its leader of allowing "Western Cultural aggression" against the Islamic Republic. President Hashemi Rafsanjani sided with the liberal forces echoed Khatami's arguments in his speeches and supported dialogue and openness rather then isolation and repression. But from the very beginning, he did not choose the cultural battle as a priority.[11] From the mid-1980s to the early 1990s, cultural policies of the Islamic Republic of Iran were primarily formulated by the "modern left" under the leadership of Khatami. Leader of the Islamic Republic, Ayatollah Khamenei sided with the conservatives. Khamenei stated in July 1991, "what the enemy is culturally engaged in is not only a cultural aggression but a cultural looting,

---

10 Mohammad Khatami, Bim-I Muj (The fear of the wave), (Tehran, 1993), PP. 188-89.
11 See Rafsanjani's interview published in the cultural monthly *Adabistan*, April May, 1991, pp. 6-9.

a cultural massacre".[12] By using the famous Islamic edict "propagation of virtue and prohibition of vice," he urged the *Hizhollah* forces to challenge that aggression. The conservatives took that speech as a signal of support and tried to reverse earlier liberal policies of the MCIG.[13] *Kayhan* editorials became more frequent implicitly and explicitly in denouncing Khatami.[14] The dailies *Abrar* and *Salam* made an attempt to counterbalance the conservative onslaught.[15] So, in the summer of 1992, Khatami resigned as the Minister of Culture and Islamic guidance that move considered a victory for the conservative. He was replaced by Ali Larijani, who had close ties to conservative.[16]

There was unanimity in adoption of Islamic tenets and principles and cultural Revolution between the conservative and liberal clerics but there was lack of consensus in only their approaches and extent. In spite of this problem, the Iranian society has been Islamised. In 1979, the monarchical authoritarian state was replaced with a religious regime whose main objective was a total reorganisation of society according to the normative rules of *shii* Islam. Many of the social references undertaken by the *Pahlavi* regime were undone by the ruling clerics. However, three major spheres in which process of Islamisation have made a more lasting impact - education, mass media, and women. For woman, new dress code was introduced and concerning marriage, divorce and job, new laws framed according to Islamic precepts. These areas were firmly guided by Khomeini, set parameters, contents and concepts; all ideas and views were eradicated in the name of Islam and unity, conformity had been imposed on intellectuals, authors, educationalists and film makers. The new regime was marked by traditional religious and anti-Western values and had developed an active legal programme to quell western influences and expedited to return traditionalism.

---

12 Quoted by Ali Larijani in his speech to the Fourth Majlis, the successor to Khatami as the Minister of MCIG. See MMMSI, *in Ruznami-yi Rasmi,* no. 13826, 11 August 1992, P.26

13 *Risalat,* 16 July 1992; *Kayhan,* 18 and 19 July 1992

14 *Kayhan,* 19, 21 and 23 July 1992.

15 *Abrar,* 19 July 1992; *Salam,* 20 and 25 July, 1992

16 Larijani has both familial and nonfamilial connections with the Qum Seminary. He is the son of Fazlullah Havadi Amuli and the son-in-law of Ayatollah Mutahhari.

Formulation of New Educational Policy in the post-Revolution

Each educational system consists of a set of social norms and values, and is attributed to a specific culture. Education is an instrument through which a culture perpetuates itself. So, education and culture are interconnected. After the Revolution, the new regime was desperate to bring major charges in the educational system of the country. Immediately after the Revolution, schools opened but universities were remained close over four years because they were centres of continued political activism, as they had been major to the Revolution. Religious leaders brought significant reforms in Iran's educational system.

The Islamisation of education was put in motion in June 1980 a part of Ayatollah Khomeini's plan to accelerate the cultural dimension of the Revolution that had already began with the acceptation of the Literacy Campaign in December of 1979. In April 1980, the Revolutionary Council ordered all the offices of political organisations on universities campuses vacated as soon as possible and the universities were closed in June in separation for Islamisation of the academic system.[17] Ayatollah Khomeini stated in this regard:

> Our universities are foreign dependent. Our universities are of the colonial type. Our university students are Westoxicated (*gharbzadeh*)... Many of our university Professors at the service of the West. They brainwash our youth... Because of their simple-mindedness the young have believed in the false education that they have received from some of their professors. Now that we want to set up an independent some of their professors. Now that we want to set up an independent university and make fundamental changes. So, that it would not be dependent on the west and communism, dependent on the Marxism, they confront us. This is in itself, shows that our universities are not Islamic and we do not have, and never have had, universities that would educate our youth. This is itself, is a proof that your youth has not received proper education... The university must become Islamic...[18]

Ayatollah Khomeini vehemently denounced the alien cultural system which influenced the Islamic educational system and culture. He thought

---

17 *Kayhan*, 17 and 19 April 1980
18 *Kayhan*, 18 April 1980.

that the exploiters began to disseminate their cultural values and norms in schools, colleges and varsities. Consequently, the whole educational system came under their influences.

Thus, the Cultural Revolution began under the powerful leadership of Imam Khomeini. The Cultural Revolution stressed, especially among the clergy, that Iran's educational system was westoxicated. The clergy argued that the subjects were taught without Islamic foundations, or even anti-Islamic in their principles, methods and procedures. The Cultural Revolution's main purpose was to revise the entire educational system. In this way, it was made an attempt to check all text books and removed any trace of un-Islamic opinion and illustration. However, there was an attempt to simplify the curriculum and make it more *maktabi*, in the old-style of clergy run schools where learning had been by rote and dutiful acceptance of the views of the teachers.

Schools

In the educational reform process, the new regime first closed the schools. All foreign-run schools were closed down and anyone suspected of an un-Islamic attitudes was sacked. Initially, nearly 40000 teachers were sacked or compulsorily retired. "But severe shortages of teachers had to many of them being reinstated at their places, some after attending courses on Islamic education".[19]

The central aim of the Cultural Revolution was the ideological purification and integrated Islamic education. But it had also to be accommodated in the context of increasing numbers of the student and deteriorating conditions in the schools. The educational system was under pressured due to financial crunch. There was shortages of schools, because birth rate was increasing by an average of 3.2 percent per year. The number of students increased very fast, but schools were not increased as birth rate pace. There was also the shortage of teachers because government was not in a position to appoint new teachers due to lack of funds. But after the end of the war, allocated funds for the schools, however, these funds were insufficient to build new schools and appoint teachers. So, the government asked the private sector to build "non-profit-making" schools. Private schools re-emerged as soon as the government allowed to reopen.

---

19 L. Zia Katouzian, "Education in Iran", *Royal Institute Conference Proceeding*, PP. 28-30.

The new regime had to encounter the westoxication by initiating changes in schools curriculum. By late 1979, primary and secondary schools used newly rewritten Islamic oriented text books. The revision of the school curricula covered five fields: humanities / social sciences, agriculture, engineering and technology, medicine, and basic science. A close scrutiny of humanities and social sciences text books at the elementary, guidance cycle (Junior High School), and High School levels, demonstrate the comprehensive and systematic character of the Revolution in the education.

First, the fundamental religious principles and precepts and the ideal pattern of state-citizen relations are introduced in the early school period. By introducing early such politico-religious notions, the regime hoped to redefine the parameters of children's intellectual realm, and strengthen its ideological hold over society. For instance, during the first year of the elementary school, concepts o god, *The Quran*, and Prophethood are introduced. In the third year, students are exposed to the *Quran*. "They are also made familiar with such important notions as *Vahdat* (unity); *Millat* (citizenship); and *Vatan* (homeland)".[20] In the fourth grade, "mosques are depicted as the centre of community where both religious and political matters should be discussed"[21] Students are also instructed to model their lives after the Prophet Mohammed and succeeding *Imams*.

Second, during the guidance cycle and high school years, more sophisticated concepts are introduced. For example, the concept of the *Velayat-e Faqih* and the over all leadership role of the clergy are taught beginning in the second grade of the guidance cycle. "At the same grade level extensive discussions of Islamic government and its features are presented"[22] "The notions of *Jehad* (holy war) and *Shahadat* (martyrdom) are introduced in the tenth grade"[23]

Third, the basic foreign policy orientation of the Islamic Republic is

---

20 M.M. Shorish, "The Islamic Revolution and Education in Iran", *Comparative Education Review,* Vol. 32, no. 1, February 1988, P-61.

21 G. Mehran, "Socialization of School Children in the Islamic Republic of Iran: A Study of Social Studies Texts" (paper presented at the Annual Meeting of the Comparative and International Education Society in 1987), P-15.

22 B. Mohsenpour, "Philosophy of Education in Post-Revolutionary Iran", *Comparative Education Review,* Vol. 32, no.1, February 1988, pp. 82-83.

23 Mehran, no. 21, p.9.

taught with a high degree of value-laden symbolism in the primary school and extended at higher grade. The West is depicted as an oppressive force whose prime purpose has always been to exploit the Muslim countries in general. The West is also portrayed as exercising cultural imperialism and hedonism.

During the first year of the guidance cycle, the basic principles of the regime's foreign policy are outlined to include various discussions on Islam as a liberating forces, "Islamisation" and "independence" from both the West and the world. The focus is put on the importance of safeguarding Islamic Revolution against the unholy intentions of the foreign powers.

Despite revision of the existing text books, the coverage of Islamic subjects was expanded through the introduction of new texts like *Binesh-e Islami: Nabovat, Quaran Va Maad* (Islamic Conception: Prophethood, Quran and Resurrection).

Universities

In the summer 1980, the administrators (religious leaders, of replaced the bureaucrats of earlier regime) in the Ministry of Education closed all colleges and universities. The closings colleges and universities gave the government an opportunity to re-organize the educational system under the correct (*Shiite*) Islamic ideology.[24] The new educational system had put emphasis on "the *Quran*, Islamic doctrines and the constitution of the Islamic Republic of Iran."[25] The architects of the new educational structure were Ayalollah Beheshti, the former Prime Minister Rajaii, and Hojat-al Islam Bahonar.[26] The effective educational restructuring was first announced by the High Council of Education Education in March 1983 that in continuation of the earlier plan which was announced in July 1980 like personal purification, curriculum development and textbook revision. But the new announcement included more that was the basic politico-ideological orientation of the Khomeini regime applied to education.

> First, to strengthen the beliefs of the student with respect to the basic theological axioms of Twelver *Shiism*, that is *Tawhid* (Oneness to

---

24 Khosrow Sobhe, "Education in Revolution: Is Iran Duplication the Chines Cultural Revolution?" *Comparative Education*, 18, no.3 1982, pp. 271-80.

25 Mehran, n. 21, P-4.

26 *Kayhan*, 7 July, 1988.

God): *Nabovat* (Prophethood): *Maad* (Ressunection): Adl (Justice of God): *Imamate* (the legitimacy of *Imam's* leadership after the Prophet Mohammad's departure). Second, to promote such sacred values like the family, Islamic brotherhood, socio-economic justices, respect for the law, and the virtues of education. Third, to promote the ideas of Pan-Islamism a political independence. Fourth, to strengthen the nations' defence capabilities through military training on school campuses. Fifth, to foster principles of legal ownership, hygiene and self- sufficiency. Finally, the new educational system was to enhance the spirit of investigation and innovation in scientific as well as cultural and Islamic fields.[27]

Universities became the first and primary targets of the Islamisation process. In the summer 1980, 200 universities and college were ordered to close. Universities, officially shut down and remained so for over four years awaiting the "Islamic rejuvenation". Almost all universities and colleges had suffered drastic cut in the size of student body, the faculty and the administrative staff. Tehran University was severely affected. The University Crusade (*Jehad-e Danishgahi*), charged with the ideological purification of the universities and accomplished its goal in less than three years.

The task for Islamic rejuvenation of universities was entrusted to the Council for Cultural Revolution.[28] Its purpose was to prepare and develop an appropriate curricula and adopt the textbooks needed to establish an Islamic University system.

At the university level, courses were re-organised into five separate groups: a. basic sciences, b. agriculture, c. engineering, and technology, d, medicine, e. humanities (including social sciences). "The curricula were designed to require all students to pass specific *Arabic-Quran* and religious studies courses beginning with the junior high school. The requirements set for university students included completion of four units (two semesters) in a subject called Islamic Knowledge."[29] The principal task of the Council was to review the humanities and social sciences, especially political science, sociology, economics, law and psychology, Among these,

---

27 Mohsenpour, no. 22, pp.85-86.
28 Ayatollah Khomeinin appointed the members of the Cultural Revolution Council on 13 June, 1980.
29 Rebert E. Rucker, "Trends in Post-Revolutionary Iranian Education", *Journal of Contemporary Asia*, Vol. 21, no. 4, 1991. P. 460.

economics was the central because defining the post-revolutionary issue in the political arena.

Just as the universities become the new regime's primary and main 'institutional target' for educational purification, social sciences and humanities became the main 'curricula target' for drastic textbook revisions. After all, it was the area where Westernization had its most toxic impact. At the general level, two criteria determined the nature of textbooks revisions. First, pre-Islamic past of Iran was to e de-emphasised and its Islamic heritage glorified. Second, Western values and culture were to be replaced by Islamic culture and values. Books and material were used in the universities were re-written strictly according to *Shiite* Islam. The clerics also succeeded in gaining centralised state control of the these schools and prohibiting co-education classes in all schools.

The responsibility to define the authentic Islamic methodology in these disciplines was delegated to the Centre for Cooperation of Seminaries and Universities (CCSU) *Daftar - e Hamkari-ye Hawzeh va Danishgah)*, headed by Mohammad Taqi Mesbah Yazdi, an instructor in a Qum Seminary. Cooperation between *Hawzeh* (Seminaries) and universities was encouraged in an effort to unify the religious and the university educational system, at least in the humanities and social sciences in which the *Hawzeh* claimed expertise. Khomeini stated in this regard,

> Islam has dealt more deeply than any one else or any school of thought with humanities and human development. You need specialists? You must ask the *Hawzeh*... Open the universities, but for humanities they must gradually ask the scholars of the *Hawzeh* in Iran, especially in Qum.[30]

The CCSU called a number of university economists to Qum to cooperate with the *mudarresin* (the instructor of seminaries) in framing an Islamic methodology fro various academic disciplines. The *mudarresin* were informed to the university professors about their discipline, in turn, the economists received a course of study in the Islamic world view and methodology.

Both the Council for Cultural Revolution and the Ministry of Culture and Higher Education promoted the translation of textbooks in various

---

30 *Kayhan*, 30 November, 1981.

fields of study. The Centre for University Publications (*Markaz-e Nashr-e Danishgahi*) of the Council of Cultural Revolution started its operation by commissioning translations of textbooks while universities were closed. The Centre for the study and Publication of Textbooks in Humanities (*Sazman-e Mutale-eh va Tadvin-e Kutub-e Ulume Insani*) of the Ministry of Culture and Higher Education had also commissioned translations and revisions of textbooks. These governmental publishing houses operated in addition to the traditional university press and the various ministries and agencies of the government that engaged in the publication of textbooks.

The University Crusade (*Jehad-e Danishgahi*) created, and entrusted the charge of the ideological purification of the universities that achieved its target very soon. Universities were permitted to reopen under the supervision of the Council of Cultural Revolution. "The University Crusade Councils were also created to ensure that all professors were familiar with and teaching according to correct *Shiite* Islamic values."[31] Crusade Councils were sent to all universities and colleges. Each Council composed of a professor, an administrative member from the particular university of college, and student.

The radical revisions and modifications of curricula of education led to deadlock and conflicts between the councils and University administrators. The conflict between the *Jehad Cadre* and the University administrator was so intense that in 1982, the Ministry of Higher Education crated Management Councils of University to sort out these problems. Councils were formed at each University, and were consisted of four Muslim faculty members, one Muslim University staff, and two Muslim students. The primary criteria for appointment was a proven record of commitment to Islam and the Revolution. "University presidents were to be appointed by the Minister of Education from among the members of the Management Council."[32]

The Management Council's prime task was faculty purification of both faculty/staff and the student body. It called for monitoring the work of present faculty and the hiring of prospective faculty members. Monitoring included examinations evaluating teachers' knowledge of Islam. If the Council found deficiencies, the instructors were required to take courses

---

31 Rucker, n. 29., p. 260
32 Sobhe, n. 24, p. 226.

in Islamic theory and ideology (including Arabic and *Farsi* literature). For newly entrant students in the universities and colleges, ideological test was held as part of the college and university entrance examination.

However, the current administrator of Iranian colleges and universities continues to include Management Council which is controlled to a large extent by the Islamic ideology. "Islamisation continued and was carried out not only in the public sphere, but in the private schools and colleges."[33] The schools and colleges included courses pertinent to Islamic values as part of their instruction. Thus, bureaucratic centralised control of Iranian education at the national level intensified in the post-Revolution era.

Overwhelming centralised control of Iran's educational system added the institutionalisation of traditional Islamic values. In the post-Revolution, strict regulations concerning life styles were enforced by the *Hezbollah* (God's party), an unofficial, religious oriented, cleric supported police force. They monitored public appearance (dress and makeup), businesses, and education (both public and private).

Educational system in Iran is centralised. The entire decision making process fro supervision to school schedule are under the Ministry of Education. All Schools follow the same pattern of curriculum, text etc. In the post-Revolution Iran, there are three types of universities: (1) Public University (2) *Islamic Azad University*, (3) International Islamic University.[34]

Some of the public universities specialise in teacher training. Their main activity is to train teacher for Education Ministry. All the public universities are financed by the Government. Some others deal with many subjects. Islamic Azad University has been especially established in the post-revolutionary Iran for an international higher education. Its purposes is to provide Islamic higher education at the international level. It is also called Imam Khomeini's international University.

At present, there are two systems of education in Iran. One is the Theological Domain (*Howzeh-e-Elmiey*), its purpose is to disseminate

---

33 Rucker, n. 29, p. 461.

34 Safar Ali Rostampur,S.M. Hamedani, Esmaeel Yahyavi, Mohammad R. Naeini, H. Mehrdad and Abdolah Najafi, "Education in the Post-Revolution Iran: some Perceptions of Educational Planners and Administrators," *Journal of Educational Planning and Administration*, Vol. 3, p. 118 nos. 1 & 2, January and April 1989.

Islamic culture and train Muslim scholars. The other is formal higher education which functions under the supervision and financial support of the government. However, after the Revolution, these two areas of higher study came to closer. Consequently, a centre was set up, known as the Bureau of Cooperation Between the Theological Domain and Universities (*Daftar-e Hamkari Hawzeh Va Danishgah*). The main duty of this bureau is to inspire the spirit of Islamic culture into the various branches of study at university level.[35]

Imam Khomeini, clerics, and their Islamic values had dominated education changes in Post-revolutionary Iran. The Revolution changed the system because of many internal pressures. These pressures came from religious and political factors which introduced both structural and behavioral changes. Religious and political struggles culminated into the clerics control of universities and schools. Islamisation covered modification of course contents, re-writing textbooks and required examinations of all faculty members concerning their academic experience and political religious point of view.

The concour is a national examination. In the pre-Revolutionary times, students were required to appear in the unified national examination called "concour" to be considered for admission in a college or university. This examination is also held in the post-Revolution period, and a new section examining students moral and ideological beliefs has been added. Students without the correct (*Shiite*) beliefs are debarred from the admission in the institutions. This new part of the concour further contributes to the Islamisation and the clerics' control.

Educational activities have been radically modified with the increasing control of the clerics. Prayers are part of the daily rituals at all educational levels. Islamic dress is compulsory for all faculty and students (males and females). University classrooms are demarcated by curtains to separate men and women.

Courses at all levels are revised to accommodate Islamic values, especially those in the humanities and social sciences. The faculties have been ideologically purified. The social-political atmosphere of learning has been completely changed in the post-Revolutionary years. The overt

---

35 Behram Mohisnpur, "Imam Khomeini's viewpoints on Education," *Mahjubah*, vol. 16, no.12 (163), December 1997, pp. 32-33.

imposition of a state ideology on the educational system has been the most fundamental changes. When the universities were reopened, there was an extensive ideological cleansing of the students and professors. Those professors who were critics of the new regime, were tagged as "non-Islamic", were retired or expelled. Those students who were recognized as political activists were expelled from the universities. Those who were seeking admission in the colleges and universities were required to pass an "ideological test" as a part of the general university entrance test examination. Moreover, 40 percent new entrant students were selected from among the sons and daughters of the martyrs of the war (with the Iranian Kurds and with Iraq), veterans of the war, and the members of the various Islamic organizations.[36] In this way, an element of ideological notion entered into the classroom.

Changing Role of the Mass Media After the Revolution

In conjunction with the Islamisation of society, mass media played an important role in the propagation of the Islamic ideology inside and outside the country. The revolutionary regime acquired political power sought to control mass media. It was an important means to spread ideology far and wide. The revolutionary leaders took control over the mass media to thwart any type of propagation against the new regime. The new regime was in the embryonic stage, so, the protection of the new regime from inside and outside onslaught was very imperative.

The regime was heavily depended upon both the print media and electronic media to disseminate its ideological message, which had to reach far beyond its political boundaries. The emergent leader of the Revolution, Imam Khomeini, categorically made clear during his visit to the Beheshte Zohra cemetery celebrating the martyrs of the Revolution in February 1979, "We are not against radio, we are against corruption. We are not against television, we are against that which is at the service of the foreigners and is used to keep our youth backward and destroy our

---

36 The students those who enter into the university through the highly competitive examination and those who enter because of their family status or political position from a highly uneven distribution of learning abilities in the university classroom; see Nadi Habibi, "Allocation of Educational Opportunities in the Islamic Republic of Iran: A Case study in Political Screening of Human Capital" *Iranian studies,* Vol. 22, no. 4, 1989, pp. 19-46.

manpower. We are against that." ³⁷ With this announcement, the stage of onslaught on the media was set to roll. Both the Persian and Western musics were banned from radio and television in July 1979. Imam Khomeini issued a decree in August 1979, which in essence allowed the authorities to gag the media. Subsequently, a press law was enacted which declared illegal the publication of any material offensive to religious personalities. Moreover, it required government-issued licenses for newspaper and magazines. By the end of August, most of the newspapers which were anti-Islamic and anti-government were closed, but those remained open, each had a "representative of *ulema*" who was entrusted with the task of ensuring the newspapers "remained true to Islamic culture and its values and defended the Revolution against the incursion of Western values."³⁸

The new regime stopped those publications which were anti- Islam and anti-government. "Only the pen and the publisher who is not actually seeking to pull down this Revolution has the right to freedom of expression. This Revolution has no room for the corrupting pen and corrupt ideas."³⁹ Various newspapers were ordered to close. However, some newspapers, such as *Ayandegan*, were allowed to resume their operation under strict guidelines set out by the government. Many Revolutionary newspapers were also set up which projected the views of popular political personalities.

Imam Khomeini several times reiterated his view concerning media that "they must not become traitors to Islam… they must not published critical and harmful material… It is their duty to block anti-governmental plots, not to encourage trouble and strife."⁴⁰ It was Khomeini's message that the media must work with the regime, and must not publish any material anti-Islam. Simultaneously, he cautioned and warned the media the consequences of publishing any material anti-Revolution and anti-Islam. "The media must align itself with the Revolution…who dares to write or publish anti-Revolutionary materials deserves the severest punishment."⁴¹

---

37 *Seda Va Sima Dar Kalam-e Imam* (Sound and Image in the Worlds of Imam Khomeini), Public Relations of the Islamic Republic's Radio and Televisión (Tehran, 1984), P. 21

38 *Kayhan*, 24 September, 1991. The duties of the representative of *Imam* were published on the appointment of the new representative.

39 Khoneini, Speaking on 11 February, 1985.

40 Homa Omid, *Islam and the Post-Revolutionary State in Iran* (London: Macmillan Press, 1994), P. 168.

41 Ibid., P. 168.

The new regime's survival was very much depended on the role of medial. If the media would have propagated against the regime then would have been detrimental for the new regime and raised its question of survival. The state had to control over the media to protect new regime from any jolt that might be proved baneful. Thus, the media came under control and was run by the state.

The state-run radio, television and press underwent an ideological screening of its employees. This process was closely watched and supervised by the conservative like Akbar Mohtashami, the representative of Ayatollah Khomeini in the Islamic Republic's Radio and Television. So, there was little room left fro any faction to disseminate its own ideology and make statement against the regime. For an institutional safeguard, the new regime set up a Council for the supervision of electronic media. Thus, the regime consolidated its institutional control on the media by appointing Mohammed Hashemi Rafsanjani, the brother of the President, Hashmi Rafsanjani, as the director of the radio and television networks. The Council coordinated the activities of the five newly-established departments: a planning unit charged with reviewing programmes; a political unit accountable for news policies; a control and evaluation unit acting as a censorship agency; a review department in charge of administrative coordination and financial affairs of the entire units, as well as investigation of complaints; and an operational unit in control of structural and functional aspects of the radio and television networks.

During 1981 and 1983, the *Majlis* enacted a series of laws to fulfill its legislative task *vis-à-vis* the mass media – called for under Article 1975 of the Constitution.[42] The most comprehensive laws were made under title, "General Policies and the Principles of the Voice Vision Organisation of the Islamic Republic of Iran", that outlined the politico-idelogical obligations and duties of electronic media. At the general level, the law emphasised on the central role of Islam and the constitution in production and broadcasting of all programmes. Moreover, the media was to advocate the principle of "Neither West, Nor East", which had become the sign that indicated the independent conduct of the Islamic Republic. At the specific level, the law emphasized the educational responsibility of the media regarding the question of the leadership, especially within the context of the principle of the *Velayat-e-Faqih*.

---

42 *Constitution of the Islamic Republic of Iran, (Tehran, 1981), P.48*

After enacting so many laws by 1984, the media had become a well-polished ideological apparatus with an extensive coverage of Islamic programmes. In addition to the domestic Islamisation of the television and radio programmes, the regime developed an extensive foreign broadcast programmes to spread its ideological message in various foreign languages to neighbouring countries and Europe. The new regime did not want that its Islamic message should confine only within the country, it was keen to spread message beyond its boundary. That is why it began broadcasting in many foreign languages.

To strengthen its control over media, codification of censorship was required. It was codified by the 1985 Media Bill, which enlisted ten major areas as a out of bounds. According to Islamic axioms, Muslim do not indulge in slander, so, banned the publication of any type of that was in any way slanderous. But the Islamic Republic went furthermore than the strict Islamic Scripture and outlawed anything that could be construed to disrespectful to Islam, or to the religious leaders, or anything that amounted to speaking ill of the dead. Thus, the censorship was strictly adopted.

Cinema and Censorship in the Post-Revolutionary Iran

The movie theatres were the target of attacks during the Revolution. Some were burned down. Many movie theatres were expropriated after the Revolution. Before the Revolution, there were 450 to 470 active theaters. In 1979, its number fell drastically to 250.[43] In the first phase of the post-Revolution, cinema was completely inactive due to stringent censorship on the media. In the post-Revolution, policy makers thought that there must be a fundamental change in every aspect of cinema, but they did not offer any clear-cut guideline on how to approach change. This lack of clarity was partially due to struggle for power and conflicting ideological point of view.[44] The confusion at the policy level and the general uncertainty, caused by the revolution, led to reluctancy on the part of the film producers to invest in movie making.

---

43 The former deputy minister incharge of cinematic affairs in the Ministry of Culture and Islamic Guidance, Fakhridin Anwar delivered speech at the 1992 Annual Meeting of the Administrators and Film Makers, published in *Mahanami-y- Sinama-yi* Film no. 140, April 1993, p.38

44 See Reza Allamihzadih, *Sarab-e Sinema-y- Islami-yi* Iran (The Mirage of the Islamic Cinema of Iran) (Saarbrucken, 1991), PP. 15-44.

The lack of clarity at policy level created shortage of movies in the domestic market. In the first year of new republic, only three movies were produced.[45] And in the second year, twenty- three movies were produced, of which only ten were screened publicly. [46] The private sector produced only the few movies, the rest were made by a few public and semi-public foundations.[47] However, finally the regime imposed strict censorship on cinema, and outlined guidelines for the movies. So, in the early years of the Revolution, a few movies were produced that created acute shortage of the movies in the domestic market. The acute shortage of the movies led to upsurge in the importation of foreign movies by the private sector in the period that immediately followed the success of the Revolution. However, objections were expressed by the clerics about the nature of the most imported films led to gradual and ultimately severe limitations on foreign films.[48]

The Ministry of Culture and Islamic Guidance was set up after the dissolution of the Ministry of National Guidance in October 1980 to formulate its ideological policies both inside and outside Iran, and especially it supervised the activities of the print media. The Ministry's operations were further expanded and streamlined. The content of the domestically produced movies and television programmes are strictly controlled so as to ensure their conformity with the Islamic precepts. It is especially true, when women are part of the cast. For example, stringent technical guidelines have been laid out in taking the image of women on the screen. The camera must not provoke lewdness in the audience.

The Ministry of Cultural and Islamic Guidance was responsible for the guidance of the cinema and television programmes, and it was also responsible for their role in society. In the course of defining the role of the cinema, the Ministry basically set forth three goals. First, it should not be anti-Islam and anti-Revolution; second, should be a national and participatory cinema; the third, should be imported only "worthwhile"

---

45 See Ghulam Haydari, *Film Shinakhti-I Iran, Vol.* (Tehran, 1992)
46 Ibid.
47 For the detail data on the number of films were produced by either private sector or the public sector, see Haydari, no. 45.
48 For detail data, see Hamid Nafisy, "Islamising Film Culture in Iran", in Samih Farsoun and Mehrdad Mashayekhi, eds; *Iran: Political Culture in the Islamic Republic* (London, 1992), PP. 178-82.

foreign movies. Cinema was considered a national wealth, so, it had to be protected by the state. [49] The media was completely under the control of the government. Ultimately, the government's role was defined concerning cinema in three ways: guidance, support, and supervision of the movie industry.[50] The Ministry took decision, the film industry would neither be completely in the hands of the government – a "natinalised" movie industry nor would be left entirely to the private sector. Concerning foreign movies, a private-sector organization, the Associations of Imports was dissolved, and the *Farabi Cinematique Foundation* a semi-governmental agency under the supervision and guidance of the MCIG was created. The new foundation acquired exclusive control over the selection and importation of foreign movies. However, the primary purpose of the foundation was to protect and promote the Iranian movies through financial support and other types of control.

There was monopoly in the film production which was enjoyed by a few wealthy film producers. To remove this monopoly, which was enjoyed by a few film producers over movie production, the cost of the movie production lowered through special tax policies and other protective measures. Subsidies, especially in regard to preferential rates of foreign exchange were made available to the film producers. This measure enabled film producers to import raw material and equipment cheaply. About forty to fifty bureaus were created throughout the country to teach photography and film-making to young people.

Between 1983 and 1987, in keeping with the revolution spirit and the populist nature of the regime,[51] the aim of democratisation[52] of movie production was actively pursued. Steps were taken to provide opportunities for anyone who were interested in this area. The stress on domestic

---

49   See statement made by Mohammed Bihishti, the former director of the Farabi Cinematique Foundation, in *Mahnami-y-Sinama-yi*, no. 142, June 1993, P. 142.

50   See Mohammad Mehdi Dadgu, *Nukati Piramun – I Iqtisadi-I Ciname – I* (Consideration about Economic Aspects of Iranian Cinema) (Tehran 1991), PP. 63-66.

51   On populism and the Islamic Republic, see Val Moghadam, "Islamic Populism, Class, and Gender in Post Revolutionary Iran," in John Foran, ed., *A Century of Revolution: Social Movements in Iran* (Minneapolis, 1994), PP. 189-220.

52   Democratisation inthis context doesnot refer to liberlisation or elimination of censorship but rather to an effort to expand film production to include a mateurs, especially youngsters from the various corners of the country – in other words, to "de-elitiese" the activity.

production and the democratistaion policy led to a quantitative spate in move production.[53] By the end of 1980s, about fifty commercial movies a year were being produced.[54] Along with quantitative growth, there were made attempts to promote quality through cultural message to the film. By the end of the 1980s, the goal of democratizing cinema was put on the back-burner, and the *Farabi Cinematique Foundation* focused mainly on promoting high quality Iranian Films at prestigious international film festivals. Consequently a great deal of international visibility was acquired by Iranian cinema.

By the end of the 1980s and in the early 1990s, the government decided to slash the subsidies, and in some cases, eradicate various subsidies. In 1992, cinema faced severe curtailment in subsidies, especially in access to preferential rates of foreign exchange. About 30 percent of the cost of each film was directly related to rate of the foreign exchange,[55] the elimination of the subsidies had bad impact on the production of films in general and high quality in particular.

One of the interesting aspect of the post-Revolutionary movie has been the position of women in the movie industry.[56] As a result of veiling and the pressure for restrictive rules concerning women in the public domain, the immediate post-Revolutionary period witnessed a drastic decline in movie scripts that contained important female roles, if any at all.[57] The restrictions imposed to avoid projecting women as object. New policy projected women as a modest in the Islamic Republic, and served to open up religiously legitimate avenues of self-expression for women in movie. Since 1993, Women's Film Festival held in order to promote women as scriptwriters, musical composers, cinematographers, editors,

---

53 The number of movies produced in 1983 was 17. Within two years the annual production increased to 27. See the speech of Sayyid Ghulam Riza Musavi, director of the Central Council of the Association of Producers and Distributors of Iranian Films, in the "Ninth Session of Reporters and Film Artists", published in *Salam*, 14 February 1993.

54 For the annual film production during the 1980s, see Haydari, no. 45

55 See *Mahname-yi Sinema-yi Film*, No. 107, June – July 1991, P.16.

56 For the evolution of womenand cinema in the post revolutionary period, see Hamid Nafisy, "Zan va Masala-yi Zan dar Sinema-yi Iran Bad az Enqelab," *Nimay* Digar, Spring 1991, pp. 123-69.

57 Hamid Nafisy, "Women and the Semiotics of Veiling and Vision in Cinema," *The American Journal of Semiotics,* Vol. 8, no. ½ , 1992, PP. 50-51.

and directors.⁵⁸

Supervision was mostly an euphemism for censorship, and the criteria for censorship were based on considerations of what was morally acceptable. For instance, for a long time the suggestion of physical love between a man and women was strictly prohibited. Themes considered either anti-revolutionary or critical of the Iran-Iraq War were also suppressed. Each film had to pass through five stage before release to the public. At each stage, the MCIG could affect everything from the script to the selection of the cast.

The relaxation of censorship had been seen towards the end of the Khatami period. But due to the existence of multiple decision making centres, this did not produce the intended result. ⁵⁹ The officially sanctioned films being taken off the screen suddenly after influential members of the elite and their supportive press complained. For instance, the *Zayandih-Rud Nights* and A Time to Love – these two movies of the religious but controversial film producer Mahsin Makhmalbaf – passed all five levels of screening and were shown at the *Fajr Festival*. But the romantic theme of the films created an uproar in the conservative press and criticized in the *Majlis*, the movies never received permission to be screened in the nation's theaters.⁶⁰

Changing Role of the Press in the post-Revolutionary Iran

In the nature of censorship of the press in the pre-and post Revolutionary period, has differed in many ways. Prior to the Revolution, the regime was more concerned with the political and economic issues, and in these areas, the publications were much more restrictive. But after the Revolution, the regime took the most censorious step in the area of chastity and public morality.

In the pre-Revolutionary period, book publication suffered from several political, economic and technical weaknesses, including censorship, high production costs, and inadequate and irrational systems

---

58 *Ayinih*, 14 January 1993.

59 For expressions of anxiety on the part of film prodncers, see *Salam*, 25 February 1993; *Mahnami-yi Sinama – Yi Film, no.* 142, June 1993, P. 34.

60 See "*Mashruh – I Muzakirat-I Majlis – I Islami*" (MMMSI), no. 13826, 11 August 1992, P. 24. For general criticism of both films and MCIG responsibility , see MMMSI, no. 13826, 11 and 12 August 1992.

of distribution.[61] The post-Revolutionary period addressed some of these problems quickly and started changes in the area of cultural development. The first impulse after the victory of the Revolution was to publish all those materials which were declared illegal by the *Pahlavi* regime. Within a year, the Publication Pamphlets (White Books) had swelled ten fold. Daily, weekly and monthly newspapers and journals proliferated, feeding up variety of viewpoints. But this period was an ephemeral, and soon most of the problems that had plagued book publication in the pre-Revolutionary period reappeared. In this period, publication was intensified, hundreds of tons of newly published White Books were burned. Heavy restrictions were imposed on publication. Substantially, the number of newspapers and journals shrunk and the revolutionary regime brought under its control many publishing houses. The average number of publication decreased in the early 1980s.[62]

The *Majlis* enacted its first press law in March 1980. It explicitly outlined the duties, entitlements, actions, licensing regulations, and penalties for the action of rules governing the operation of the press. The new law concerning press was necessary because Revolution's social and ethical values had been defined in new social paradigm. The constitution of the Islamic of Iran explicitly states, "the press is free to the everything, except that which goes against the interests of the nation or Islamic principles or is defined as possible by law."[63] The law in essence banned publication of material that undermined Islam and the Revolution.[64]

Moreover, it banned the publication of secret military materials, and secret decisions of the *Majlis*. The press was instructed not to publish immoral material and pictures, that unveil women were not to be shown at all.

In August 1988, after three years codification of the media, the Supreme

---

61 To get detail on books and articles that published in different periods of the pre-Revolutionary era, see Abdul Hussayan Azarang, *"kand-U Kavi darllatha va Rishiha-yi Buhran-I Nashr Kitab dar Iran"* (An Investigation into the Causes and Roots Books Publications Crises in Iran), in the monthly *Nigah-I Nu,* no – 26, 1995, PP. 80-95.

62 See Ali Rizai, *"Vaziyat-l Iqtisadi-yi Nashr dar Iran"* (The Economic Circumstances of Publication in Iran), in the monthly *Anat-i Chap,* no. 114, 1992, PP. 9-14.

63 Article 21.

64 Article 24.

Council of Cultural Revolution (*Shoray-eh Enqelab*), issued a further list of prohibitions. Publication of any material could be defined anti-Islamic or anti-regime, or anything that denied religion anyway, supported irreligiousity, or atheism, as well as any trial that could be considered as socially or politically disruptive or like to undermine the unity and gritty of the country. Furthermore, any material supporting western culture and values, or indicating any sort of superiority for the Western culture and values was prohibited. Anything that was to be considered lewd and provocative and gender freedom or feminist activities, was also strictly banned. The purpose of the ban was to show the women are not merely the object of pleasure but they have more role than it. The Supreme Council of the Cultural Revolution appointed a five-man committee to ensure that the media obey the rulings.

Imam Khomeinin had firm attitude on the censorship of the media. He wanted strict censorship on the media as had been reflecting from his various statements. He stated,

> my dying words to the *Majlis* and the Council of Guardians is to warn them never to permit the media, and news agencies and reporters, to waver from the Revolutionary path and the defence of Islam... the government be unrelenting in its condemnation and punishment of anything that threatened the public face of Islam... All such things must be firmly dealt with and eradicated. Any one who fails in this duty is responsible for the death and destruction of our Revolution that would surely follows.[65]

There were server restrictions on the media. Those papers were pro-Revolution enjoyed a degree of freedom, even they could publish against official and highlight failures of civic personalities and municipal civil servants whose manoeuvre capacity was much more restricted.

But by mid- to late-1980s, the situation started to improve, and number of titles and published books increased. The Ministry encouraged and funded the publication of books on religious matters. It is reported that during 1984-85 period, a total of 1986 religious titles were published which was almost six times higher then the titles released in 1975.[66] Out of total titles published 4873 during 1987-88, of which 2301 titles or approximately

---

65 Khomeini's Will, Published in Tehran (1990).
66 *Plan and Budget Organization, Annual Statistical Yearbook* (1989) P. 173.

49 percent were religious in orientation.[67]

The MCIG gave subsidies to the publishers. Like cinema, publishing industry benefited from low rates of foreign exchange. It was necessary when paper and offset presses had to be imported. They also controlled the book prices, providing them affordable to a greater number of readers. A rational distribution system was also set up with formation of about twenty book distribution agencies in which many became actively involved in introducing and promoting newly written or translated titles. By the beginning of 1990s, the number of titles published annually had swelled to 8000 almost twice as many as in the best year of the pre-Revolutionary period.[68]

The MCIG classified books in four categories: religious, children's, scientific, and art and literature. The number of titles of religious and children's books were remarkably increased. The greatest increase had been in the number of titles of children's books. By the end of 1992, the annual number of children's books titles published, comprising translations, averaged 1500 titles, and the total number of copies printed surpassed all other categories, averaging about 15 million.

The Minister of Guidance, Mohammed Khatami clearly stated about the "freedom of the press" and declared "the media is free in the Islamic Republic and is willing serving to educate and inform the Islamic society and facilitate its development.[69] He further explained the particular sense of freedom that had become operative in the post-Revolutionary state. "The press in this country is free to follow the general climate of popular opinion and to reflect the policies of the Islamic government."[70] Khatami was a liberal clergy who sought to give relaxation to the press. In October 1991, the Minister of Guidance, Khatami announced the removal of strict censorship of books. But he declared that any material would go against the national interest would be dealt with harshly.

During the tenure of Khatami, particularly in his last days, the MCIG showed a greater degree of tolerance, although it was limited and erratic.

---

67 Ibid., P. 142.
68 See the Quarterly *Kitabnameh*, published by MCIG. Data collected from Winter 1990 and Spring and Summer 1991 issues.
69 *Kayhan*, 30 August 1986.
70 *Kayhan*, 30 August 1986.

But since his resignation in 1992 and the removal of his supporters from positions of power at the MCIG, censorship became more extensive. The conservative newspapers and *Majlis* deputies publicly attacked the MCIG's policies concerning cinema and books. Deputy Maryam Bihruzi accused Khatami and MCIG of allowing public distribution of a variety of "anti-Islamic," "immoral", and "anti-human" materials and asked Larijani to "set things right".[71]

Position and Status of Women after the Islamic Revolution

When we throw light on the social spectrum, the issue of women was the most contentious issue after the Revolution. The new regime entirely reversed the pre-Revolution notion regarding women and brought drastic changes in all spheres of women's lives. Women's relation *vis-à-vis* society has been redefined in the post-Revolution period. Their role, activities, and appearance in society have been defined in accordance with the Islamic precepts. The post-Revolution regime was determined to redefine women's lives and behaviours *vis-à-vis* society in the Islamic paradigm because previous regime mixed up numerous western social norms and values with Iranian norms and values, cosequently degraded the society as a whole, and women in particular.

Imam Khomeini just after a month of his return in March 1979, dismissed all female judges and ordered the compulsory veiling to all women. According to Islamic dictum, a women can not sit as a judge, that is why, Imam Khomeini in the process of implementation of the *Sharia* sacked all female judges. In schools, colleges, and universities co-education was banned in May 1979, and furthermore in June, married women were debarred from attending schools. Government started to close down work-place and nurseries. In July, sea resorts were sexually segregated and women flogged publicly for transgression of these rules. Morality codes were defined and declared, and for the first time women were executed on the charges of bad behaviour and indulgent into bad activities in society.

Many changes were brought in the Personal Law. Just after the Revolution, the regime outlawed the Family Protection Law which was introduced in 1967 and 1975. Men regained the right to polygamy, unilateral divorce at will, and the right to prevent their wives from entering into paid employment. The legal age of marriage for female had been

---

71   See MMMSI, no. 13826, P.23.

reduced to 13 from 18 years and 15 years for male. Men also regained the automatic custody of their children after divorce.

The annulment of Family Protection Law was felt necessary because it did not conform with the *Sharia*. So, in February 1979, the new regime ordered that "the application of the Family Protection Law had been stopped by ordered of the leader and competent special courts had been dissolved by fiat of the Bureau of the Leader"[72] This annulment of the Family Protection Law created hue and cry among women, they met Imam Khomeini in this regard. Imam Khomeini softly interacted with them and issued statement.

> If women when concluding marriage set it as a condition that in matters of divorce they are authorized representatives (of their husband) in absolute terms. i.e., that they may divorce him whenever they wish, or in relatives terms, i.e. if he mistreats them or, for instance, takes another wife, then they are no other obstacles for them; they may obtain a divorce.[73]

Even after issuing such a statement, did not pacify women and could not solve the problem. He again declared that "the jurists had the right to issue a divorce If a husband mistreat his wife and she lodged a complaint with them against him." [74] The government gave only some relaxation regarding Family Protection Law to women but did not reverse its earlier decisions which had been already taken, and the marriage and divorce issue have had to deal with according to the *Sharia*. It was the first step after the Revolution toward the Islamisation of the Law.

Immediately coming into power, the clergy began to campaign to enforce a public dress code for women. In the process of Islamisation of society, the government was bound to introduce Islamic dress code. Imam Khomeini delivered a speech on 6 March, 1979 in Qum, prior to International Women's Day, in which he called for the mandatory public veiling to all women. The speech was widely hailed in the media during the days, however, it instigated a strong reaction among intellectuals and educated women. Women who were leery of the implementation of Islamic law, assumed a more aggressive stance. Their opposition to the compulsory

---

72 Asghar Schirazi, The Constitution of Iran: Politics and the State in the Islamic Republic, trnas. by John O'Kane, (London, New York: I. B. Tauris, 1997), PP. 216-17

73 Ibid; P. 247.

74 Ibid; P. 274.

dress code culminated into a series of demonstrations in Tehran and other cities.

Despite of demonstrations in Tehran and other cities against imposition of public veiling to women, the government was determined to implement it, because it was an ideological battle in which the new regime had little option to drop this idea. Public veiling was strictly imposed to all women. In support of the regime, the official Muslim Women's organization issued a statement, "the unveiling programme…was a murderous and disgusting project… It was an inhuman plan to turn Muslim women into painted dolls all the books and journals and the media colluded the corrupt women and erode the very foundations of the families."[75] Women should not be portrayed as an object of pleasure like west and they must be projected to play a role of chaste wife and good mother. Shahla Habibi, the President's advisor on women's issues stated,

> women are the guarantors of culture and educations in our country. The enemies of revolution seek to undermine us and rule us through the cultural subversion of our women. But our Revolutionary women must retain their cultural identity (expressed by doning the veil) and must go to men for help. It would be a mistake to assume feminine self-reliance and superiority.[76]

However, the new regime did not bend on the issue of public veiling and did not compromise on the issue of veil, because it further might be led to the degradation of society. The imposition of the veil was an ideological triumph, so, there was no question of retreating on this issue. The veil suggests not only that women's bodies are the subject of ideological control but also that eye contact must be regulated in women's relations with men. While state was imposing the veil, argued that the freedoms that *Pahlavi* regime granted women, including the right to unveil, were colonial in nature. The veil, or more precisely the women's issue became the point of contention between the western modernity and Islam. Iran did not want further exploitation of women in the name of modernity, freedom and feminism, so, veil became mandatory in the public life.

The veil has been clearly defined by the government. In the course of the discussion of *hejab* (veil), the interpretation of *bad-hejab* (loosely

---

75   Omid, n. 40, P. 183

76   Ibid; P. 183.

covered) and *bi-hejab* (without cover), have become significant. There must not be *bad-hejab* because the sense and purpose of the veil will be defeated. So, the government has clearly set out guidelines for the veil. Official dress required public consists of the full Islamic garment (*lebaseh-Kamil-e Islami*), which involves long dark trousers and a head scarf which covers the head, hair, and neck, leaving only the face exposed. Moreover, the meaning of *ba-hijab* was also defined in terms of thickness, design, colour, and quality of the covering cloth, and one's social manner. The light colour and transparent *hejab* might be used on less formal family occasions but, not official purposes and *Howzeh* (seminaries).

In schools, colleges and universities co-education was banned, and was strictly implemented. The government ordered that the boys and girls should not be mixed up and both should get separate education. Even curtain was drawn in the classroom to segregate boys and girls when rooms were not available to attend the classes separately. The segregation policy was adopted in the educational system by the government in the process of the Islamisation of the education. Gender segregation was actively promoted by the state, and gender became a major criterion, according to which social roles were defined.

Restrictions are introduced in women's appearance, activities, and even in their choice of occupation. For example, it is legally ban on women's higher education in the fields that were considered unwomanly like Agricultural, Mining, Geology, and Mechanical Engineering.[77]

Women are getting jobs in limited sectors, their employment is primarily confined to the health and education sectors. It is argument of the government that women are not fit physically and psychologically for all jobs. Islam itself has defined nature and role different from men. Hojatoleslam Abdelmajid Moadikhen, the Minister of Guidance, in 1992 stated, "since Islam deals with men and women with two different perspectives it assigns specific roles to each and they develop in their different ways."[78] Concerning women employment, Rafsanjani pointed out, it is natural that the women should perform, "only those fruitful activities that suit them and permissible namely in the health and education

---

77 The Status of Women in Iran, *Women International Network News*, Vol.13, no.4, 1987, PP.40-42.

78 *Zaneh Rouz*, 19 April, 1992.

sectors."[79] As such women's employment was banned in various sectors.

It is reflected in the various government directives that it prohibited female recruitment, "in 1987 the government extended the ban on new employment of women in all except the health sector."[80] The government wanted that the women should be confined to home and family. Supreme Council of Cultural Revolution also favoured the women's first priority was to remain with the home and family. The Article 1 gives the sanctity of motherhood and the importance of raising the next generation and home management. The material and spiritual value of women's role in the family must retain its paramount position. Their main role in society is a chaste wife and good mother.

Even the constitution itself asserts the women's role in the public life. The Article 5 A, employment which is desirable for women such as midwifery and similar medical posts as well as teaching. According to Article 5B, employment which best suits the nature and temperament of women such as laboratory work, electronic engineering, pharmacology, welfare work and translation work. These Articles explicitly state that the women are not fit for all works physically, psychologically, and temperamentally. One of the fundamental features of Islam's gender discourse, is its praise of motherhood.

The new Islamic regime not only banned the old regime's Family Protection Law but also imposed gender segregation in every aspect of society and compulsory veiling. The Islamic religious codes were formulated by the government to regulate women's behaviour in virtually every respect.[81] The ideal roles for a women are those of chaste wife and good mother, even if out of necessity they have to participate in social and economic activities. Moreover, according to the clerics, veiled women

---

79 *Zaneh Rouz*, 24 July, 1984.

80 Omid, no. 40, P. 192

81 According to these laws, women may be stonned if they commit adultery. For merely ppearing in public without veil, a women may be imprisoned for at least forty five days, given seventy-six lashes, or fined. A women charged with improper dress can also lose her job if she is working in the civil services. Strictly speaking, the law forbids social contact between the sexes and regulates sexual a conduct. For information about he Islamic punishment codes see *"Qanun-I Mujazat-I Islami Majmuah –I Qavanin-I Sal-I* 1370," *Ruznameh-I Rasmi (Summer 1992)*, PP. 593-654.

symbolize Muslim virtue and the rejection of the west.[82]

Society has been redefined in new paradigm in the post-Revolution Iran. Imam Khomeini's vision was to build the Iranian society a thorough Islamic society through implanting Islamic ethos, values and defined its own method and approach to achieve Islamic society within Islamic parameter. But only conservative faction's interpretation of Islam got triumph, and subsumed and overshadowed other factions method and approach. The dominance of the conservatives marginalised other factions, and a liberal elegy, Khatami, who was the Minster of Culture and Islamic Guidance resigned in 1992.

The massive reform in the educational system in the post-revolution was a sign of transformation of society into a new phase. Islam penetrated in every aspect of life and left profound impact on the society as a whole. Besides changes in the educational system along Islamic line, the mass media and press had also come under the influence of Islam. The heavy censorship was imposed to restrict any activity against the new regime and any type of opposition was eliminated in the name of Islam. The press came under censorship not to publish any materials which were considered anti-Islam and anti-Iran. The Personal Law was reformulated in the aftermath of the revolution and the marriage and divorce law was redefined. Women's activities and appearance are restricted at places and public veiling has been made compulsory. Women's choice of job has been also restricted. These moves have led society toward traditionalism.

Mohammad Khatami (1997-2005) initiated changes in people's social life and restrictions were eased. He lifted many restrictions on social activities and encouraged people interaction in social affairs. He eased regulations on women activities and cultural interactions. He lifted restrictions on press and media, and encouraged free expression of views. He allowed all to air their views in society which was resisted by the conservatives. Mahmoud Ahmedinejad (2005-2013) imposed restrictions on free expression, closed down night clubs, and restaurants. He suppressed domestic dissidents.

---

82 It was not the first time that the image of women offered such symbolic significance to the development of a Revolution. The image of women was used in the Shah's White Revolution. It was also used in the French Revolution. See Caire Moses, *French Feminism in the Nineteenth Century* (Albany: State University of the New York Press, 1984).

Ideology continues to play major role in deciding policy issues in the post-revolution period. Islam has penetrated in all aspects of society and its role will be continuing in deciding social issues. The penetration of Islam into society has far-reaching implications. Ayatollah Khamenei is playing the same role in deciding social issues as Ayatollah Khomeini did in the 1980s. Society experienced some changes during the Khatami period, but Ahmedinejad reversed those changes. Iran's society will remain under influence of Islam that the *ulema* sought for long. Iranian society seeks to protect and preserve cultural identity that desired in the past.

CONCLUSION

The Islamic Revolution 1979 is the latest manifestation in the history of Islam which brought revolution in the name of religion through employing its various symbols and precepts by depicting the existing order as incompatible with Islam. The galvanisation of Islamic idioms into action shocked the entire world who ignored Islam as a political religion. The use of Islamic idioms and signs and its conversion into action indicated that Iran is heading toward a Cultural Revolution which was envisioned by the people for long. The revolutionary leaders used Islamic symbols and idioms during the course of revolution. Islam reinforced its greater role and became only source of authority. Islam's greater role in the movement marked the beginning of the Islamic Revolution where diverse sections of society came together in the name of Islam, and depicted the Shah as their common enemy.

The Islamic idiom's conversion into Islamic ideology marked the beginning of the Islamic Revolution in which divers sections of society sank their differences at least for time being against the despotic monarch. The polarisation of society in the name of religion against the Shah was engendered by the *ulema*. Their successful mass mobilization proved fatal for the monarchy and Mohammad Reza Shah. The Shah could not contain and curb the activities of the ulema, though he made attempts to do.

The Islamic appeal was not only confine within Iran but it affected neighbouring countries also. The neighbouring countries felt insecure as a result of unrest and discontent in their own countries. The Islamic Revolution and Iran-Iraq War infested sense of insecurity that caused the formation of a new regional alliance, like the Gulf Cooperation Council (GCC) in May 1981. The regimes in the Arab became nervous. Saudi Arabia perceived threat fron Iranian policy of 'Export of Revolution' which was detrimental to the survival of the regime. Thus, Saudi Arabia felt uneasiness since disturbances began in the country. The massacre of Iranian *Hajii* during *Haj* was a clear indication that the Saudis would not allow any opposition. Particularly, Saudi Arabia suspected the activities and movements of the Iranians. With introduction of a new brand of Islamic government, Iran sought Islamic solidarity among Muslim countries. Imam Khomeini issued *fatwa* against Salman Rushdie to show himself as a champion of the Muslim cause. Saudi Arabia and Iran struggled to acquire the leadership of the Islamic world. Saudi Arabia succeeded in isolating Iran regionally and beyond and acquired much more influence among the Muslim countries than Iran.

The *ulema* played dual role in society: (a) guardians of traditions of the Prophet and the Imams; (b) protectors of the resources of the community against exploitation by non-believers and struggle against suppression and repression policy of the state. The *ulema* used their social position in the form of protests and demonstrations against the Shah as seen in the Reuter Concession in 1872 and Tobacco Concession in 1891-92. The two economic concessions to foreigners were perceived by the religious section as infidel penetration in their political, social, and economic life. On both occasions, the *ulema* opposed the Iranian rulers.

The *ulema* continued to project themselves as protectors and defenders of the national interests against growing foreign encroachment. They used their social position in the form of protests and demonstrations against the Shah as demonstrated in the Reuter Concession 1872 and the Tobacco Concession 1891-92. The Reuter Concession became the focal point for many elements of unrest and discontent. Sectional grievances were subsumed under a single protest voiced in religious terms. The protest against the Reuter Concession marked the beginning of a much wider protests against mounting foreign influence.

The protest against the Tobacco Concession was different both in quality and extent from earlier display of the clerical power. The expression of unrest and discontent was greater and its direction was more unified and firmer. The *ulema* played and acted as *de facto* leaders of nation against the state and defender against foreign encroachment. This agitation was far more than the expression of personal or sectional discontent in religious terms through the medium of the *ulema*.

The Constitutional Revolution in the early twentieth century was the culmination of the earlier events. The unrest and discontent of the nineteenth century against the state burst into the form of the Constitutional

Revolution (1905-06) that threatened the foundation of monarchy. The *ulema* protest to reform became inevitable since it threatened their prerogatives. The complex relationship between the *ulema* and the Bazaaris (native merchant community) acquired a new socio-political expression in the form of a clerical led movement against Western economic and ideological penetration.

In the nineteenth and early twentieth century, the clergy bid for greater power and influence in society, and asserted themselves. They called strikes against the Shah and foreign intrusion in Iran. The power of the *ulema* was based on their institutional influence as well as their sociological links with the urban classes. Urban areas were the main bases from where they could use their influence, and organised protest against the Shah.

The successive reforms threatened social fabric that existed for years. It created social problems. Social crisis continued due to reforms since it was resisted by the *ulema* to defend social order. This crisis was in fact the cultural identity crisis. The bureaucratization policy of the Pahlavi regimes severely affected the clergy class. The bureaucratisation restricted clergy's jobs, revenues, and shrines.

The monarchy was always under question since Islam did not allow any form of monarchical government. The legitimacy of monarchy was always a bone of contention throughout the Iranian history. But the monarch always tried to assert as legitimate ruler of the country. Despite monarch's claim as a legitimate ruler, the *ulema* assumed the leadership and mobilized masses against the Shah as had been demonstrating throughout the Iranian history.

Ayatollah Khomeini's notion of the *Velayat-e- Faqih* is based on the Imamate system that incorporated in the constitution of the Islamic Republic of Iran. It manifests that Islam is a political religion that cannot be ignored as redundant or peripheral force in politics as was ignored by the West before the dawn of the Islamic Revolution. Islam has become a political ideology. The revolutionary leaders derived legitimacy from religion. Nonetheless, the institutinalised role of the *ulema* has restricted their powers and positions. It will have deep impact on their position and status in future.

Ayatollah Khomeini's notion of the *Velayat-e Faqih* is derived from

Conclusion

the Imamate system. The *Faqih* has all temporal and spiritual powers and he is the only legitimate and rightful ruler of society. Constitutionally, the position and status of the *Velayat-e Faqih* is so elevated that no one is above him. He is the leader of the nation. He is an infallible leader because he is the representative of the Hidden Imam who is into occultation.

Iran has been changing since the Islamic Revolution 1979. The grip of the conservatives over administration is slowly and steadily dwindling. The moderate factions are prevailing and their views are considered in functioning of the government. The revolutionary euphoria has declined as the revolution is turning into history its grip over society is losing. The May 1997 presidential election illustrated the declining base of the conservatives where Modammad Khatami won a landslide victory over his conservative rival. But the moderates could not hold power for long and the hardliner conservative candidate, Moahmoud Ahmedinejad won the June 2005 presidential elections and he was again re-elected in the June 2009 presidential elections.

The victory of Hassan Rouhan in June 2013 presidential elections reflects that Iranian polity has been changing. Hassan Rouhani was considered as moderate during the presidential election and received supports of the moderates-reformists and Hashemi Rafsanjani faction, though be belongs to the conservatives side. It is clear that Iran is not these days as was just after the revolution. The new generation prefers that Islam must have a liberal face. The struggle between the conservatives and moderates has been continuing and would be.

It is clear that conservatism cannot always work in all matters, so there must be a balance between the conservatives and moderates otherwise fighting between these two factions may lead to upheaval in society and the entire system will be adversely affected. The two centres of powers, the *Velayat-e Faqih* and the President will have to work consciously and cautiously otherwise the whole system may get adverse effects.

When Ayatollah Khomeini was alive, there was also fighting between the conservatives and moderates. But it did not erupt into a major crisis because Khomeini's personality overshadowed whole things. The lack of charismatic leadership in Iran may create difficulty in resolving important issues effectively. Imam Khomeini was the natural leader of the revolution, and no one can be compared with him. Ayatollah Khamenei has been performing the same role in policy formulations and implementations as Ayatollah Khomeini. Islam continues to play major role in deciding policy issues even in the absence of Ayatollah Khomeini.

The economic performance of Iran in the 1980s was affected by political, institutional, and policy changes in the Post-Revolution period; policy crisis and intra-governmental conflicts; the Iran-Iraq war; fluctuations of oil-export revenues due to price and production changes; and international trade and economic sanctions against the country. All these factors in addition to structural weaknesses of the Iranian economy, i.e., one-sided economic dependence upon the world market system, distorted and fragmented nature, stagnation in production of industrial commodities, many services and some agricultural commodities, disruption of distribution process, rising inflation and unemployment, a decline in the real per-capita income, the standard of living, and growing poverty.

The Revolution led to migration of many businessmen and skilled workers, and increase in government ownership of production and distribution. The Iran-Iraq War and increasing government intervention led to new regulations price, distribution and external sector. Factional infighting prevented the implementation of a clear economic policy.

The Iranian economy in the 1980s can be categorised as 'war managed' economy rather than 'centrally-planned' command economy. The intervention of the government in the economy was required. It was dictated by immediate circumstances, and used as short-term crisis management policy rather than being based on a well and coherent economic plan.

The populist-state control economy was adopted during the post-revolutionary period. *Mostazaffin's* (deprived) participation forced the state to adopt populist schemes for them. The revolutionary regime introduced various schemes to provide them economic benefits. However, the proponents of this notion were forced to retreat from their past position and gradually toned down their promises and initial commitments to the rule of *Mostazaffin*.

Nationalisation in economic affairs introduced, as a result the state played a dominant role in the sphere of economy after nationalising the

CONCLUSION

means of production. Despite expanded government role in domestic economic affairs, private sector led service sector. The government's expanded role in domestic trade was in reaction to US embargo of 1980s and the Iran-Iraq War that created shortage of foreign exchange revenues, imported commodities, rising prices, and hoarding. The government played a major role in supervising the distribution of essential commodities through a limited number of co-operatives and distribution centres.

The process of economic reforms in post-Khomeini period indicated that the Islamic state would allow the private sector, legally and ideologically. The nationalisation of industries and services, and the control of the economy were activated by ideological purposes. Although it was also a spontaneous since at that time Iran had been facing economic embargo and the Iran-Iraq War.

The economic hardship compelled the government to initiate reforms in the post-war and post-Khomeini period. The government pursued nationalization policy immediately after the revolution but reversed and process of denationalization started. Introduction of some restrictions, including a degree of controls, trade regulations and currency transfer restrictions in 1993 and 1994 occurred in the post-Khomeini period. The government policy of privatization and at the same time imposition of restrictions are quite indicative of government attitudes towards economic reforms and high level of autonomy the state continued to enjoy.

Inflation rose as a result of privatisation that adversely affected the individual house-holds. The government's taxation policy pushed the cost of living higher. However, depreciation of the *rial* had left adverse impact on society as a whole. It caused to increase unemployment and hardship for those on fixed and low-incomes. It also fuelled inflation.

The First-Five-year plan reflected a compromise between the two trends. But at the time it also reflected a retreat on the part of the populist state control tendency. First, the state's direct involvement in the economy was, however, explicitly restricted in certain areas. Second, the over ambitious targets were toned down. Both were compromises on the part of the populist state control tendency. The state control over economy during the Rafsanjani period and the Khatami period decreased. But state's control over economy increased during the Ahmedinejad period. The state control tendency retreated and preferred moderate tendency during Hashemi and

Khatami periods. It demonstrates that the populist-state control tendency has not completely retreated and rebounds time to time.

Islamisation of society was one of the main issues before the new regime. The government initiated reforms in society. The educational system, mass-media, publications and women were the major spheres where Islam's presence was perceived *sine qua non*. The cultural decadence due to intrusion of the Western culture and norms in society was the main issue before the revolutionaries prior to the revolution. In the process of modernisation of society, the Western culture's influx into Iranian society and mixing up with it, caused in deterioration of the Islamic culture and morality which was always opposed by the *ulema* who considered themselves the custodians of the culture. The *ulema* viewed that Iranian culture deteriorated after coming into contact with the Western culture, values, and norms

The government brought many changes in the educational system of the country because it was the sphere where ideology had deep and profound impact in making a new society. Islmaistion of education was an ideological triumph, to hold over education meant to hold over society. Education is a means that infuses ideas in souls and minds of the people and children. It was an ideological battle that the new regime was bound to do. But it has had also negative impact because new learning methods and ideas outside Islam were not included in the curricula. The entire educational system has been centrailised in the process of centrailsiation of power.

Islamisation of mass-media was not only essential but prerequisite for the survival of the post-Revolution regime. Mass-media forms opinion for and against the government. Hence, immediately after the revolutionary upheaval, the government controlled the mass-media and restricted those publications which were considered anti-Islam and anti-revolution. Through media Islam was exalted and Western norms and ideas were shown as devil norms and corrupt ideas. In the process of Islamisation of mass media, the freedom of speech and expression had been curtailed and suppressed. The pragmatist leaders like Mohammad Khatami expressed desire to loosen the restrictions in many areas. Changes in policy and promotion of liberal ideas would adversely affect current power structures.

Mohammad Khatami introduced some changes in social spheres

which were resisted bb the conservatives. He brought changes in social activities and lifted restrictions clubs and cultural interactions. But Mahmoud Ahmedinejad imposed restrictions on such social activities which he considered as anti-Islam, and banned restaurants, night clubs, and alcohol. He started to regulate people activities. Thus, ideological battle continues in deciding policy issues in Iran and will be continuing.

The Islamic Revolution of Iran has pushed the women into traditional role. In the post-Revolution Iran, women's appearance and activities have been restricted. They have been regarded as dignified women and must play traditional role. They are publicly segregated, and in schools and colleges, coeducation is prohibited. Dress law has been imposed and veiling at public places has been mediatory. They are debarred from joining various jobs which have been considered unfit for them. Women should perform their traditional role as good mothers and good wife. The Iranian society is changing such restrictions will lose its relevance in future.

The Revolution 1979 transformed Iran's society, polity and economy and the country came under influence of Islam. Religion coalesced with politics in 1979 that transformed political culture consequently a new political system was born. Introduction of *Velayat-e Faqih* into political system reflects importance of Islam in Iran. This institution was institutionalized in July 1989 and its powers, functions, and duties were incorporated in the constitution. Society was transformed in Islamic lines that had far-reaching implications. Restrictions were imposed on social activities in the name of Islam and people's life and activities were regulated. Iran's economy was transformed and ideology played major in managing economic affairs of the country. Ideological contest began in deciding polity, economy and society in the 1980s that has been still continuing. Islam continues to remain omnipresence in polity, economy and society despite ideological battle. Thus, Islam has played major role in all spheres of society and will be continuing.

BIBLIOGRAPHY

Primary Sources:

Abolhasna, Ali, *Shahid Mutahhari: Efshagar-e Towtieh* (Tehran: Daftre-e Entesharat-e Eslami, 1984

Al-e Ahmad, Jalal, *Gharb Zadigi* [Tehran, 1341 (1962)]

Allamizadih, *Sarab-e Sinama-yi Islami-yi Iran* (Saarbrucken, 1991

Sadre, Abolhasan, *Vaziat – I Iran Va Naqsh-I Modarres* (Tehran, 1977). *The Fundamental Principles And Precepts of Islamic Government* (Tehran: Anjuman Amir Kabir, 1981).

Bazargan, Mehdi, *Bazyabi-e Arzesh-ha* (Tehran: n. p., 1983) "Marz Mianeh Madheb va Omoureh Ejtamayi," *Madhab dar Ourupa* (Tehran; 1965)

Central Bank of the Islamic Republic of Iran

The constitution of the Islamic Republic of Iran (Tehran: Islamic Propagation Organization, n.d.)

The Constitution of the Islamic Republic of Iran, trans. By H. Algar (Berkeley: Mizan press, 1980)

Dadga, Mohammad Mehdi, *Nukati Piramum-I Iqtisadi-I Cinema-I Iran* (Tehran, 1991)

Dihkhuda, Ali Akbar, *Lughatnameh* (Tehran, 1947)

Encyclopaedia of Iranica (Costa Mesa, Califarnia: Mazda Publishers, 1993)

The Encyclopaedia of Islam (London: Europa Publication Ltd. 1998).

Government Finance Statistics, IMF

International Financial Statistics IMF

Iqbal, Abbas, Khandan-I Naubakhti (Tehran, 1933)

Kasravi, Ahamad, *Tarikh-I Mashruta-e Iran* (Tehran, 1961) *Shiagari* (Tehran: Noor Publication, n.d.)

Khalili, Akbar, *Gam be Gam ba Enqelab* (Tehran: Soroush, 1981).

Khatami, Mohammad, Bim-I Muj (Tehran 1993)

Khomeini, Ayatollah Rouholla, *Hokumateh Eslami* (Islam Government) (Tehran, 1971) *Payam-I Inqilab: Majmu-yi Payamha Va Bayanat-I Hazrat-I Imam Khomeini* (Tehran, 1941)

Shaifeh-e Nur, Vol.2 (Tehran: Markaz-e Madarek-e Farhanghi-e Enqelab-e Eslami, 1983)

Mashruh-I Muzakerat-I Majlis-I Islami

Maududi, Sayyid Abul Ala, *The Islamic Law and Constitution,* (Lahore: Islamic Publications Ltd. 1960).

The Process of Islamic Revolution (Lahore, 1955)

The Political Theory of Islam (Lahore, 1939)

The Middle East and North Africa (London: Europa Publications Ltd. 1998)

Mutahhari, Ayatollah Murtada, *Barresiyeh Ejmali-e Manabi-e Eqtesad-e Eslami* (Tehran: Estesharat-e Hekmat, 1982)

Fundamental of Islamic Thought (Berkeley and California: Mizan Press, 1982)

Naqdi bar Marxixm (Tehran: Entesharat-e Sadra, 1984)

Piramun-e Enqelabeh Eslami (Tehran: World Organisation for Islamic Services, 1981)

Mustavfi, Abdullah, *Tarikh-I Idari-I Va Ijtamai-yi Daura-yi Qajariya Sharh-I Zindagani-yi Man, Vol. I* (Tehran, 1942-43)

Nehzat-e Azadi-ye Iran; Tafsil Va Tahil-e Velayat-e Motlaq-e Faqih (Tehran: Nehzat-e Azadi-e Iran, 1988).

BIBLIOGRAPHY

Office of Revolutionary Project, "Summary of the preliminary Report on Determination of the Economic Social Policies in the Islamic Republic of Iran", *Murdad(1358)* (August, 1979).

Plan and Budget organisation of the Islamic Republic of Iran

Al-Quran, text and translation

Report of United States Congress, Committee on Banking, Finance an Urban Affairs, 1981

Al-Sadr, Mohammed *Baqir, Eqtisaduna (Our Economics), Vol. I & 2* (Tehran: World Organisation for economic Services, 1982).

"Al-hanib al-Iqtisadi mim al-Nizam al-Islam" (The Economic Perspective of Islamic System) in Ikhtarnalak

Shariati, Ali, Tashiiyeh Alavi va Tashiiyeh Safavi (Tehran: Hoseinieh Irshad Publication, n. d.)

Shia (Tehran: Hasayniya-I Irsha, 1978)

Islam Shenai (Tehran, 1972)

Bazghast (Tehran: 1978)

Mazheb Aleyh-e Mazheb (np, n.d)

Emmat va Imamate (Tehran, 1977)

Eqbal Mamar, Tajdid Bana-ye Tafakur-e Islami (Tehran: Forough Publications, 1973).

Tabatabao. A. S. M. H., Usul-I Falsaf va Rawish-I Realism (Qum 1953)

Taymuri, Ibrahim, *Tahriam-I Tanbaku-e Avalin Muqavamat-I Manfi dar Iran* (Tehran, 1949)

Women's International Network News, Vol. 13, 1987

Secondary Sources:

Books

Abdelman, Jonathan R., ed., *Super powers and Revolution* (New York: Praeger, 1986)

Abedi, Mehdi and Gray Legenhausen, ed., *Jehad and Shahadat: Struggle and Martyrdom in Islam* (Housten: Institute of Research and Islamic Studies, 1986).

Abidi, A.H.H., *Iran at the Corossroads: The Dissent Movement* (New Delhi: Patriot Publishers, 1989).

Abrahamian, Ervand, *Radical Islam:* The Iranian Mojahedin (London: I. B. Tauris, 1989)

Afkhami, Mahnaz, *ed., Faith and Freedom: Women's Human Right in the Muslim World* (London & New York: I B. Tauris, 1995)

Ahmed, Alkar S., *Postmodernism and Islam: Predicament and Promise* (New York: Routledge, 1992).

Ahmed, Akbar S., *Discovery of Islam: Making Sense of Muslim History and Society* (new York: Routledge, 1988)

Akhavi, Sharough, Religion and *Policitcs in contemporary Iran: Clergy State Relations in the Pahlavi Period* (Albany: State Univ. of New York Press, 1969).

Algar, Hamid *Religion and State in Iran 1785-1906: The role of the Ulama in the Qajar Period* (Berkeley and Los Angeles: Univ. Of California Press, 1969).

Mirza Malkum Khan: A study in the History of Iranian Modernism (Berkeley: Univ. of California Press, 1973).

Arjomand, Said Amir, *The Turban for the Crown: Islamic Revolution in Iran* (Oxford and New York: Oxford Univ. Press, 1988)

The Shadow of God and the Hidden Imam: Religion, Political Order and Social Change in Shiit Iran from the Beginning to 1890 (Chicago: Univ. of Chicago Press, 1984).

BIBLIOGRAPHY

Ashraf, Haleh, ed., *Women in the Middle East: Perceptions, Realities and Struggles for Liberation* (London: Macmillan Press, 1993)

Avery, Peter, *Modern Iran* (London: Ernest Benn, 1965)

Ob, Mohammad, ed., *The Politics of Islamic Reassertion* (New Delhi: Vikas Publishing House, 1982)

Fakhreddin, Iran: *The Crisis of Democracy* (London: I.B. Tauris, 1989)

Salem, ed., *Islam and Contemporary Society (London:* Longman, 1982)

Khash, Shaul, *The Reign of the Ayatollah: Iran and the Islamic Revolution* (new York: Basic Books, 1984)

Herman, Patrick, *Islam in Perspective: A Guidance to Islamic Society, Politics and Law* (London & New York: Routledge, 1988)

Hazizi, Ali and Winder, Myron, ed.s, *The State, Religion and Ethnic Politics: Afghanistan, Iran and Pakistan* (New York: Syracuse Univ. Press, 1986).

Daniel G. and Rassam, Amal, eds., *Peoples and Cultures of the Middle East* (New Jersey: Prentice – Hall, 1983)

Dor, Gabriel *State and Conflict in the Middle East: Emergence of the Post Colonial State* (New York: Praeger, 1983)

Hjamin, S. G. W., Persia (Londong: T. fisher Unwing, 1920)

James A. And Roger, W. M. Louis, eds *Musaddiq, Iranian Nationalism, and Oil* (Londong: I B. Tauris, 1988)

Bonine, Michael E. and Keddie, Nikki R., eds., *Modern Iran: The Dialectics of Continuity and Change* (Albany: State Univ. of New York Press, 1981)

Cordesman, Anthony H. and Hashim, Ahmed, S., eds. Iran: Dilemmas of Dual Containment (Oxford: Westview Press, 1997)

Kedourie, Elie and Haim, Sylvia G., eds,. Towards A modern Iran: Studies in Thought, Politics and Society (London: Frank Cass, 1980)

Khan, Chandri Nazir Ahamad; *Commonwealth of Muslim States: A plea for Pan-Islamism* (Lahore Al-Ahibba, 1972)

Korany, Bahgat and Dessouki, Ali, E. Hillal, eds., *The Foreign Policies of Arab States* (Boulder: Westivew Press, 1984)

Kirk, George, E., A *Short History of the Middle East: From the Rise of Islam to Modern Times* (London: Methnen & Co. Ltd., 1957)

Kramer, Martin, ed., *Shiism, Resistance and Revolution* (Boulder Westview Press, 1987).

Kurdi, Abdulrahman Abdulkadir, *The Islamic State: A Study Based on the Islamic Holy Constitution* (London & New York: Mansell Publishing Ltd., 1984).

Landaun, Jacob M., *The Politics of Pan-Islam: Ideology and Organization* (Oxford: Clarendon press, 1990)

Legum, Colin, ed., *Crisis and Conflicts in the Middle East, The Changing Strategy: From Iran to Afghanistan* (New York, London: Holmes & Meimer Publishers, 1981).

Lengyel, Email, *The Changing Middle East* (New York: Van Rees Press, 1960)

Lewis, Bernard, *Islam in History: Idea, Men and Events in the Middle East* (London: Alcove Press Ltd., 1973)

Limbert, John W., *Iran: At War with History* (Colorado: Westview Press, 1987).

Mac Eoin, Denis and Shahi, Al-Ahmed, eds., *Islam in the Modern World* (London: Croom Helm 1983).

Karl, *Ideology and Utopia: An Introduction to the Sociology of Knowledge* (New York: Routledge, 1936)

Field, Peter, *The Middle East: A Political and Economic Survey* (Oxford & Yrok: oxford Univ. Press, 1980)

Moshe and Pappe, IIan, eds. *Middle Eastern Politics and Ideas: A history form Within* (London: Tauris Academic Studies, 1997)

Keith, ed., *The Boundaries of Modern Iran* (London: University College London press, 1994)

BIBLIOGRAPHY

Mohsen M., *The Making of Iran's Islamic Revolution: From Monarchy to Islamic Republic* (San Francisco and Oxford: Westview Press, 1994).

Kamran, *The Economic Consequences of the Gulf War* (London: Routledge, 1991)

James, *Islam Inflamed: A Middle East Picture* (New Yorkd: Pantheon Books, 1957)

Portimer, Edward, *Faith and Power: The Politics of Islam* (London: Faber and Faber Ltd., 1982)

Caire, *French Feminism in the Nineteenth Century* (Albany: State Univ. of the New York Press, 1984)

Mottahedeh, Roy, *The Mantle of the Prophet: Religion and Politics in Iran* (New York: Pantheon Books, 1985).

Masih, *Islamic Revolution Future Path of the Nations* (Tehran: Jihad-e Sazandegi, 1982)

Mutalib, Hussin and Hashmi, Taj ul-Islam, eds., *Islam, Muslims and the Modern State: Case Studies of Muslims in Thirteen Countries* (New York: St. Martin's Press, 1994)

Nomani, Farhad and Rahnema, Ali, eds., *Islmaic Economic System* (London: Zed Books, 1994)

Omid, Homa, *Islam and the Post-Revolutionary State in Iran* (London: Macmillan Press, 1994)

Pipes Daniel, *In the Path of God: Islam and Political Power* (New York: Basic Books, 1982)

Radji, Parviz C., *In the Service of the Peacock Throne: The Diaries of the Shah's last Ambassador to London* (London: Hamish Hamilton, 1983)

Rahnema, Ali, ed., *Pioneers of Islamic Revival* (London: Zed Book, 1994)

Rahnema, Ali and Nomani, Farhad, eds., *The Secular Miracle: Religion, Politics and Economic Policy in Iran* (London: Zed Books, 1990)

Rahnema, Saeed and Behdad, Sohrab, eds., *Iran After the Revolution: Crisis of an Islamic State* (London: I. B. Tauris, 1996)

Ravands, M., *Tarikh-e Ijtama-e Iran, Vol. 3* (Tehran, 1978)

Richard, Yaun, *Shiite Islam: Polity, Ideology, and Creed*, Trans. By Antonia Nevill (Cambridge: Massachusetts, 1995)

Robinson, Joan, *Economic Philosophy* (Chicago: Aldiene, 1962)

Rossevelt, Kermit, *Counter Coup: The Struggle for the Control of Iran* (New York: Mc Grow-Hill Book Company, 1979)

Ross, Sir E. Denison, *The Persians* (Oxford: Clarendon Press, n. d.)

Rowlinson. H., *England and Russian in the East* (London: 1875)

Rubin, Barry, *Paved with Good Intensions: The American Experience and Iran* (New York: Oxford Univ. Press, 1980)

Sanlogi, Hajjat ul-Islam Mohammad, *Qadar dar Islam* (Tehran, 1959-60)

Schirazi, Asghar, *The Constitution of Iran: Politics and the State in the Islamic Republic*, Trans. By John O Kane (London and New York: I. B. Tauris, 1997)

Shariati, Ali, *Civilization and Modernisation* (Iranian Student Islamic Association North India, n. d.)

Yar-Shater, Ehsan, eds., *Iran Faces the Seventies* (New York: Praeger, 1971)

Shawcross, William, *The Shah's Last Pride: The Story of the Exile, Misadventures and Death of the Emperor* (London: Chatto and Windus Ltd., 1989)

Siavoshi, Sussan, *Liberal Nationalism in Iran: The Failure of a Movement* (Boulder: Westview Press, 1990)

Sick, Garry, *All Fall Down America's Fateful Encounter with Iran* (London: I. B. Tauris, 1985)

Simpson, John, *Behind Iranian Lines* (London: Fontana, 1989)

Smith, Wilfred Cantwell, *Islam in Modern History* (New York: The New American Library, 1957)

Stoddard, Philip H., David C. Cuthel and Margaret W. Sallivan, eds.,

Change and the Muslim World (Syracuse: Syracuse Univ. Press, 1981)

Ali-Sawaidi, Jamal S., ed., *Iran and the Gulf: A Search for Stability* (Abu Dhabi: The Emirates centre for Strategic Studies and Research 1996)

Skyes, Brigedier-General Sir Perey, *A History of Persia* (London: Routledge, 1969)

Turner, Baryan S.., *Max Waber: From History to Modernity* (London and New York: Routledge, 1993)

Vatikiotis, P. J., The Middle East: From the end of Empire to the end of the Cold War (London: Routledge, 1997)

Weiner, Myron and Banuazizi, Ali, eds., *The Politics of Social Transformation in Afghanistan, Iran and Pakistan* (Sycaruse, 1994)

Watt, William Montgomery, *Islamic Fundamentalism and Modernity* (London and New York, Routledge, 1988)

Wiber, Donald, *Reza Shah: The Resurrection and Reconstruction of Iran* (New York, 1975)

Zabih, Sepehr, *The Left in Contemporary Iran: Ideology, Organisation and the Soviet Connection* (London: Croom Helm, 1986)

Zonis, Marvin, *The Political Elite of Iran* (New Jersey: Princeton Univ. Press, 1971)

Zinos, Marvin and Daniel Brumber, eds., *Khomeini, The Islamic Republic of Iran, and The Arab World* (USA, 1987)

Articles

Abdelnassir, Walid M., "Islamic Organisations in Egypt and the Iranian Revolution 1979: The Experience of the First Few Years", Arab Studies Quarterly, vol. 19, no. 2 , Spring 1997.

"Achievements of Islamic Revolution", The Message Quarterly, vol. 45, no. 2, December 1995 – February 1996.

Afshar, Haleh, "Women and Work in Iran", Political Studies, vol. 45, no. 4, September 1997.

Agenor, P. R., "Parallel Currency Markets in developing Countries: Theory, Evidence, and Policy Implications", IMF Working Paper, WP/90/114

Akhavi, Shahrough, "Ideology and Praxis of Shiism in the Iranian Revolution", Comparative Studies in Society and History, vol. 25, 1983.

Amirahmadi, Hooshang, "Iran's Develolpment: Evolution and Challenges", Third World Quarterly, vol. 17, no. 1, March 1996.

Amuzegar, Jahangir, "Iran's Economy and the US Sanctions", The Middle East Journal, vol. 51, no. 2, Spring 1992.

Anjum, Mohammad Iqbal, "An Islamic Scheme of Equitable Distribution of Income and Wealth", The American Journal of Social Sciences, vol. 12, no. 2, Summer 1995.

Arjomand, Said Amir, "Shiite Islam and the Revolution in Iran", Government and Opposition, Vol. 6, Summer 1981.

"Iran's Islamic Revolution in Comparative Politics", World Politics, vol. 38, 1986.

"Iran's Islamic Revolution in Comparative Politics", World Politics, vol. 38, 1986

Avery, Peter, "Balancing Factors in Irano-Islamic Politics and Society", Middle East Journal, vol. 50, no. 2, Spring 1996

Azarang, Abdul Hussayn, "Kand-u Kavi Darllatha vo Rishia-ye Buhran-e Nashr Kitab dar Iran", Nigah-e Nu, no. 26, 1995

Aziz, Mohammad Mehdi, "Evaluation of Urban Land Supply Policy in Iran", International Journal of Urban and Regional Research, vol. 22, no. 1, March 1998

Aziz, T. M., "An Islamic Perspective of Political Economy: The Views of Martyr Mohammad Baqir al-Sadr", Al-Tawhid: A Quarterly Journal of Islamic Thought and Culture, vol. 10, no.1, July-September 1992

Bahgat, Gawdat, "New Iran: A Myth or a Reality?", Asian Affairs, vol. 29, no. 2, June 1998

Bahmani-Oskooee, Mohsen, "Decline of the Iranian Rial During the Post-

Revolution Period: A Productivity Approach", Journal of Developing Areas, vol. 30, no. 4, July 1994

"Sources of Stagflation in Oil-Producing Country: Evidence from Iran", Journal of Post- Keynesian Economics, vol. 18, no. 4, Summer 1996

"Black Market Exchange Rate and Demand for Money in Iran", Journal of Macroeconomics, vol. 18, no. 1, Winter 1996

Bayat, Asef, "Workerless Revolutionaries: The Unemployed Movement in Revolutionary Iran", International Review of Social History, vol. 42, no. 2, August 1997

Behdad, Sohrab, "A Disputed Utopia: Islamic Economy in Revolutionary Iran", Comparative Studies in Society and History, vol. 36, no. 4, October 1994

"Property Rights in Contemporary Islamic Thought: A Critical Perspective", Review of Social Economy, vol. 47, no. 2, 1989

"Winers and Losers of the Iranian Revolution: A Study of Income Distribution", International Journal of Middle East Studies, vol. 21, 1989

"Foreign Exchange Gap, Structural Constraints, and the Political Economy of Exchange Rate Determination", International Journal of Middle East Studies, vol. 20, 1989

"Islamisation of Economics in Iranian Universities", International Journal of Middle East Studies, vol. 27, no. 2, May 1995

"Islamic Utopia in Pre-Revolutionary Iran: Navab Safavi and the Fadian-e Islam", Middle Eastern Studies, vol. 33, no. 2, April 1997

Behrooz, Maziar, " Islamic State and the Crisi of Marjayiat in Iran", Comparative Studies of South Asia, Africa and the Middle East, vol. 16, no. 2, 1996

Bill, James A., "Power and Religion in Revolutionary Iran", Middle East Journal, Winter 1982

Burns, Gene, "Ideology, Culture, and Ambiguity: The Revolutionary Process in Iran", Theory and Society: Renewal and Critique in Social Theory, vol. 25, no. 3, June 1996

Chase, Anthony, "Comparative Religious Politics: Iran and India", Journal of South Asian and Middle Eastern Studies, vol. 19, no. 4, Summer 1996

Chiachian, Mohammad A., "First generation Iranian Migrants and the Question of Cultural Identities: The Case of IOWA", International Migration Review, vol. 31, no. 3, Fall 1997

Chubin, Shahram and Tripp, Charles, eds., "Iran-Saudi Arabia relations and Regional Order", Adelphi Papers, no. 304, 1996

Dadwal, Shebonti Ray, "Iranian Presidential Election: A Second Revolution", Strategic Analysis, vol. 20, no. 4, July 1997

Dronbusch, R., "Multipule exchange rates for commercial transactions", in Edward, S. and I. Ahmad, eds., Economic Adjustment in Developing Countries (Chicago: University of Chicago Press, 1986)

Dronbusch, R., "Special Exchange Rates for Capital Account Translations", The World Bank Economic Review, vol. 1, 1986 A

Dorraj, Manochehr, "Symbolic and Utilitarian Political value of a Tradition: Martyrdom in Iranian Political Culture", The Review of Politics, vol. 59, no. 3, Summer 1997

Etemad, Mohsen Azimi, "Political Thought in Islam", The Message Quarterly, vol. 5, no. 2, December 1995- February 1996

Farhi, Frideh, "State Disintigration and Urban-Based Revolutionary Crisis: A Comparative Analysis of Iran and Nicaragua", Comparative Political Studies, vol. 21, 1988

Geiling, Saskia, "Marja'iya in Iran and the Nomination of Khamenei in December 1994", Middle Eastern Studies, vol. 33, no. 4 October 1997

Goldstone, "Ideology, Cultural Frameworks, and the Process of Revolution", Theory and Society: Renewal and Critique in Social Theory, vol. 20, 1991

Habibi, Nadi, "Allocations of Educational Opportunities in the Islamic Republic of Iran: A Case Study in Political Screening of Human Capital", Iranian Studies, vol. 22, no. 4, 1989

Haghayehghi, Meherdad, "Politics and Ideology in the Islamic Republic of Iran", Middle Eastern Studies, vol. 29, no. 1, January 1993

Halliday, Fred, "An Elusive Normalisation: Western Europe and the Iranian Revolution", Middle East Journal, vol. 48, no. 2, Spring 1994

Ismail, J. S., "Social Change in Islamic Society: The Political Thought of Ayatollah Khomeini", Social Problems, vol. 27, no. 5, 1980

Karmer, Martin, ""Real Islamic Threat", Survival, vol. 38, no. 4, Winter 1996-97

Karshenas, Massoud and Pesaran, M. Hashem, "Economic Reform and the Reconstruction of the Iranian Economy", The Middle East Journal, vol. 49, no. 1, Winter 1995

Kazem, Farhad, "Iranian Enigma", Current History, vol. 96, no. 606, January 1997

Kia, Mehrdad, "Persian nationalism and the Campaign for Language Purification", Middle Eastern Studies, vol. 34, no. 2, April 1998

"Pan-Islamism in Late Nineteenth Century Iran", Middle Eastern Studies, vol. 32, no. 1, January 1996

Kurzman, Charles, "Structural Opportunity and Perceived Opportunity in Social-Movement Theory: The Iranian revolution of 1979", American Sociological Review, vol. 61, no. 1, February 1996

Larijani, Mohammad Javad, "Islamic Society and Modernism", The Iranian Journal of International Affairs, vol. 7, no. 1, Spring 1995

Madelung, W., "A Treaties of the Sharif al-Murtada on the Legality of Working for the Government", Bulletin of the School of Oriental and African Studies, vol. 43, 1980

Martin, Vanessa, " A Comparison Between Khumaini's Government of the Jurist and the Commentary on Plato's Republic of Ibn Rushd", Journal of Islamic Studies, vol. 7, no. 1, January 1996

Mazarei, Adnan, "Iranian Economy under the Islamic Republic: Institutional Change and Macroeconomic Performance (1979-1990)", Cambridge Journal of Economics, vol. 20 no. 3, May 1996

Mehrpur, Husayn, "The Guardian Council of the Constitution of the Islamic Republic of Iran", Al-Tawhid: A Quarterly Journal of Islamic Thought and Culture, vol. 4, no. 3, April- June 1987

Moadel, Mansoor, "Ideology as Episodic Discourse: The Case of the Iranian Revolution", American Sociological Review, vol. 57, 1991

"Social Bases and Discursive Context of the Rise of Islamic Fundamentalism: The Case of Iran and Syria", Sociological Inquiry, vol. 66, no. 3, Summer 1996

Mohsenpur, Bahram, "Imam Khomeini's Viewpoints on Education", Mahjubah vol. 16, no. 12, December 1997

"Philosophy of Education in Post-Revolutionary Iran" Comparative Educational Review, vol. 32, no. 1, 1988

Muttahari, "Ijtihad in the Imamiyyah Tradition", Al-Tawhid: A Quarterly Journal of Islamic Thought and Culture, vol. 4, no. 1, Muharram-Rabial-Awwal 1407 (Sep-Nov 1986)

Nafisy, Hamid, "Women and the Semiotics of Veiling and Vision in Cinema", The American Journal of Semiotics, vol. 8, no ½, 1992

"Zan va Masla-yi Zan dar Cinama-yi Iran bad az Enqelab", Nimay Digar, Spring 1991

"No Class in an Islamic Society", The Message Quarterly, vol. 5, no. 2, December 1995- February 1996

Nonneman, Gerd, "Iran After the Elections: The Future Under Khatami", Middle East International, vol. 27, no 553, June 1997

Ocampo, J. A., "Collapse and (Incomplete) Stabilisation of the Nicaraguan Economy", in Dorubusch, R. and S. Edwards, eds., The Macroeconomics of Populism in Latin America (Chicago: University of Chicago Press, 1991)

Pasler, Karen, "Concessions, Repression, and Political Protest in the Iranian Revolution", American Sociological Review, vol. 61, no. 1, February 1996

Rezaii, Mohammad Mehdi, "Tahavalate Arz az Didgah-e Kalan-e Eqtesadi", Rouznameh-e Ettela'at Vizeh-e Kharji az Keshvra, 6 Mordad, 1373 (1994)

Rizai, Ali, Vaziyat-e e Eqtesadi-e Nashr dar iran" Sanat-e Chap, no. 114, 1992

Rostampur, Safar Ali, S. M. Hamedani, Esmaeel Yahyavi, Mohammad R. Naini, H. Mehrdad and Abdollah Najafi, eds., Education in the Post-revolution Iran: Some Perceptions of Educational of Planners and Administrators", Journal of Educational Planning and Administration, vol. 3, no. 1&2, January and April 1989

Rucker, Robert E., "Trends in Post-Revolutionary Iranian Education", Journal of Contemporary Asia, vol. 21, no. 4, Spring 1995

Sabet, Amr, "Islamic Iran: A Pragmatic Response to Modernity", The Iranian Journal of international Affairs, vol. 7, no. 1, Spring 1995

"Welayat al-Faqih: An Islamic Theory of Elite Hegemony or, Assabiyyat al-Khawass", The Iranian Journal of International Affairs, vol. 7, no. 2, Summer 1995

Safi, Louay, "Leadership and Sub-Ordinance: An Islamic Perspective", The American Journal of Islamic Social Sciences, vol. 12, no. 2, Summer 1995

Shahabi, Sohrab, "Investment Policy in Iran", Iranian Journal of International Affairs, vol. 7, no. 4, Winter 1996

Shorish, M. M., "The Islamic revolution and Education in Iran", Comparative Education Review, vol. 32, no. 1, 1988

Siavoshi, Sussan, "Cultural Policies and the Islamic Republic: Cinema and Book Publication", International Journal of Middle East Studies, vol. 29, no. 4, November 1997

Sirageldin, Ismail, "Islam, Society and Economic Policy", The Pakistan Development Review: An International Journal of Development Economics, vol. 34, no. 4, Winter 1995

Skocpol, Theda, "Rentier State and Shia Islam in the Iranian Revolution", Theory and Society: Renewal and Critique in Social Theory, vol. II, 1982

Sobhe, Khosrow, "Education in Iran: Is Iran Duplicating the Chinese Cultural Revolution", Comparative Education, vol. 18, no. 3, 1982

Swidler, Ann, "Culture in Action: Symbols and Strategies" American Sociological Review, vol. 51, 1986

Talattaf, Kamran, "Iranian Women's Literature: From Pre-Revolutionary Social Discourse to Post-Revolutionary Feminism", International Journal of Middle East Studies, vol. 29, no. 4, November 1997

Talqani, "Nazre Islam dar Bara-yi Malkiat", Guftar-e Mah dar Nameyandan-e Rafi Ras Din, vol. III, (Tehran 1962)

Tashakkori, Abbas and Thompson, Vaida, "Social Change and Changes in Intentions of Iranian Youth Regarding Education, Marriage, and Careers", International Journal of Psychology, vol. 26, no. 2, 1991

Wright, Robin and Bakhash Shaul, eds., "US and Iran: An Offer They Cannot Refuse", Foreign Policy, no. 108, Fall 1997

Zeghal, Malika, "Religion and Politics: The Complete Relationship Between Islamism and the State", Middle East Studies Association Bulletin, vol. 32, no. 1, Summer 1998

Zonis, Marvin, "Iran: The Theory of Revolution from Accounts of the Revolution", World Politics, vol. 25, 1983

Newspapers and Periodicals

Abrar (Tehran)

Ayinih (Tehran)

British Broadcasting Corporation (BBC) Summary of World Broadcasts

Enqelab Eslami (Tehran)

Etteta'at (Tehran)

Foreign Broadcasting Information Service (FBIS)

Bibliography

Iran Times (Tehran)

Iran News (Tehran)

Kayhan (Tehran)

Mahnammi-e Sinama-e Film (Tehran)

Middle East Economic Survey (MEES)

Middle East Economic Digest (MEED)

The New York Times (New York)

Risalat (Tehran)

Razuami-e Rasmi (Tehran)

Salam (Tehran)

The Sunday Times (Tehran)

Tehran Times (Tehran)

Zaneh Rouz (Tehran)

INDEX

A

Abbasid 31, 32

Ali Larijani 160

Ali Shariati 1, 3, 10, 11, 12, 13, 14, 15, 16, 23, 24, 29, 57, 81, 88, 199, 204

Al-millah 10

Anglo-Iranian Oil Company (AIOC) 48

Aql (reason) 95

Architect of Islamic Ideology in Iran

  Ali Shariati 1, 3, 10, 11, 12, 13, 23, 24, 29, 81, 88

  Ayatollah Khomeini vii, 1, 19, 23, 49, 51, 57, 60, 68, 109, 114, 154, 155, 156, 161, 172, 187, 190, 191, 192

  Jalal Al-e Ahmad 9, 10, 13

  Mehdi Bazargan 17, 18, 23, 84

  Murtada Mutahhari 3, 13, 14, 15, 16, 28, 82, 96

  S. Hassan Modarres 16

Architects of the revolutionary pan-Islamists

  Abd al-Hakim Khalifa 1

  Hasan al-Banna (1906-49) 1

  Jamal al-Din al-Afghani (1865-1935) 1

  Mohammad Abduh (1849-1905) 1

  Rasid Rida (1865-1935) 1

Armed struggle 11. *See also* Jehad

Army of Uthman 79

Ashura march 106

Ayatollah Khomeini vii, viii, ix, 1, 3, 4, 13, 16, 19, 20, 21, 22, 23, 25, 28, 49, 51, 52, 55, 56, 57, 58, 59, 60, 61, 62, 63, 64, 68, 70, 71, 72, 73, 75, 77, 78, 80, 81, 82, 83, 84, 86, 87, 88, 90, 91, 92, 95, 96, 102, 105, 109, 110, 114, 124, 153, 154, 155, 156, 160, 161, 162, 164, 166, 168, 169, 170, 171, 172, 179, 181, 182, 186, 187, 189, 190, 191, 192, 193, 198, 205

Ayatollah Motahhari 96

B

Bilateral real exchange rate 119

C

Concour 169

Constitutional Revolution 2, 37, 38, 41, 43, 44, 45, 48, 189

Cossek Brigade 2

Cultural Revolution vii, ix, 162, 164, 165, 166, 167, 179, 185, 188

D

Divine Unity 108

E

Ebadat 12

F

Faqih vii, viii, 19, 22, 23, 61, 63, 65, 68, 69, 70, 71, 72, 73, 74, 75, 76, 78, 79, 81, 82, 83, 84, 85, 86, 87, 88, 89, 90, 91, 92, 93, 96, 103, 104, 105, 163, 172, 190, 191, 195, 198, 211, 217

Farabi Cinematique Foundation 175, 176

Fatawa 21, 43, 48, 71, 86, 114

Freedom Movement of Iran 19, 81

Fuqaha 68, 72, 73, 74, 75, 76, 77, 78, 79, 80, 82, 83, 99

G

Gharb-Zadigi 10

Guftar-e Mah 24. *See also* monthly lectures

H

Hasan al-Askari 31

Hashemi Rafsanjani 136, 159, 172, 191

Hassan Rouhan 191

Hawzaeh 166

Hawzeh 166, 169

Hukumat-e Islami 22, 64, 70, 82

Husayniyah Irshad 24, 52

I

Ideology-e Islami 1. *See also* Islamic Ideology

Ijtihad (qiyas) 95

Imam-al Zaman 67

Imamate system vii, 63, 66, 68, 104, 190, 191

International Islamic University 168

International Monetary Fund 107, 146

Iran-Iraq War 107, 110, 115, 120, 128, 131, 152, 153, 177, 188, 192, 193

Islamic Azad University 168

Islamic Economic Organisation 124

Islamic ideology vii, ix, 1, 5, 6, 10, 11, 13, 14, 15, 24, 25, 164, 168, 170, 188

Islamic Republican Party 25, 87

Islamic Republic News Agency 157

Islamic Revolution 1979 vii, ix, 1, 9, 23, 24, 46, 56, 59, 60, 63, 65, 106, 108, 155, 156, 157, 163, 164, 181, 188, 190, 191, 195, 198, 200, 201, 203

Islamic Revolutionary Guard Corps 89, 136

J

Jalal Al-e Ahmad 1

Jalal Al-e Ahmad 9, 10, 13

INDEX

Jamal al-Din al-Afghani 1

Jehad 11, 22, 28, 38, 42, 43, 136, 163, 165, 167, 200. *See also* Armed Struggle

K

Kashful Asrar 19, 20, 96

M

Madarssa 47, 51, 52, 55, 69

Madarssa-e Fayziah 25

Mahmoud Ahmedinejad 136, 186, 187, 191, 193, 195

Majlis 45, 47, 49, 63, 64, 88, 90, 92, 93, 94, 95, 96, 97, 102, 143, 158, 160, 172, 177, 178, 179, 181, 198

Majlis Shorayeh Islami 95

Majmaeh Tashkhiseh Maslehateh Nezam 101, 102

Maktabi (Followers of the Imam's Line) viii, 109, 216

Maktabi School viii

Masjid-i Shah 39

Mehdi Bazargan 17, 18, 19, 23, 57, 81, 84, 197

Ministry of Cultural and Islamic guidance 157

Mohammad Abduh 1, 17

Mohammad Khatami 136, 159, 186, 194

Monetary Reform 142

Mujtahids 20, 34, 35, 36, 39, 44, 49, 55, 68, 70, 71, 83, 92, 93, 96

Multi-lateral real exchange rate 119

Murtada Mutahhari 3, 13, 14, 15, 16, 24, 25, 28, 82, 96, 160, 197, 198

Muzaffar ud-Din Shah 38

N

Nasir ud-Din Shah 26, 37, 38, 40, 41, 42, 43, 46

National Iranian Industry Organisation 135

O

Office of Revolutionary Project 108, 199

Organization of the Petroleum Exporting Countries 115, 116, 117, 143

Ottoman Turks 26

P

Pahlavi Dynasty 45, 46, 51, 58, 60, 216

Pahlavi Family 110, 111

Pahlavi regime 52, 149, 160, 178, 183

Pak Dini Movement 20

Para-satatal 110, 134

Personal Law 155, 181, 186

Perso-Russian war 37, 38, 39

Prophet Mohammad 1, 5, 11, 20, 30, 65, 66, 68, 72, 73, 79, 82, 165

Public University 168

Q

Qajar dynasty 2, 34, 62

Qarz al-hasanah 123, 124

Quran 2, 3, 5, 6, 10, 11, 16, 17, 18, 20, 30, 35, 36, 64, 68, 69, 72, 76, 79, 81, 95, 163, 164, 165, 199

R

Reuter Concession 2, 40, 61, 189

Reuter Concession in 1872 2, 61, 189

Reza Khan 2, 46, 58

Reza Shah 2, 16, 19, 46, 47, 48, 51, 62, 188, 205

S

Safavid dynasty 26, 32, 34

Safavids 2, 12, 26, 32, 33, 34, 36, 37, 61, 81

Shah Ismail 26, 32, 34

Sharia 18, 20, 38, 49, 51, 64, 73, 89, 94, 102, 103, 105, 181, 182

Sharia courts 69

Shariatmadari Kazim 44, 56, 58, 84, 85

S. Hassan Modarres 16, 17, 197

Shia vii, 7, 11, 31, 32, 35, 57, 65, 66, 67, 68, 69, 70, 80, 96, 199, 212

Shiism vii, 2, 7, 8, 11, 12, 19, 26, 28, 31, 32, 33, 34, 35, 45, 56, 57, 65, 68, 71, 80, 81, 82, 164, 202

Shiite phenomenon 1, 61

Shorayeh Negahaban (Council of Guardians) 97

Structural Adjustment Programme 134

Sunna 3, 6, 16, 30, 64, 68, 81, 95

Sunnis 94

T

Tobacco Concession 1892 2

Treaty of Gulistan (1813) 38

Twelfth Imam viii, 1, 2, 31, 32, 63, 67, 70, 73, 82, 104

Twelver Imami Shii theory 31

Types of Universities

International Islamic University 168

Islamic Azad University 168

Public University 168

U

Ulema vii, 1, 2, 3, 12, 17, 19, 20, 22, 23, 29, 30, 33, 34, 35, 36, 37, 38, 39, 40, 41, 42, 43, 44, 45, 46, 47, 48, 49, 50, 51, 52, 53, 54, 55, 56, 57, 58, 60, 61, 62, 63, 65, 67, 69, 71, 79, 80, 81, 82, 85, 87, 92, 171, 187, 188, 189, 190, 194

Umayyads 31

Umma 1, 12, 89

V

Velayat vii, viii, 19, 22, 23, 63, 65, 68,

69, 70, 71, 73, 75, 81, 82, 83, 84, 85, 86, 87, 88, 89, 91, 92, 93, 104, 105, 163, 172, 190, 191, 195, 198, 217

Velayat-e Faqih vii, viii, 19, 22, 23, 63, 65, 68, 70, 71, 73, 81, 82, 83, 84, 85, 86, 87, 88, 89, 91, 92, 93, 104, 105, 163, 190, 191, 195

W

Westoxication 10, 163

White Revolution 3, 49, 51, 52, 53, 186

Z

Zaban-e mushtaraka 11. *See also* Common Language

www.ingramcontent.com/pod-product-compliance
Lightning Source LLC
Chambersburg PA
CBHW031812220426
43662CB00007B/616